One Thousand and One
Thoughts from My Library

D. L. MOODY

BAKER BOOK HOUSE
Grand Rapids, Michigan

Reprinted 1974 from the original
edition published in 1898 by
Fleming H. Revell Company
ISBN: 0-8010-5951-8

The Mission of a Good Book

It will go anywhere, sea or land,
Gets into cabin or palace,
Reaches those otherwise unreachable,
Waits its time to be heard,
Is never tired of speaking.

Travels further and cheaper than any other;
Is unaffected by climate, untouched by fever.

Once started off, calls for no salary,
Costs nothing to feed or clothe.

Never changes its voice, and lasts
Forever—until the fire comes!

By Way of Preface

Why are not more gems from our great authors scattered over the country? Great books are not in everybody's reach; and though it is better to know them thoroughly than to know them only here and there, yet it is a good work to give a little to those who have neither time nor means to get more. Let every book-worm, when in any fragrant scarce old tome he discovers a sentence, a story, an illustration, that does his heart good, hasten to give it to others.

COLERIDGE.

One Thousand and One Thoughts
from My Library

And God said, Let there be light: and there was light. GEN. i. 3.
God said, Let there be light: and there was light.
How simple! And yet how Godlike! "He spake,
and it was done. He commanded, and it stood fast."
Infidelity may ask, "How? where? when?" The
answer is, "By faith we understand that the worlds
were framed by the word of God, so that things which
are seen were not made of things which do appear."

C. H. McINTOSH.

The Lord God planted a garden . . . and there GEN. ii. 8, 9.
he put the man whom he had formed. And out of
the ground made the Lord God to grow every tree
that is pleasant to the sight, and good for food.
By one man sin entered into the world.—Rom. v. 12.
The doctrine of environment had its deathblow in
the garden of Eden.   G. CAMPBELL MORGAN.

A river went out of Eden to water the garden. GEN. ii. 10.
A pure river of water of life . . . proceeding out
of the throne of God and of the Lamb.—Rev. xxii. 1.
The Bible is a circle, in describing which the Divine
hand begins in Paradise and ends there. In Genesis
God dwells with men, and He does so in Revelation.
In Genesis man is in Eden, with the river that watered
the garden, and the trees yielding their pleasant fruits,

and in Revelation man is in the garden of God once more, with this advantage, that no serpent is there to beguile, and no forbidden fruit to allure.

JOHN HALL.

GEN. iii. 8. *Adam and his wife hid themselves from the presence of the Lord God, amongst the trees of the garden.*

We also, when like to be obtruded on by the presence of God to our conscience or our thoughts, do, by a movement almost instinctive, flee to hide ourselves. We too have our gardens of vain security, our places of sweet and soothing forgetfulness, which serve, to ourselves at least, the temporary purpose of a hiding-place from God. If they do not hinder Him from seeing us, they at least hinder us from seeing Him; and this does in the meantime, for a respite from all those troublesome awakenings, which might else have haunted our spirits, and rifled away from them the rest and the enjoyments which we are so fain to prolong.

CHALMERS.

GEN. iv. 8. *Cain rose up against Abel his brother, and slew him.*

On the summit of a hill in a Western State is a courthouse, so situated that the raindrops that fall on one side of the roof descend into Lake Erie, and thence, through the St. Lawrence, into the Atlantic. The drops on the other side trickle down from rivulet to river, until they reach the Ohio and Mississippi, and enter the ocean by the Gulf of Mexico. A faint breath of wind determines the destination of these raindrops for three thousand miles. So a single act determines, sometimes, a human destiny for all time and for eternity.

CUYLER.

Death did not first strike Adam, the first sinful man;

nor Cain, the first hypocrite; but Abel, the innocent and righteous. The first soul that met with death overcame death: the first soul that parted from earth went to heaven. Death argues not displeasure; because he whom God loved best died first; and the murderer was punished while living.   BISHOP HALL.

The bow shall be in the cloud ; and I will look upon it, GEN.
that I may remember the everlasting covenant.   ix. 16.

The whole creation rests, as to its exemption from a second deluge, on the eternal stability of God's covenant, of which the bow is the token; and it is happy to bear in mind, that when the bow appears, the eye of God rests upon it; and man is cast, not upon his own imperfect and most uncertain memory, but upon God's. "I," says God, "will remember." How sweet to think of what God will, and what He will not, remember! He will remember His own covenant, but He will not remember His people's sins.   The cross, which ratifies the former, puts away the latter.
                                        C. H. McINTOSH.

Get thee out . . . unto a land that I will show thee. GEN.
This same voice has often spoken since. It called xii. 1.
Elijah from Thisbe, and Amos from Tekoa; Peter from his fishing nets, and Matthew from his tollbooth; Cromwell from his farm in Huntingdon, and Luther from his cloister at Erfurt. It ever sounds the perpetual summons of God. "Come out from among them, and be ye separate, saith the Lord, and touch not the unclean thing." Has it not come to you? Strange, if it has not. Yet, if it has, let nothing hinder your obedience; strike your tents, and follow where the God of glory beckons; and in that word "Come,"

understand that He is moving on in front, and that if
you would have His companionship, you must follow.

F. B. MEYER.

GEN.
xii. 2.
I will bless thee . . . and thou shalt be a blessing.
It is good for us to think that no grace or blessing is
truly ours till we are aware that God has blessed
some one else with it through us. PHILLIPS BROOKS.

GEN.
xiii. 9.
*If thou wilt take the left hand, then I will go to the
right; or if thou depart to the right hand, then I will
go to the left.*
The man of faith can easily afford to allow the man
of sight to take his choice. He can say, "If thou wilt
take the left hand, then I will go to the right; or if
thou wilt depart to the right hand, then I will go to
the left." What beautiful disinterestedness and moral
elevation we have here! and yet what security! It is
certain that let nature range where it will, let it take its
most comprehensive grasp, its boldest and highest
flight there is never the slightest danger of its laying
its hand upon faith's treasure. It will seek its portion
in quite an opposite direction. Faith lays up its treasure in a place which nature would never dream of ex-
amining, and, as to its approaching thereto, it could
not if it would; and it would not if it could. Hence,
therefore, faith is perfectly safe, as well as beautifully
disinterested, in allowing nature to take its choice.

C. H. McINTOSH.

GEN.
xiii. 14.
*The Lord said unto Abram . . . Lift up now thine
eyes, and look . . . northward, and southward,
and eastward and westward.*
It is difficult to read these words, "northward, and

southward, and eastward, and westward," without being reminded of "the breadth, and length, and depth, and height" of "the love of Christ which passeth knowledge." Much of the land of Canaan was hidden behind the ramparts of the hills, but enough was seen to ravish that faithful spirit. Similarly, we may not be able to comprehend the love of God in Christ, but the higher we climb the more we behold. The upper cliffs of the separated life command the fullest view of the measureless expanse.

F. B. MEYER.

The word of the Lord came unto Abram.
GEN. XV. 1.

He did not need to go to search for it; it *came* to him. And so it will come to you. It may come through the Word of God, or through a distinct impression made on your heart by the Holy Ghost, or through circumstances; but it will find you out, and tell you what you are to do. . . . There is no spot on earth so lonely, no cave so deep and dark, that the word of the Lord cannot discover and come to us.

F. B. MEYER.

And it came to pass, that when the sun went down, GEN. *and it was dark, behold, a smoking furnace, and a* XV. 17. *burning lamp that passed between those pieces.*

When the ancients wanted to take an oath they would slay an animal, divide it lengthwise, and lay the pieces opposite to each other. Then the parties would advance from opposite points, and midway between the pieces take the oath. God wished to take an oath. He ordered a heifer and some birds slain and divided, and the pieces lain opposite to each other; then between the pieces passed first a *furnace,* typical of suffering, and then a *lamp*, emblem of deliverance.

So it is in the history of individuals, cities, and nations.   First the awful furnace, then the cheerful lamp. The *furnace* of conviction, the *lamp* of pardon.   The *furnace* of trial, the *lamp* of consolation.   The *furnace* of want, the *lamp* of prosperity.   The *furnace* of death, the *lamp* of glory.   TALMAGE.

GEN. *Thou God seest me.*

xvi. 13.   When no eye seeth you except the eye of God, when darkness covers you, when you are shut up from the observation of mortals, even then be ye like Jesus Christ.   Remember His ardent piety, His secret devotion—how, after laboriously preaching the whole day, He stole away in the midnight shades to cry for help from His God.   Recollect how His entire life was constantly sustained by fresh inspirations of the Holy Spirit, derived by prayer.   Take care of your secret life; let it be such that you will not be ashamed to read it at the last great day.   SPURGEON.

GEN. *Walk before me, and be thou perfect.*

xvii. 1.   In other words, Christian perfection is a spiritual constellation, made up of these gracious stars,—perfect repentance, perfect faith, perfect humility, perfect meekness, perfect self-denial, perfect resignation, perfect hope, perfect charity for our visible enemies as well as for our earthly relations, and, above all, perfect love for our invisible God through the explicit knowledge of our Mediator Jesus Christ.   And as this last star is always accompanied by all the others, as Jupiter is by his satellites, we frequently use, as St. John, the phrase "perfect love," instead of the word "perfec-

14

tion "; understanding by it the pure love of God shed abroad in the hearts of established believers by the Holy Ghost, which is abundantly given them under the fullness of the Christian dispensation.

J. FLETCHER.

Shall not the Judge of all the earth do right?
   Resignation is putting God between one's self and one's grief. MADAME SWETCHINE.

GEN. xviii. 25.

While he lingered.
   Lot was the Pliable of the earliest Pilgrim's Progress.

F. B. MEYER.

GEN. xix. 16.

In Isaac shall thy seed be called.
Take . . . Isaac . . . and offer him . . . for a burnt-offering.—Gen. xxii. 2.
   "In Isaac shall thy seed be called"—there was a promise. "Offer Isaac for a burnt-offering"—there was a command. How did Abraham reconcile them? He did not, he could not. He simply obeyed the command, and God fulfilled the promise. The reconcilement was complete. HECTOR HALL.

GEN. xxi. 12.

It came to pass after these things, that God did tempt Abraham.

GEN. xxii. 1.

God sends us no trial, whether great or small, without first preparing us. Trials are God's vote of confidence in us. Many a trifling event is sent to test us, ere a greater trial is permitted to break on our heads. We are set to climb the lower peaks before urged to the loftiest summits with their virgin snows; are made to run with the footmen, before contending with horses;

are taught to wade in the shallows, before venturing into the swell of the ocean waves.   F. B. MEYER.

Temptation is that which puts to the test. Trials sent by God do this. A test is never employed for the purpose of injury. A weight is attached to a rope, not to break, but to prove it. Pressure is applied to a boiler, not to burst it, but to certify its power of resistance. The testing process here confers no strength. But when a sailor has to navigate his ship under a heavy gale and in a difficult channel; or when a general has to fight against a superior force and on disadvantageous ground, skill and courage are not only tested, but improved. The test has brought experience, and by practice is every faculty perfected. So, faith grows stronger by exercise, and patience by the enduring of sorrow. Thus alone it was that "God did tempt Abraham."   NEWMAN HALL.

GEN. xxii. 16.

Because thou . . . hast not withheld thy son . . . I will bless thee.

It is from the dark clouds in our sky that the showers of blessing come.

GEN. xxiv. 12.

Good speed this day.

To live for to-day is in the noblest sense to live for eternity. To be my very best this very hour, to do the very best for those about me, and to spend this moment in a spirit of absolute consecration to God's glory, this is the duty that confronts me.   D. J. BURRELL.

GEN. xxiv. 48.

I bowed down my head, and worshipped the Lord, and blessed the Lord God.

Worship is the overflowing of a full heart; prayer is the craving of an empty heart.

16

Thoughts from My Library

Isaac said unto Jacob, Come near, I pray thee, that I may feel thee, my son, whether thou be my very son Esau. GEN. xxvii. 21.

Only one man in the Bible wanted to *feel,* and he was deceived.

I am with thee, and will keep thee in all places whither thou goest, and will bring thee again into this land. GEN. xxviii. 15.

"With thee," companionship; "Keep thee," guardianship; "Bring thee," guidance.

Now then, whatsoever God hath said unto thee, do. GEN. xxxi. 16.

Every hard duty that lies in your path that you would rather not do, that it will cost you pain, or struggle, or sore effort to do, has a blessing in it. Not to do it, at whatever cost, is to miss the blessing. Every heavy load that you are called to lift hides in itself some strange secret of strength.

A negro preacher once said, "Bredren, whateber de good God tell me to do in dis blessed Book, dat I'm gwine to do. If I see in it dat I must jump troo a stone wall, I'm gwine to jump at it. Going *troo* it belongs to God; jumpin' *at* it 'longs to me."

Mahanaim (two hosts). GEN. xxxii. 2.

"Mahanaim" is still the name of every place where a man who loves God pitches his tent. We may be wandering, solitary, defenceless, but we are not alone. Our feeble encampment may lie open to assault, and we be all unfit to guard it, but the other camp is there too, and our enemies must force their way through it before they get at us. McLAREN.

One Thousand and One

GEN.
xxxii.
10. *I am not worthy of the least of all thy mercies.*

Measure your mercies by the foot rule of your deserts.　　　　　　MARK GUY PEARSE.

GEN.
xxxii.
25, 28. *He touched the hollow of his thigh . . . And he said, Thy name shall be called no more Jacob, but Israel.*

In the ancient times, a box on the ear given by a master to a slave meant liberty: little would the freedman care how hard was the blow. By a stroke from the sword the warrior was knighted by his monarch: small matter was it to the new-made knight if the hand was heavy. When the Lord intends to lift His servants into a higher stage of spiritual life, He frequently sends them a severe trial; He makes His Jacobs to be prevailing princes, but He confers the honor after a night of wrestling, and accompanies it with a shrunken sinew. Be it so: who among us would wish to be deprived of the trials, if they are the necessary attendants of spiritual advancement?

SPURGEON.

GEN.
xxxii.
26. *I will not let thee go except thou bless me.*

It was on his knees that Jacob became a prince; and if we would become princes, we must be more upon our knees.　　　　　WILLIAMS.

GEN.
xxxvii
28. *They . . . sold Joseph to the Ishmeelites.*

Those birds soar the highest that have had the hardest upbringing. . . . Even so, God usually nurses those amid difficulties and hardships who are destined to rise to eminence, and accomplish great deeds on earth.　　　　　　GUTHRIE.

18

Thoughts from My Library

He left all that he had in Joseph's hand; and he knew GEN.
not ought he had, save the bread which he did eat. xxxix.
6.

If you are a servant, make your employer feel that
you are the most reliable person about the place.
Joseph in jail was as reliable as when governor of
Egypt. Cream rises to the top even if it is in a wash-
hand basin. CHAMPNESS.

He was there in the prison, but the Lord was with Joseph. GEN.
xxxix.
God never places us in any position in which we can-
20, 21.
not grow. We may fancy that He does. We may
fear we are so impeded by fretting petty cares that we
are gaining nothing; but when we are not sending
any branches upward, we may be sending roots
downward. Perhaps in the time of our humiliation,
when everything seems a failure, we are making the
best kind of progress. E. PRENTISS.

The Lord . . . showed him mercy. GEN.
xxxix.
Oh! wondrous revelation! Joseph did not stand in
21.
a niche on the mountain side, as Moses did, whilst the
solemn pomp swept past; and yet the Lord showed
him a great sight—He showed him His mercy. The
prison cell was the mount of vision, from the height
of which he saw, as he had never seen before, the
panorama of Divine loving-kindness. It were well
worth his while to go to prison to learn that. When
children gather to see the magic lantern, the figures
may be flung upon the sheet, and yet be invisible, because the room is full of light. Darken the room,
and instantly the round circle of light is filled with
brilliant color. God our Father has often to turn
down the lights of our life because He wants to show
us mercy. Whenever you get into a prison of cir-

cumstances, be on the watch. Prisons are rare places for seeing things. It was in prison that Bunyan saw his wondrous allegory, and Paul met the Lord, and John looked through heaven's open door, and Joseph saw God's mercy. God has no chance to show His mercy to some of us except when we are in some sore sorrow. The night is the time to see the stars.

F. B. MEYER.

GEN. xlix. 24. *The arms of his hands were made strong by the hands of the mighty God of Jacob.*

The old legend tells us that Ulysses, returning home after long years, proved his identity by bending a bow which had defied the efforts of the stoutest heroes who had tried it in his absence. There are a good many of these defiant bows lying all around us. Tasks that deride our puny efforts; empty churches that will not fill; wicked neighborhoods that will not yield; hardened soils that will not admit the plough-share to cut into their crust. The one thing of which we need to assure ourselves is—whether it be God's will for us to take them in hand: if not, it is useless to attempt the task; we may as well husband and re-serve our strength. But if it is made clear to us that we are to take up armor, methods, instrumentalities, once wielded by giant hands, but now as unbefitting these poorer times as the armor of the age of chivalry mocks at the smaller make of modern warriors—let us not hesitate for a single moment, let us assume the armor of defence and the weapons of attack; and, as we do so, we shall become aware of a strength being infused into us—not ours, but His: "the arms of our hands will be made strong by the hands of the mighty God of Jacob." F. B. MEYER.

Thoughts from My Library

She took for him an ark of bulrushes; and she laid it EX.
in the flags by the river's brink. ii. 3.

The mother of Moses laid the ark in the flags by the
river's brink. Ay, but before doing so she laid it on
the heart of God! She could not have laid it so cour-
ageously upon the Nile, if she had not first devoutly laid
it upon the care and love of God. We are often surprised at the outward calmness of men who are called
upon to do unpleasant and most trying deeds; but could
we have seen them in secret we should have known the
moral preparation which they underwent before coming
out to be seen of men. Be right in the sanctuary if you
would be right in the market-place. Be steadfast in
prayer if you would be calm in affliction. Start your
race from the throne of God itself, if you would run
well, and win the prize. JOSEPH PARKER.

Come now . . . and I will send thee unto Pharaoh EX.
that thou mayest bring forth my people . . . out iii. 10.
of Egypt.

None of us can tell for what God is educating us.
We fret and murmur at the narrow round and daily
task of ordinary life, not realizing that it is only thus
that we can be prepared for the high and holy office
which awaits us. We must descend before we can
ascend. We must suffer, if we would reign. We
must take the *via crucis* (way of the cross) submis-
sively and patiently if we would tread the *via lucis*
(way of light). We must endure the polishing if we
would be shafts in the quiver of Emmanuel. God's
will comes to thee and me in daily circumstances, in
little things equally as in great: meet them bravely;
be at your best always, though the occasion be one of

the very least; dignify the smallest summons by the greatness of your response.   F. B. MEYER.

EX. *I am that I am.*
iii. 14.
     God *gives* to the body,—He *is* to the soul.
                                                    JOHN KER.

EX. *The Lord said unto him, What is that in thine hand ?*
iv. 2.   *And he said, A rod.*

It was probably only a shepherd's crook. What a history, however, awaited it! It was to be stretched out over the Red Sea, pointing a pathway through its depths; to smite the flinty rock; to win victory over the hosts of Amalek; to be known as the rod of God. When God wants an implement for His service He does not choose the golden sceptre, but a shepherd's crook; the weakest and meanest thing He can find— a ram's horn, a cake of barley meal, an ox-goad, an earthen pitcher, a shepherd's sling. . . . A rod with God behind it is mightier than the vastest army.
                                                    F. B. MEYER.

EX. *And he said, O my Lord, send, I pray thee, by the*
iv. 13. *hand of him whom thou wilt send.*

It was a very grudging assent. It was as much as to say, "Since Thou art determined to send me, and I must undertake the mission, then let it be so; but I would that it might have been another, and I go because I am compelled." So often do we shrink back from the sacrifice or obligation to which God calls us, that we think we are going down to our doom. We seek every reason for evading the Divine will, little realizing that He is forcing us out from our quiet home into a career which includes, among other things, the song of victory on the banks of the Red Sea; the two lonely sojourns for forty days in converse with God; the shining face; the vision of glory; the burial by the hand of Michael; and the supreme honor of standing beside the Lord on the Transfiguration Mount.

F. B. MEYER.

Thou shalt speak all that I command thee. EX. vii. 2.

To every one of us God gives something that He wants us to say to others. We cannot all write poems or hymns, or compose books which will bless men; but if we live near the heart of Christ, there is not one of us into whose ear He will not whisper some fragment of truth, some revealing of grace or love, or to whom He will not give some experience of comfort in sorrow, some new glimpse of glory. Each friend of Christ, living close to Him, learns something from Him and of Him which no one has learned before, which he is to forth-tell to the world.

J. R. MILLER.

Take heed to thyself. EX. x. 28.

Art thou a traveller, like him who prayed, "Guide my footsteps"? Take heed to thyself lest thou wander from the way, lest thou turn to the right or left. Walk on the King's highway. Art thou an architect? Lay firmly the foundation of faith, which is Jesus Christ. Art thou a builder? Look how thou buildest and what,—not wood, grass, stubble; but gold, silver, and precious stones. A pastor? Take heed lest any of the duties belonging to thine office are omitted. A husbandman? Dig round the barren fig-tree, and supply it with what is needed to produce fruitfulness. Art thou a soldier? Endure hardship for the Gospel,

engage in the good warfare against the spirits of darkness, against the affections of the flesh. Entangle not
thyself with the affairs of this life, that thou mayest
please Him who has called thee to be a soldier. Art
thou an athlete? Take heed to thyself lest thou trans-
gress any of the laws of the contest, for no one is
crowned unless he strive lawfully. BASIL THE GREAT.

EX.
xiii. 13.
Every firstling of an ass thou shalt redeem with a lamb.

Little things are made important in the Scriptures.
This is an apparently out-of-the-way incident. Out of
the way! What way? Out of our way, possibly; but
what is our way? a little path leading nowhere: a
road we have made with which to please ourselves to
go up and down upon, and suppose to be the universe. JOSEPH PARKER.

EX.
xiv. 2.
*Speak unto the children of Israel that they encamp
. . . between Midgol and the sea, over against
Baal-zephon.*

Often God seems to place His children in positions
of profound difficulty—leading them into a wedge
from which there is no escape; contriving a situation
which no human judgment would have permitted had
it been previously consulted. The very cloud conducts them thither. You may be thus involved at this
very hour. It does seem perplexing and mysterious
to the last degree. But it is perfectly right. The
issue will more than justify Him Who has brought you
hither. It is a platform for the display of His almighty
grace and power. He will not only deliver you, but
in doing so He will give you a lesson that you will
never forget; and to which, in many a psalm and
song in after days, you will revert. F. B. MEYER.

Thoughts from My Library

EX.
xiv. 19.

The pillar of the cloud.

"It was a cloud and darkness to the Egyptians, but "it gave light by night" to Israel. How like the cross of our Lord Jesus Christ! Truly that cross has a double aspect, likewise. It forms the foundation of the believer's peace; and, at the same time, seals the condemnation of the guilty world. The self-same blood which purges the believer's conscience and gives him perfect peace, stains this earth and consummates its guilt. The very mission of the Son of God which strips the world of its cloak, and leaves it wholly without excuse, clothes the Church with a fair mantle of righteousness, and fills her mouth with ceaseless praise. The very same Lamb who will terrify, by His unmitigated wrath, all tribes and classes of earth, will lead, by His gentle hand, His blood-bought flock, through the green pastures, and beside the still waters forever.   C. H. McINTOSH.

EX.
xiv.
19, 20

And the angel of God, which went before the camp of Israel, removed and went behind them; and the pillar of the cloud went from before their face, and stood behind them. And it came between the camp of the Egyptians and the camp of Israel; and it was a cloud and darkness to them, but it gave light by night to these; so that the one came not near the other all the night.

Jehovah placed himself right between Israel and the enemy—this was protection indeed. Before ever Pharaoh could touch a hair of Israel's head, he should make his way through the very pavilion of the Almighty—yea, through the Almighty Himself. Thus it is that God ever places Himself between His people and every enemy, so that "no weapon formed against them can prosper." He has placed Himself between us and our sins; and it is our happy privilege to find Him between us and every one and everything that could be against us. . . . The believer may institute a diligent and anxious search for his sins, but he cannot find them. Why? Because God is between him and them. He has cast all our sins behind His back; while, at the same time, He sheds forth upon us the light of His reconciled countenance.

C. H. McINTOSH.

EX.
xiv.20.

It was a cloud and darkness to (the Egyptians) but it gave light by night to (Israel).

The nearer the moon draweth into conjunction with the sun, the brighter she shines toward the heavens and the earth; so, the nearer the soul draws into communion with Jesus Christ, the comelier it is in the eye of the Spouse, and the blacker it appears in the sight of the world. He that is a precious Christian to the Lord is a precious puritan to the world; he that is glorious to a heavenly saint is odious to an earthly spirit. But it is a sign thou art an Egyptian, when that cloud which is a light to an Israelite is darkness to thee. It is a sign thou movest in a terrestrial orb, when thou seest no lustre in such celestial lights.

EX.
XV. 2.

The Lord is my . . . song.

This is the fullness and perfection of knowing God— so to know Him that He Himself becomes our delight; so to know Him that praise is sweetest and fullest and freshest and gladdest when we sing of Him. He who has learned this blessed secret carries the golden key

26

of heaven—nay, he hath fetched heaven down to earth, and need not envy the angels now.

MARK GUY PEARSE.

So Moses brought Israel from the Red Sea; and they went out into the wilderness of Shur: and they went three days in the wilderness, and found no water. EX. XV. 22.

It is when we get into wilderness experience, that we are put to the test as to the real measure of our acquaintance with God, and with our own hearts. There is a freshness and an exuberance of joy connected with the opening of our Christian career, which very soon receives a check from the keen blast of the desert; and then, unless there is a deep sense of what God is to us, above and beyond everything else, we are apt to break down, and "in our hearts, turn back again into Egypt." The discipline of the wilderness is needful, not to furnish us with a title to Canaan, but to make us acquainted with God and with our own hearts; to enable us to enter into the power of our relationship, and to enlarge our capacity for the enjoyment of Canaan when we actually get there.   C. H. McINTOSH.

They could not drink of the waters of Marah, for they were bitter. EX. XV. 23.

Hast thou come, my friend, in thy wilderness way, to the place of bitter waters? Canst thou not drink of the stream, even though thy thirst be burning and thy strength be wasted? Know thou, there is a tree the leaves of which are for the healing of the nations! A tree? Truly so; but a tree as yet without a leaf,—a tree bare as the frosts and the winds of the winter can make it,—the great, grim, dear, sad, wondrous cross of the Son of God! Some have sought to touch the wells of life with other trees, but have only aggravated the disease which they sought to cure. By the grace of heaven, others have been enabled to apply the Cross to the bitter wells of their sin and grief, and behold the waters have become clear as the crystal river which flows fast by the throne of God! JOSEPH PARKER.

EX.
xv. 25.

The Lord shewed him a tree, which when he had cast into the waters, the waters were made sweet.

Beside each bitter Marah pool there grows a tree, which, when cast into the waters, makes them palatable and sweet. It is ever so. Poison and antidote, infection and cure, pain and medicine, are always close together. The word which saves is nigh even in the mouth and in the heart. We do not always see the "sufficient grace"; but it is there. Too occupied with our disappointment, we have no heart to seek it; but when we cry, it is shown to our weary longing eyes.

F. B. MEYER.

EX.
xvi.29.

The Lord hath given you the Sabbath.

Through the week, we go down into the valleys of care and shadow. Our sabbaths should be hills of light and joy in God's presence; and so, as time rolls by, we shall go on from mountain-top to mountain-top, till at last we catch the glory of the gate, and enter in to go no more out forever. BEECHER.

EX.
xvi.31.

The manna . . . was . . . white; and the taste of it was like wafers made with honey.
The manna was . . . as the color of bdellium . . . and the taste of it was as the taste of fresh oil.—Num. xi. 7, 8.

How could a soul which has tried again to satisfy

28

itself with Egypt's food, find manna the *same* thing after restoration? The pure and sweet manna which has sustained the *virgin* soul which has unwaveringly followed the guiding pillar, must for the *restored* soul, have its color changed into that of *tried* gold, and its taste to that of *healing* oil. Nothing else would supply its need now.

Thou shall smite the rock, and there shall come water out of it. EX. xvii. 6.

This is strange! A rock would seem the last place to choose for the storage of water. But God's cupboards are in very unlikely places. Ravens bring food. The Prime Minister of Egypt gives corn. Cyrus lets go the people of Israel from Babylon. The Jordan heals the leper. Meal makes poisoned pottage wholesome. Wood makes iron swim. . . . It is worth while to go to Rephidim to get an insight into the fertility and inventiveness of God's providence. There can be no lack to them that fear Him, and no fear of lack to those who have become acquainted with His secret storehouses. "Eye hath not seen, nor ear heard . . . the things which God hath prepared for them that love Him; but God hath revealed them unto us by His Spirit." F. B. MEYER.

Thou shalt have no other gods before me. EX. XX. 3.

If you find yourself beginning to love any pleasure better than your prayers, any book better than the Bible, any house better than the House of God, any table better than the Lord's table, any person better than Christ, or any indulgence better than the Pope of Heaven—take alarm. GUTHRIE.

29

One Thousand and One

EX.
XX. 21. *Moses drew near unto the thick darkness where God was.*

How wonderfully life loses all fear to the soul that has been called apart, alone, into some darkness and has found God there. "Morning dawns from His face," and what light is like the light that rises upon those who touch God's right hand in the darkness and are lifted up and strengthened? G. GUINNESS.

EX.
xxviii.
1. *Take . . . Aaron . . . that he may minister unto me in the priest's office.*
And Aaron . . . made . . . a golden calf.
—Ex. xxxii. 2, 4.

Do we not see how God's purposes are thwarted and deferred by human perversity? . . . At the very time when God had determined upon the election and consecration of Aaron to the priesthood, Aaron was spending his time in moulding and chiselling the golden calf. . . . We might have been crowned fifty years ago, but just as the coronation was about to take place we were discovered in the manufacture of an idol. . . . The Lord was just ready to make kings of us when we made fools of ourselves.

JOSEPH PARKER.

EX.
xxviii.
2. *Thou shalt make holy garments for Aaron . . . for glory and for beauty.*
Ye are . . . a royal priesthood.—1 Peter ii. 9.

And have we no ornaments? The ornaments of the meek and quiet spirit is in the sight of God of great price. And have we no garments of blue, and purple, and beautiful suggestiveness? We have garments of praise; we are clothed with the Lord Jesus. And have we no golden bells? We have the golden bells of holy actions. Our words are bells, our actions are bells, our purposes are bells; wherever we move our motion is thus understood to be a motion toward holy places, holy deeds, holy character. JOSEPH PARKER.

Moses . . . went down from the mount. . . .
    As soon as he . . . saw the calf and the danc-
ing . . . Moses' anger waxed hot. EX. xxxii. 15, 19.

When you have been sitting in a well-lighted room, and are suddenly called into the outer darkness, how black it seems; and thus, when a man has dwelt in communion with God, sin becomes exceeding sinful, and the darkness in which the world lieth appears like tenfold night. SPURGEON.

My presence shall go with thee. EX. xxxiii. 14.

Some of us think and say a good deal about "a sense of His presence"; sometimes rejoicing in it, sometimes going mourning all the day long because we have it not; praying for it, and not always seeming to receive what we ask; measuring our own position, and sometimes even that of others by it; now on the heights, now in the depths about it. And all this April-like gleam and gloom instead of steady summer glow, because we are turning our attention upon the *sense* of His presence, instead of the changeless *reality* of it! FRANCES RIDLEY HAVERGAL.

Come up in the morning . . . and present thyself
unto me in the top of the mount. EX. xxxiv. 2.

God wishes me to be alone with Him. How solemn will the meeting be! Father and child; Sovereign and subject; Creator and creature! The distance between us will be infinite, unless He shorten it by

His mercy! Oh! my poor broken and weary heart, think of it and be glad; God wants thee to meet Him alone! He will heal thy wounds; He will shed His light upon thy tears, and make them shine like jewels; He will make thee young again. Oh that I might be on the mountain first, and that praise might be waiting for God! I will be astir before the sun; I will be far on the road before the dew rises; and long before the bird sings will I breathe my sweet hymn. Oh, dark night, flee fast, for I would see God and hear still more of His deep truth! Oh! ye stars, why stay so long? Ye are the seals of night, but it is for other light I pine, the light that shows the way to the Mount of God. My Father, I am coming; nothing on the mean plain shall keep me away from the holy heights: help me to climb fast, and keep Thou my foot, lest it fall upon the hard rock. At Thy bidding I come, so Thou wilt not mock my heart. Bring with Thee honey from heaven, yea, milk and wine, and oil for my soul's good, and stay the sun in his course, or the time will be too short in which to look upon Thy face, and to hear Thy gentle voice. Morning on the mount! It will make me strong and glad all the rest of the day so well begun! JOSEPH PARKER.

The morning is the time fixed for my meeting the Lord. What meaning there is in the *time* as well as in the place! This very word *morning* is as a cluster of rich grapes. Let me crush them and drink the sacred wine. In the morning—then God means me to be at my best in strength and hope; I have not to climb in my weakness; in the night I have buried yesterday's fatigue, and in the morning I take a new lease of energy. Give God thy strength—*all* thy

Thoughts from My Library

strength; He asks only what He first gave. In the morning—then He may mean to keep me long that He may make me rich! In the morning—then it is no endless road He bids me climb, else how could I reach it ere the sun be set? Sweet morning! There is hope in its music.

Blessed is the day whose morning is sanctified. Successful is the day whose first victory was won by prayer. Holy is the day whose dawn finds thee on the top of the mount! Health is established in the morning. Wealth is won in the morning. The light is brightest in the morning. "Wake psaltery and harp, I myself will awake early." JOSEPH PARKER.

Moses wist not that . . . his face shone EX. xxxiv. 29.

I charge you, be clothed with humility, or you will yet be a wandering star, for whom is reserved the blackness of darkness forever. Let Christ increase, let man decrease. Remember, "Moses wist not that the skin of his face shone." Looking at our own shining face is the bane of the spiritual life, and of the ministry. Oh for closest communion with God, till soul and body, head and heart, shine with divine brilliancy! But oh for a holy ignorance of their shining! M'CHEYNE.

The fire shall ever be burning upon the altar: it shall never go out. LEV. vi. 13.

As the fire never went out on the altar of burnt-offering, so Christians ought to be continually engaged in the service of God. CAWDRAY.

The Urim (light) *and the Thummim* (perfection). LEV. viii. 8.

What the Urim and the Thummim actually were no

man has been able to find out. But whatever they were, there can be no doubt as to what our Urim and Thummim are. We are not left without light and perfection. . . . Our Urim and Thummim are the Old and New Testaments. Keep these in the heart; be at home with them in all their wondrous variety of speech, of doctrine, of song, of inspiration, and of instruction of every kind; and then you never can stray far from the path providential that makes its own course straight up to the God who started the mysterious outgoing. JOSEPH PARKER.

LEV. X. 10. *That ye may put difference between holy and unholy, and between unclean and clean.*

A holy calling will never save an unholy man.
RYLE.

LEV. xi. 44. *Ye shall be holy, for I am holy.*

Prove your godliness by your Godlikeness.
PUNSHON.

LEV. xxiii. 44. *Moses declared unto the children of Israel the feasts of the Lord.*

The feasts of the Lord. This was their true character, their original title; but in the Gospel of John, they are called *"feasts of the Jews."* They had long ceased to be Jehovah's feasts. He was shut out. They did not want Him; and hence, in John vii., when Jesus was asked to go up to *"the Jews' feast of tabernacles"* He answered, "My time is not yet come"; and when He did go up it was "privately," to take His place outside of the whole thing, and to call upon every thirsty soul to come unto Him and drink. There is a solemn lesson in this. Divine in-

Thoughts from My Library

stitutions are speedily marred in the hands of man; but, oh! how deeply blessed to know that the thirsty soul that feels the barrenness and drought connected with a scene of empty religious formality, has only to flee to Jesus and drink freely of His exhaustless springs, and so become a channel of blessing to others. C. H. McINTOSH.

The consecration of His God is upon his head. NUM.

Consecration is going out into the world where God vi. 7. Almighty is, and using every power for His glory.

At the commandment of the Lord the children of Israel NUM. *journeyed, and at the commandment of the Lord* ix. 18. *they pitched.*

This is the secret of peace and calm elevation. If an Israelite in the desert, had taken it into his head to make some movement, independent of Jehovah; if he took it upon him to move when the cloud was at rest, or to halt while the cloud was moving, we can easily see what the result would have been. And so it will ever be with us. If we move when we ought to rest, or rest when we ought to move, we shall not have the divine presence with us. " At the commandment of the Lord they rested in the tents, and at the commandment of the Lord they journeyed." They were kept in constant waiting upon God, the most blessed position that any one can occupy; but it must be occupied ere its blessedness can be tasted. It is a reality to be known, not a mere theory to be talked of. May it be ours to prove it all our journey through! C. H. McINTOSH.

Trumpets of silver . . . for the calling of the NUM. *assembly, and for the journeying of the camps.* X. 2.

The silver trumpet ordered and settled every movement for Israel of old. The testimony of God ought to settle and order everything for the Church now. A Christian has no right to move or act apart from divine testimony. He must wait upon the word of his Lord. Till he gets that he must stand still. When he has got it he must go forward. God can and does communicate His mind to His militant people now, just as distinctly as He did to His people of old. True, it is not by the sound of a trumpet, or the movement of a cloud, but by His Word and Spirit. It is not by aught that strikes the senses that our Father guides us, but by that which acts in the heart, the conscience and the understanding.   C. H. McINTOSH.

NUM. *And when the dew fell upon the camp in the night, the*
xi. 9. *manna fell upon it.*

The manna was so pure and delicate that it could not bear contact with earth. It fell upon the dew, and had to be gathered ere the sun was up. Each one, therefore, had to rise early and seek his daily portion. So it is with the people of God now. The heavenly manna must be gathered fresh every morning. Yesterday's manna will not do for to-day, or to-day's for to-morrow. We must feed upon Christ every day, with fresh energy of the spirit, else we shall cease to grow. Moreover, we must make Christ our primary object. We must seek Him "early."   C. H. McINTOSH.

NUM. *I am not able to bear all this people alone, because it is*
xi. 14. *too heavy for me.*

It is most needful for all servants of Christ to remember, that whenever the Lord places a man in a position of responsibility, He will both fit him for it and maintain him in it. It is, of course, another thing

altogether if a man *will* rush unsent into any field of
work, or any post of difficulty or danger. In such a
case, we may assuredly look for a thorough break
down, sooner or later. But when God calls a man to
a certain position, He will endow him with the needed
grace to occupy it. He never sends any one a warfare
at his own charges; and therefore all we have to do is
to draw upon Him for all we need. This holds good in
every case. We can never fail if we only cling to the
living God. We can never run dry, if we are drawing
from the fountain. Our tiny springs will soon dry up;
but our Lord Jesus Christ declares that, "He that believeth in me, as the Scripture hath said, out of his belly
shall flow rivers of living water." C. H. McINTOSH.

We saw the giants, . . . and we were in our own   NUM.
sight as grasshoppers, and so we were in their sight.   xiii. 33.

The ten spies differed from Caleb and Joshua in their
report of the land of Canaan. There are three words
here beginning with G—the word "God," the word
"giant," and the word "grasshopper." Now, note,
these spies made a great mistake as to the position of
these three words; they compared themselves with the
people of the land and said, "And in their sight we
were as grasshoppers." If they had compared the
people of the land with God, they would have come
back, as Caleb and Joshua did, who said in effect,
"We have compared the giants with God, and the
giants are as grasshoppers." F. B. MEYER.

The daughters of Zelophehad speak right.   NUM.
They always do so. Their words are words of   xxvii.
faith, and, as such, are always right in the judgment   7.
of God. It is a terrible thing to limit "the Holy One

37

of Israel." He delights to be trusted and used. It is utterly impossible for faith to overdraw its account in God's bank. God could no more disappoint faith than He could deny Himself. He can never say to faith, "You have miscalculated; you take too lofty,—too bold a stand; go lower down, and lessen your expectations." Ah! no; the only thing in all this world that truly delights and refreshes the heart of God is the faith that can simply trust Him; and we may rest assured of this, that the faith that can trust Him is also the faith that can love Him, and serve Him, and praise Him.   C. H. McINTOSH.

DEUT. *Now therefore hearken, O Israel, unto the statutes and*
iv. 1. *unto the judgments which I teach you, for to do them,*
        that ye may live, and go in and possess the land
        which the Lord God of your fathers giveth you.

"Hearken" and "do," that ye may "live" and "possess." This is a universal and abiding principle. It was true for Israel and it is true for us. The pathway of life and the true secret of possession is simple obedience to the holy commandments of God. We see this all through the inspired volume, from cover to cover. God has given us His Word, not to speculate upon it or discuss it, but that we may obey it. And it is as we, through grace, yield a hearty and happy obedience to our Father's statutes and judgments, that we tread the bright pathway of life, and enter into the reality of all that God has treasured up for us in Christ. "He that hath my commandments, and keepeth them, he it is that loveth me; and he that loveth me shall be loved of my Father, and I will love him, and will manifest myself to him."   C. H. McINTOSH.

Thoughts from My Library

Observe and hear all these words which I command DEUT.
thee, that it may go well with thee. xii. 28.

The constitution of man and the law of God are
fitted into each other like lock and key. ARNOT.

The Lord your God proveth you, to know whether ye DEUT.
love the Lord your God with all your heart and with xiii. 3.
all your soul.

We may observe in this the difference between
Christ and the Tempter. Christ hath His fan in His
hand, and He fanneth us: the Devil has a sieve in his
hand, and he sifteth us. Now, a fan casteth out the
worst, and keepeth in the best; a sieve keepeth in the
worst, and casteth out the best. So Christ and His
trials purgeth chaff and corruption out of us, and
nourisheth His graces in us. Contrariwise, the Devil,
what evil soever is in us, he confirmeth it: what faith
or good thing soever, he weakeneth it. TRAPP.

Ye are the children of the Lord your God. DEUT.

A child of God should be a *visible beatitude*, for joy xiv. 1.
and happiness, and a *living Doxology* for gratitude and
adoration. SPURGEON.

As for thee, the Lord thy God hath not suffered thee so DEUT.
to do. xviii.

We give thanks often with a tearful, doubtful voice 14.
for our spiritual mercies *positive ;* but what an almost
infinite field there is for mercies *negative !* We cannot
even imagine all that God has suffered us *not* to do,
not to be. FRANCES RIDLEY HAVERGAL.

The secret things belong unto the Lord our God. DEUT.

Be not curious to search into the secrets of God; xxix.
29.

pick not the lock where He hath allowed no key. He that will be sifting every cloud may be smitten with a thunderbolt; and he that will be too familiar with God's secrets may be overwhelmed in his judgments. Adam would curiously increase his knowledge; therefore Adam shamefully lost his goodness: the Bethshemites would needs pry into the ark of God; therefore the hand of God slew about fifty thousand of them. Therefore hover not about this flame, lest we scorch our wings. For my part, seeing God hath made me His secretary, I will carefully improve myself by what He has revealed, and not curiously inquire into or after what He hath reserved.   ADAMS.

DEUT. *Moses made an end of speaking.*
xxxii.
45.   So we all shall do some day. Moses knew it was the end for him; we may not know when our end is at hand. Any word of ours, spoken amid glee and merriment, may be our last. If we always thought of this would it not make us more careful? Would we ever say an unkind word to a friend, if we felt that we may never have an opportunity to unsay it or atone for it? Would we ever utter an angry, untrue, or unclean word, if we only remembered that it may be the last utterance our lips shall give forth? We want to have beautiful endings to our life, to leave sweet memories behind us in the hearts of those who love us. We want our names to be fragrant in the homes on whose thresholds our footfalls are wont to be heard. We want the memory of our last words in our friends' ears to live as a tender joy with them as the days pass away. We can be sure of all this only by making every word we speak beautiful enough to

be our last word.   For with any sentence we may come to the end of our speaking.   J. R. MILLER.

The beloved of the Lord.

Who is the beloved of the Lord?   It is one who believes in the love that God has toward him.   . . . Peter had a great idea of his own love to Christ; "though all men forsake thee, yet will I not forsake thee"; but John was content to speak of himself as the beloved of the Lord.   "O Daniel, greatly beloved," said the angel to that man of God.   . . . Do you hesitate to class yourself with Daniel and John?   Tell me, is there any greater expression of the love of God, than was given in the surrender of His Son to Gethsemane, Gabbatha, and Calvary?   Did Daniel or John ever receive any more affecting love token than this?   Be only bold enough to know the love that was expressed when Christ tasted death for you, and you may without hesitation sit down beneath the same tree with Daniel and John, and expect them to listen while you speak of the Crucified One.

BOWEN.

DEUT. xxxiii. 12.

Thy shoes shall be iron and brass; and as thy days so shall thy strength be.

Each of us may be sure that if God sends us on stony paths He will provide us with strong shoes, and will not send us out on any journey for which He does not equip us well.   ALEX. McLAREN.

DEUT. xxxiii. 25.

As thy days so shall thy strength be.

Watch your way, as a cautious traveller; and don't be gazing at that mountain or river in the distance, and saying: "How shall I ever get over them?" but keep

DEUT. xxxiii. 25.

to the present *little inch* that is before you, and accomplish *that* in the little moment that belongs to it. The mountain and the river can only be passed in the same way; and when you come to them, you will come to the light and strength that belong to them.

M. A. KELTY.

DEUT. xxxiii. 25. *As thy days so shall thy strength be.*
I can do all things through Christ which strengtheneth me.—Phil. iv. 13.

He will not impose upon you one needless burden; He will not exact more than He knows your strength will bear; He will ask no Peter to come to Him on the water, unless He impart at the same time strength and support on the unstable wave; He will not ask you to draw water if the well is too deep, or withdraw the stone if too heavy. But neither at the same time will He admit as an impossibility that which, as a free and responsible agent, it is in your power to avert. He will not regard as your misfortune what is your crime.

MACDUFF.

DEUT. xxxiii. 27. *The eternal God.*

Time is the age of the visible world; but eternity is the age of God. CHRISTMAS EVANS.

DEUT. xxxiii. 27. *The eternal God is thy refuge.*

God is a perpetual refuge and security to His people. His providence is not confined to one generation; it is not one age only that tastes of His bounty and compassion. His eye never yet slept, nor hath He suffered the little ship of His church to be swallowed up, though it hath been tossed upon the waves; He hath always been a haven to preserve us, a house to secure us; He hath always had compassion to pity us, and power to protect us; He hath had a face to shine, when the world hath had an angry countenance to frown. He brought Enoch home by an extraordinary translation from a brutish world; and when He was resolved to reckon with men for their brutish lives, He lodged Noah, the phœnix of the world, in an ark, and kept him alive as a spark in the midst of many waters, whereby to rekindle a church in the world; in all generations He is a dwelling-place to secure His people here or entertain them above.　　　　CHARNOCK.

Moses was an hundred and twenty years old when he died. 　　　DEUT. xxxiv. 7.

Moses' life consisted of one hundred and twenty years, divided into three forties.

In the first forty years, he was learning to be somebody.

In the second forty years, he was learning to be nobody.

In the third forty years, he was proving what God could do with a man who had learned those two lessons.

Arise, go over this Jordan. 　　　JOSH. i. 2.

The supreme enquiry for each of us, when summoned to a new work, is—not whether we possess sufficient strength or qualification for it, but—if we have been called to it of God; and when that is so, there is no further cause for anxiety.—If it is in His plan that we should march through a river, or attack a walled town, or turn to flight an army, we have simply to go forward. He will make the mountains a way. Rivers will dry up; walls will fall down; armies shall be scattered as snow in Salmon. There is no such thing as impossibility when God says, "Forward, soul; arise, go over this Jordan!"   F. B. MEYER.

JOSH. *Every place that the sole of your foot shall tread upon,*
i. 3. *that have I given unto you.*

But though this was so, each square mile of it had to be claimed from the hand of the peoples that possessed it. "The soul of the foot" had to be put down to claim and take. The cities were theirs, but they must enter them; the houses which they had not built were theirs, but they must inhabit them. The cornfields in the rich vales, and vineyards on the terraced slopes were theirs, but they must possess them. It is not difficult for us to realize these things, for spiritually we occupy a precisely similar position. God our Father hath blessed us with all spiritual blessings in Christ Jesus; but they are not ours to enjoy, until we have claimed and appropriated them by a living faith. They are only ours as we avail ourselves of them. Hence the need to "be strong and very courageous."   F. B. MEYER.

JOSH. *Only be thou strong and very courageous.*
i. 7.   Man is larger and stronger than his environment. No burden was ever heavy enough to crush manhood out. No sorrow was ever greater than the heart can bear. God never made a coward, nor has He anywhere held up as a model a nature that would break under sorrow. The whole Book of Job centres around this single test: that no affliction or evil could crush him. Man is not a worm to be trodden down, but a child of God. He is made to have dominion, to put all things under his feet. The agonies of Gethsemane may fall with frightful weight, but they cannot crush him. The cross will hurt, but cannot harm.   D. O. MEARS.

44

Thoughts from My Library

JOSH. ii. 18.

This line of scarlet thread.

In the British navy there is a scarlet thread running through every line of cordage, and though a rope be cut into inch pieces, it can be recognized as belonging to the government. So is there a scarlet thread running all through the Bible—the whole book points to Christ. In the promise made to Adam appears, as it were, the first twig of the tree. Twig after twig is added, till we can count not only 200 direct promises of the Messiah, but 1,500, direct and indirect. Then as history comes to fulfill these predictions, each little twig in turn is set on fire, yet not consumed, till finally the whole tree becomes a great burning bush, and we take off our shoes and stand in awe, for it is holy ground. A. T. PIERSON.

JOSH. iii. 15, 16.

As . . . the feet of the priests that bare the ark were dipped in the brim of the water . . . the waters . . . rose up . . . and were cut off; and the people passed over right against Jericho.

Keep in fellowship with the Apostle and High Priest of your profession. Consider Him. Look away from all else to Him. Follow Him. It may seem as if He is leading thee into certain destruction; but it shall not be so. When thou comest to the dreaded difficulty, be it what it may, thou wilt find that because His feet have been dipped in its brink, it has dwindled in its flow. Its roar is hushed; its waters are shrunken; its violence is gone. The iron gate stands open. The stone is rolled away from the sepulchre. The river-bed is dry. Jericho is within reach. "They passed over right against Jericho." F. B. MEYER.

One Thousand and One

JOSH.
vii. 4.
They fled before the men of Ai.

The defeats that we incur in the Land of Promise are not necessary. They are due entirely to some failure in ourselves, and they cause grief to the immortal Lover of our souls. There is no reason for defeat in the Christian life; always and everywhere we are meant to be more than conquerors. The course of the Christian warrior should be as the sun when he goeth forth in his strength, and in regular gradients drives his chariot from the eastern wave up the steep of heaven. Child of God, never lay the blame of thy failure on God; seek for it within!   F. B. MEYER.

JOSH.
vii. 13.
Thou canst not stand before thine enemies until ye take away the accursed thing from among you.

No rush to battle atones for sin in the tent.

G. CAMPBELL MORGAN.

JOSH.
xxiii.
10.
One man of you shall chase a thousand: for the Lord your God, he it is that fighteth for you, as he hath promised you.

If God fought for victory He need never fight; He fights that He may teach.   JOSEPH PARKER.

JOSH.
xxiv.
15.
Choose you this day whom ye will serve.

CHOICE and SERVICE—these were demanded of the Israelites, these are demanded of you, these only. Choice and service—in these are the whole of life.

MARK HOPKINS.

JUDG.
v. 23.
Curse ye Meroz, said the angel of the Lord; curse ye bitterly the inhabitants thereof; because they came not to the help of the Lord . . . against the mighty.

"Curse ye Meroz. By whose authority? The angel

46

of the Lord's. What has Meroz done? Nothing.
Why then is Meroz to be cursed? Because he did
nothing. What ought Meroz to have done? Come
to the help of the Lord. Could not the Lord do without Meroz? The Lord did do without Meroz. Did
the Lord sustain, then, any loss? No, but Meroz did.
Is Meroz then to be cursed? Yes, and that bitterly.
Is it right that a man should be cursed for doing nothing? Yes, when he ought to do something. Who
says so? The angel of the Lord. 'That servant which
knew his Lord's will, and did it not, shall be beaten
with many stripes.'"

Bring them down unto the water, and I will try them JUDG.
for thee there. vii. 4.

The way the men drank water from the brook was
the test of their fitness for the work of conquering the
Midianites. It seemed to make the smallest difference
in the world whether a soldier drank by bowing down
with his face in the water, or by lapping up the water
with his hand as he stood; yet it was a difference
that settled the question of fitness or unfitness for the
great work before the army. It is in just such little
ways, and in such matters of everyday and commonplace action, conduct, and manner, that God is always
testing us and deciding whether we are fit or unfit for
the greater work for which He is seeking men. .
. . We cannot know what future honor may depend on the way we do the simplest, most commonplace thing to-day. J. R. MILLER.

(Hannah) . . . *prayed unto the Lord, and wept* I SAM.
sore . . . *she spake in her heart.* i. 10,
For real business at the mercy-seat give me a home- 13.

47

made prayer, a prayer that comes out of the depths of my heart, not because I invented it, but because God the Holy Ghost put it there, and gave it such living force that I could not help letting it out. Though your words are broken, and your sentences disconnected, if your desires are earnest, if they are like coals of juniper, burning with a vehement flame, God will not mind how they find expression. If you have no words, perhaps you will pray better without them than with them. There are prayers that break the backs of words; they are too heavy for any human language to carry. SPURGEON.

I SAM. ii. 3.
The Lord is a God of knowledge, and by him actions are weighed.

Regard not how *full* hands, but how *pure* hands you bring to God. TAYLOR.

God does not measure what we bring to Him. He *weighs* it. MARK GUY PEARSE.

I SAM. ii. 6.
He bringeth down to the grave.

The grave is the great city. It hath mightier population, longer streets, thicker darknesses than any other. Cæsar is there, and all his subjects. Nero is there, and all his victims. City of kings and paupers! City of silence! no voice, no hoof, no wheel, no smiting of hammer, no loom, no whisper. Of all its million million hands, not one is ever lifted. Of all its million million eyes, not one ever sparkles. Of all its million million hearts, not one ever pulsates. TALMAGE.

I SAM. xvi. 14.
An evil spirit from the Lord troubled him.
My peace I give unto you.—John xiv. 27.

Let God once wound a heart, all the world cannot

48

heal it; but let Christ speak peace to it, all the world cannot disturb it. CHARLES BRADLEY.

There is but a step between me and death. I SAM. XX. 3.

The *nearness* of heaven is suggested by the epithet " veil." Christians, there is only a veil between us and heaven! A veil is the thinnest and frailest of all conceivable partitions. It is but a fine tissue, a delicate fabric of embroidery. It waves in the wind; the touch of a child may stir it, and accident may rend it; the silent action of time will moulder it away. The veil that conceals heaven is only our embodied existence; and, though fearfully and wonderfully made, it is only wrought out of our frail mortality. So slight is it, that the puncture of a thorn, the touch of an insect's sting, the breath of an infected atmosphere, may make it shake and fall. In a bound, in a moment, in the twinkling of an eye, in the throb of a pulse, in the flash of a thought, we may start into disembodied spirits, glide unabashed into the company of great and mighty angels, pass into the light and amazement of eternity, know the great secret, gaze upon splendors which flesh and blood could not sustain, and which no words lawful for man to utter could describe! Brethren in Christ, there is but a step between you and death; between you and heaven there is but a veil!

C. STANFORD.

It came to pass in the morning that David wrote a let- II SAM. *ter to Joab.* xi. 14.

We sleep: but the loom of life never stops; and the pattern which was weaving when the sun went down is weaving when it comes up to-morrow.

BEECHER.

49

One Thousand and One

II SAM.
XV. 15. *Thy servants are ready to do whatsoever my Lord the king shall appoint.*

If we are really and always and equally ready to do whatsoever the king appoints, all the trials and vexations, arising from any change in His appointments, great or small, simply do not exist. If He appoints me to work there, shall I lament that I am not to work here ? If He appoints me to wait indoors to-day, am I to be annoyed because I am not to work out of doors ? If I meant to *write* His messages this morning, shall I grumble because He sends interrupting visitors, rich or poor, to whom I am to *speak* them, or "show kindness" for His sake, or at least obey His command "Be courteous" ? If all my members are really at His disposal, why should I be put out if to-day's appointment is some simple work for my hands, or errands for my feet, instead of some seemingly more important doing of head or tongue ?

FRANCES RIDLEY HAVERGAL.

II SAM.
xviii.
9. *The mule that was under him went away.*

The things of this world, like Absalom's mule, run away and leave us when we have most need of them.

VENNING.

II SAM.
xxii.
19. *The Lord was my stay.*

When I first amused myself with going out to sea, when the winds arose and the waves became a little rough I found a difficulty to keep my legs on the deck, for I tumbled and tossed about like a porpoise on the water. At last I caught hold of a rope that was floating about, and then I was enabled to stand upright. So when in prayer a multitude of troublous thoughts invade your peace, or when the winds and waves of temptation arise, look out for the rope, lay hold of it, and stay yourself on the faithfulness of God in His covenant with His people and in His promises. Hold fast by that rope, and you shall stand. SALTER.

Who is a rock save our God?

God is a rock for a *foundation*. Build your lives, your thoughts, your efforts, your hopes there. The house founded on the rock will stand though wind and rain from above smite it, and floods from beneath beat on it like battering rams. God is a rock for a *fortress*. Flee to Him to hide, and your defence shall be the "munition of rocks," which shall laugh to scorn all assault, and never be scorned by any foe. God is a rock for *shade* and *refreshment*. Come close to Him out of the scorching heat, and you will find coolness, and verdure and moisture in the clefts, when all outside that grateful shadow is parched and dry.

McLAREN.

II SAM. xxii. 32.

Although my house be not so with God; yet he hath made with me an everlasting covenant.

An old commentator says " There is an 'although' in every man's lot and life." Paul was the mightiest of preachers, the noblest of spiritual heroes, but he had his "although," for "there was given to" him "a thorn in the flesh." Jonah was "exceeding glad of the gourd," but a vile insect lurked unseen at its root. Ezekiel soared as few prophets did, with bold wing, amid the magnificent visions of Providence and Grace, but "the desire of" his "eyes" was taken away "with a stroke." . . . But the "althoughs" of life are generally qualified by some "yet." Listen to the psalmist's testimony again. "All thy waves and

II SAM. xxiii. 5.

thy billows are gone over me. *Yet* the Lord will command His loving kindness in the daytime and in the night His song shall be with me." Habbakuk mourns over the fig-tree without blossom, vines withered and fruitless. " *Yet,*" he adds, "will I glory in the Lord and rejoice in the God of my salvation." And is it not so with all God's true people? The *"yets"* outbalance and overbalance the " *althoughs.*" The bitter cup has its sweet drops, the dark night its clustering stars of consolation and solace, the "valley of Baca" its wells of joy. MACDUFF.

I KINGS ii. 38.

As my lord the king hath said, so will thy servant do.

What God wants is men great enough to be small enough to be used. H. WEBB-PEPLOE.

I KINGS vi. 7.

There was neither hammer, nor axe, nor any tool of iron, heard in the house while it was in building.

You know that in Solomon's temple there was no sound of hammer heard; for the stones were made ready in the quarries, and brought all shaped and marked so that the masons might know the exact spot in which they were to be placed; so that no sound of iron was needed. All the planks and timbers were carried to their right places, and all the catches with which they were to be linked together were prepared, so that there might not be even the driving of a nail—everything was ready beforehand. It is the same with us. When we get to heaven, there will be no sanctifying us there, no squaring us with affliction, no hammering us with the rod, no making us meet there. We must be made meet here; and blessed be His name, all *that* Christ will do beforehand.

SPURGEON.

Thoughts from My Library

Elijah . . . said unto Ahab, As the Lord God of Israel liveth, before whom I stand, there shall not be dew nor rain these years, but according to my word.   I KINGS xvii. 1.

Our boldness for God before the world must always be the result of individual dealing with God in secret. Our victories over self, and sin, and the world, are always first fought where no eye sees but God's. . .

If there be the daily work going on within us, unseen and unnoticed by any but God Himself, then we may depend upon certain victory in our conflicts before the world—then may we stand before an Ahab, and realize a living God at our side. . . . And if we have not these secret conflicts, well may we not have any open ones. The *outward* absence of conflict betrays the *inward* sleep of the soul.   WHITFIELD.

Hide thyself by the brook.   I KINGS xvii. 3.

Not by the *river*, but by the *brook*. The river would always contain an abundant supply, but the brook might dry up at any moment. What does this teach us? God does not place His people in luxuriance here. The world's abundance might withdraw their affections from Him. He gives them not the river but the brook. The brook may be running to-day, to-morrow it may be dried up. And wherefore does God act thus! To teach us that we are not to rest in His gifts and blessings, but in Himself. This is what our hearts are always doing—resting in the gift instead of the Giver. Therefore God cannot trust us by the river for it unconsciously takes up His place in the heart. It is said of Israel, that when they were full they forgot God.   WHITFIELD.

One Thousand and One

I KINGS xvii. 10.

So he arose and went to Zarephath.

Let it be equally said of you to whatever duty the Lord may call you away, "He arose and went!" Be the way ever so laborious or dangerous, still arise, like Elijah, and go. Go cheerfully, *in faith*, keeping your heart quietly dependent on the Lord, and in the end you will assuredly behold and sing of His goodness. Though tossed on a sea of troubles, you may anchor on the firm foundation of God, which standeth sure. You have for your security His exceeding great and precious promises, and may say with the psalmist, "Why art thou cast down, O my soul? and why art thou disquieted within me? hope thou in God: for I shall yet praise Him who is the health of my countenance and my God!" F. W. KRUMMACHER.

I KINGS xvii. 16.

The barrel of meat wasted not, neither did the cruse of oil fail.

God never leaves us in His debt. He takes care to pay for His entertainment, royally and divinely. He uses Peter's fishing smack, and gives it back, nearly submerged by the weight of the fish which He had driven into the nets. He sits down with His friends to a country marriage-feast, and pays for their simple fare by jars brimming with water turned to wine. He uses the five barley loaves, and two small fishes; but He fills the lad with an ample meal. He sends His prophet to lodge with a widow, and provides meal and oil for him and her for many days. F. B. MEYER.

I KINGS xviii. 17, 18.

Ahab said unto (Elijah) Art thou he that troubleth Israel? And he answered, I have not troubled Israel; but thou and thy father's house.

A minister without boldness is like a smooth file, a

knife without an edge, a sentinel that is afraid to let off his gun. If men will be bold in sin, ministers must be bold to reprove.   GURNALL.

Fill four barrels with water and pour it on the burnt sacrifice and on the wood.   I KINGS xviii. 33.

Few of us have faith like this! We are not so sure of God that we dare to pile difficulties in His way. We all try our best to make it easy for Him to help us. Yet what Elijah had, we too may have, by prayer and fasting.   F. B. MEYER.

Elijah . . . cast himself down upon the earth, and put his face between his knees.   I KINGS xviii. 42.

The man who is to take a high place before his fellows must take a low place before his God.

F. B. MEYER.

The men who stand straightest in the presence of sin bow lowest in the presence of God.

F. B. MEYER.

Elijah went up to the top of Carmel; and he cast himself down upon the earth, and put his face between his knees. . . . And the hand of the Lord was on Elijah: and he girded up his loins, and ran before Ahab to the entrance of Jezreel.   I KINGS xviii. 42, 46.

In driving piles, a machine is used by which a huge weight is lifted up and then made to fall upon the head of the pile. Of course the higher the weight is lifted the more powerful is the blow which it gives when it descends. Now, if we would tell upon our age and come down upon society with ponderous blows, we must see to it that we are uplifted as near to God as possible. All our power will depend upon the elevation of our spirits. Prayer, meditation, devotion, communion, are like a windlass to wind us up aloft: it is not lost time which we spend in such sacred exercises, for we are thus accumulating force, so that when we come down to our actual labor for God, we shall descend with an energy unknown to those to whom communion is unknown.

SPURGEON.

I KINGS *He arose and went for his life.*
xix. 3. *Anoint . . . Elisha . . . to be prophet in thy room.—1 Kings xix. 15, 16.*

What might have been! If only Elijah had held his ground he might have saved his country, and there would have been no necessity for the captivity and dispersion of his people. The seven thousand secret disciples would have dared to come forth from their hiding-places and avow themselves, and would have constituted a nucleus of loyal hearts by whom Baal had been replaced by Jehovah. . . . Elijah's influence in Israel never recovered from that one false step. He missed a chance which never came again. And though God in His mercy treated him lovingly and royally as a child, He never again reinstated him as a servant in just the same position which he so thoughtlessly flung away. It is a solemn thought for us all. As children, we may be forgiven; as servants, we may never be reinstated or trusted quite as we were once. . . . As children, God will never cast us away; but as His servants He may, employing us only in some humble ministry, or to anoint our successors. . . . Others shall finish our uncompleted task.

F. B. MEYER.

Thoughts from My Library

He lay and slept under a juniper tree. I KINGS xix. 5.

Even in the midst of the desert our gracious God is able to provide for us a place of repose; the storm does not rage incessantly; peaceful hours intervene unawares, and the burden upon our shoulders becomes for a while a resting pillow to our heads, upon which we insensibly gather recruited strength. . . . The very days of storm and tempest have their hours of repose and mercy. Therefore let no one be anxious, however steep and thorny his path, however rough and dreary his road. When the weary knees are ready to sink, God will know how to provide him a resting-place, and he shall be able to say, "I laid me down and slept; I awaked, for the Lord sustained me." And although these may be only short pauses; still they remind us how easily He could, if He pleased, at any moment, deliver us out of every trouble. And a believing assurance of this is sufficient to overcome every anxiety and fear.   F. W. KRUMMACHER.

What doest thou here, Elijah? I KINGS xix. 9.

The wanderer was alone, yet not alone. A voice he could neither mistake nor misinterpret had sounded in his ears the thrilling question, "What doest thou here, Elijah?" Every syllable was pregnant with meaning and rebuke. "What *doest* thou here?" Life (and none should know better than thee) is a great *doing;* not hermit inaction, inglorious repose. "What doest *thou*"—thou, my viceregent in these degenerate days —thou whom I have honored above thy fellows, and who hast had proof upon proof of my faithfulness? "What doest thou *here*"—here in this desolate spot; away from duty; the Baal altars rebuilding; my own altar in ruins; the sword of persecution unsheathed, and the bleating flock left by thee, coward shepherd, to the ravening wolf? "What doest thou here, Elijah?" Thy very name rebukes thee! Where is God, thy strength! Where are the prayers and vows of Carmel? Child of weakness, belying thy name and destiny, "*What—doest—thou—here?*"   MACDUFF.

I KINGS *Elisha . . . was plowing . . . and Elijah*
xix. 19. *passed by him, and cast his mantle upon him.*

The more God empties your hands from other work, the more you may know that He has special work to give them.   E. H. GARRETT.

II KINGS *Behold, . . . a chariot of fire, and horses of fire.*
ii. 11.   It was in a chariot of *fire* Elijah was taken to heaven. Is it not in a similar chariot, in a figurative sense, God takes many of His people still? He brings them, as He did Elijah, to the brink of Jordan; keeps them for years hovering amid the rough, rugged glens and gorges of trial; seats them in a flaming equipage; reins in the fiery horses until, *in the fire*, they are refined and purified as gold, and fitted for their radiant crowns. . . . It is *the chariot of fire.* As God's loved ones enter it, He whispers in their ear, "Through much tribulation ye shall enter into the kingdom."
                MACDUFF.

II KINGS *Go and wash in Jordan seven times.*
v. 10.   The waters of God's blessings flow downward, and he who would drink them must stoop.   A. C. DIXON.

II KINGS *As the Lord liveth, before whom I stand.*
v. 16.   Here is our defence against being led away by the gauds and shows of earth's vulgar attractions, or being

terrified by the poor terrors of its enmity. Go with this talisman in your hand, "The Lord liveth before whom I stand," and everything else dwindles down into nothingness, and you are a free man, master and lord of all things, because you are God's servant, seeing all things aright, because you see them all in God, and God in them all. McLAREN.

Elisha prayed . . . and, behold, the mountain was full of horses and chariots of fire. II KINGS vi. 17.

The Christian on his knees sees more than the philosopher on tiptoe.

When the man was let down and touched the bones of Elisha, he revived, and stood up on his feet. II KINGS xiii.21.

When men thought him dead, one of Elisha's bones was worth a whole army of ordinary men. So, if we live with God, and for God, we, too, shall possess a deathless influence, and a spiritual immortality. Our lives will not cease with our funerals, but when men are saying, "He is dead" here, voices shall be calling yonder, "Blessed are the dead who die in the Lord, for they rest from their labors, and their works do follow them."

A daily rate for every day. II KINGS xxv. 30.

The acts of breathing which I performed yesterday will not keep me alive to-day: I must continue to breathe afresh every moment, or animal life ceases. In like manner, yesterday's grace and spiritual strength must be renewed, and the Holy Spirit must continue to breathe on my soul from moment to moment, in order to my enjoying the consolations, and to my working the works, of God. TOPLADY.

I CH.
iv. 23.
These were the potters, and those that dwelt among plants and hedges; there they dwelt with the king for his work.

Anywhere and everywhere we may dwell "with the King for His work." We may be in a very unlikely or unfavorable place for this; it may be in a literal country life, with little enough to be seen of the "goings" of the King around us; it may be among hedges of all sorts, hindrances in all directions; it may be, furthermore, with our hands full of all manner of pottery for our daily task. No matter! The King who placed us "there" will come and dwell there with us; the hedges are all right, or He would soon do away with them; and it does not follow that what seems to hinder our way may not be for its very protection; and as for the pottery, why, that is just exactly what He has seen fit to put into our hands, and therefore it is, for the present, "His work."

FRANCES RIDLEY HAVERGAL.

I CH.
xvii. 7.
I took thee from the sheepcote . . . that thou shouldest be ruler over my people Israel.

David was keeping sheep in the wilderness with no eye upon him but God's. In prompt obedience to his father, he went to the valley of Elah, taking loaves and cheeses to his brethren: if we are content to serve God in mean things, God will bring us forth in greater. In the valley of Elah was Goliath ready for David's sling.

I CH.
xxix. 2.
David . . . said . . . I have prepared . . . for the house of my God.
Then spake Solomon . . . I have built an house for the . . . Lord God of Israel.—1 Kings viii. 12, 20.

We should so live and labor in our time that what

came to us as seed, may go to the next generation as blossom, and what came to us as blossom, may go to them as fruit.

We rest on thee.

II CH.
xiv. 11.

The ship that is anchored is sensitive to every change of wind or tide, and ever turns sharply around to meet and resist the stream, from what direction soever it may flow. A ship is safest with her head to the sea and the tempest. In great storms the safety of all often depends on the skill with which the sailors can keep her head to the rolling breakers. Life and death have sometimes hung for a day and a night in the balance, whether the weary steersman could keep her head to the storm until the storm should cease. Even a single wave allowed to strike her on the broadside might send all to the bottom. But to keep the ship in the attitude of safety, there is no effort and no art equal to the anchor. As soon as the anchor feels the ground, the vessel that had been drifting broadside, is brought up, and turns to the waves a sharp prow that cleaves them in two and sends them harmless along the sides. Watch from a height any group of ships that may be lying in an open roadstead. At night when you retire they all point westward; in the morning they are all looking to the east. Each ship has infallibly felt the first veering of the wind or water, and instantly veered in the requisite direction, so that neither wind nor wave has ever been able to strike her on the broadside. Thereby hangs the safety of the ship. Ships not at anchor do not turn and face the foe. The ship that is left loose will be caught by a gust on her side, and easily thrown over. As with ships, so with souls.

ARNOT.

II CH.
xxiv.
13.

The workmen wrought and the work was perfected by them.

The life tabernacle is a wondrous building; there is room for workers of all kinds in the uprearing of its mysterious and glorious walls. If we cannot do the greatest work, we may do the least; our heaven will come out of the realization of the fact that it was God's tabernacle we were building, and under God's blessing that we were working. JOSEPH PARKER.

II CH.
xxxiii.
12, 13.

When he was in affliction, he besought the Lord his God . . . and he was entreated of him, and heard his supplication.

Have you ever noticed the great clock of St. Paul's? At midday, in the roar of business, how few hear it but those who are close to it! But when the work of the day is over, and silence reigns in London, then it may be heard for miles around. That is just like the conscience of an impenitent man. While in health and strength, he will not hear it; but the day will come when he must retire from the world, and look death in the face; and then the clock of conscience—the solemn clock—will sound in his ears, and, if he has not repented, will bring wretchedness and misery to his soul. RYLE.

II CH.
xxxiv.
12.

The men did the work faithfully.

You cannot set the world right, or the times, but you can do something for the truth; and all you can do will certainly tell if the work you do is for the Master, Who gives you your share, and so the burden of responsibility is lifted off. This assurance makes peace, satisfaction, and repose possible even in the partial work done upon earth. Go to the man who is

Thoughts from My Library

carving a stone for a building; ask him where is that stone going, to what part of the temple, and how is he going to get it into place, and what does he do? He points you to the builder's plans. This is only one stone of many. So, when men shall ask where and how is your little achievement going into God's plan, point them to your Master, Who keeps the plans, and then go on doing your little service as faithfully as if the whole temple were yours to build.

PHILLIPS BROOKS.

The king said unto me, For what dost thou make request? So I prayed to the God of heaven. And I said unto the king . . . NEH. ii. 4, 5.

Ejaculatory prayer has this advantage—it flies up to heaven before the devil can get a shot at it.

ROWLAND HILL.

We made our prayer unto our God, and set a watch. NEH. iv. 9.

Don't wait for some work to turn up but go and turn up some work. You may work without praying but you can't pray without working.

HUDSON TAYLOR.

So did not I, because of the fear of God. NEH. v. 15.

Doubtful amusements are like doubtful eggs—so likely to be bad that it is safest to let them alone.

The joy of the Lord is your strength. NEH. viii. 10.

The mass of Christians make a little dark world of their own, and live there. They build the walls of their houses out of their troubles and sorrows. They put stained glass in their windows. They keep the doors locked. It is all dark about them. No sunshine comes into their chambers, and no fire burns on the hearth. They have no pictures on their walls but the pictures of their dead joys. And there they live, from year to year, in gloom and sadness, because they will not let God's sunshine in. I meet many persons who can talk for hours of their troubles, sorrows and cares, who seem to forget that God ever made a flower, or a star, or a sunbeam, or did a single kind, tender thing for them. J. R. MILLER.

NEH. ix. 17. *Thou art a God ready to pardon, gracious and merciful, slow to anger, and of great kindness.*

It is observable, that the Roman magistrates, when they gave sentence upon any one to be scourged, had a bundle of rods, tied hard with many knots, laid before them. The reason was this,—that whilst the beadle was untying the knots, which he was to do by order, and not in any other hasty or sudden way, the magistrate might see the deportment and carriage of the delinquent,—whether he was sorry for his fault, and showed any hope of amendment,—that then he might recall his sentence, or mitigate his punishment: otherwise, he was corrected so much the more severely. Thus God in the punishment of sinners,— how patient is He! how loath to strike! how slow to anger! SPENCER.

JOB i. 8. *My servant Job . . . there is none like him.*

We see in a jeweller's shop, that, as there are pearls and diamonds and other precious stones, there are files, cutting instruments, and many sharp tools for their polishing; and, while they are in the workhouse, they are continual neighbors to them, and come often under them. The Church is God's jewel; His workhouse, where His jewels are polishing for His palace and house;

and those He especially esteems, and means to make the most resplendent, He hath oftenest His tools upon.

LEIGHTON.

He disappointeth the devices of the crafty.

JOB V. 12.

During the siege of Sebastopol a Russian shell buried itself in the side of a hill outside the city, and opened a spring. A little fountain bubbled forth where the missile of death had fallen, and afforded to the weary troops encamped there an abundance of pure cold water during all the rest of the siege. What enemies mean shall do us evil often becomes a spring in the desert of privation and persecution.

He taketh the wise in their own craftiness.

JOB V. 13.

A Russian fable tells of a man who wished to accomplish a journey over the snow and ice, through an inhospitable region infested with ravenous wolves. The distance was so great that it could only be traversed in a day by the strongest and swiftest horse to be found. Thus furnished, the traveller set forth to cross the steppe. When well on his way a huge wolf sprang upon the horse and devoured him. The wolf then became entangled in the harness and sped forth at a rapid rate, and soon drew the traveller to the very place he sought. Rev. Wm. Taylor says the devil has often attacked him in this way, and the result has only been to take him the quicker over the rough roads to the place desired. The devil himself becomes the Lord's servant to save and help His people.

Happy is the man whom God correcteth.

JOB V. 17.

Happy, because the correction is designed to bring him into paths of blessedness and peace.

Happy, because there is no unnecessary severity in it.

Happy, because the chastisement is not so much against us, as against our most cruel enemies—our sins.

Happy, because we have abundant words of consolation.

Happy, because whom the Lord loveth He chasteneth.

Happy, because our light affliction is but for a moment.   BOWEN.

JOB xiv.14, 15. *All the days of my appointed time will I wait, till my change come. Thou shalt call, and I will answer thee.*

When shall this change come? I know not, the patriarch replies, but I am content to wait for it "all the days of my appointed time." Faith and Hope then express themselves in prayer, "Hide me in the grave," he says, "keep me secret till Thy wrath be past," and the day of peace and glory come—"appoint me a set time and remember me—then Thou shalt call and I will answer." How beautiful is all this! The child lying down to rest asks the parent to remember him in the morning, and call him at the appointed time. And when the sun casts his glad beams over the earth, and all nature is awakening to joy, the father withdraws the curtains and bids his child arise. So shall it be with the blessed God and His children in the glad resurrection morning. He will remember to call them at the "time appointed," and at His well-known voice they shall awake to sleep no more.   TAIT.

JOB xxii. 10. *Snares are round about thee.*

There is not a place beneath which a believer walks

that is free from snares. Behind every tree there is the Indian with his barbed arrow; behind every bush there is the lion sneeking to devour; under every piece of grass there lieth the adder. Everywhere they are.

SPURGEON.

He knoweth the way that I take.

When you are doubtful as to your course, submit your judgment absolutely to the spirit of God, and ask Him to shut against you every door but the right one. . . . In the meanwhile, continue along the path which you have been already treading. It lies in front of you; pursue it. Abide in the calling in which you were called. Keep on as you are, unless you are clearly told to do something else. Expect to have as clear a door out as you had in; and if there is no indication to the contrary, consider the absence of indication to be the indication of God's will that you are on His track. . . . Be not afraid to trust Him utterly. As you go down the long corridor you will find that He has preceded you, and locked many doors which you would fain have entered; but be sure that beyond these there is one which He has left unlocked. Open it and enter, and you will find yourself face to face with a bend of the river of opportunity, broader and deeper than anything you had dared to imagine in your sunniest dreams. Launch forth on it; it conducts to the open sea.

F. B. MEYER.

JOB xxiii. 10.

When he hath tried me, I shall come forth as gold.

When David was fleeing through the wilderness, pursued by his own son, he was being prepared to become the sweet singer of Israel. The pit and the dungeon were the best schools at which David ever

JOB xxiii. 10.

graduated. The hurricane that upset the tent and killed Job's children prepared the man of Uz to write the magnificent poem that has astounded the ages. There is no way to get the wheat out of the straw, but to thresh it. There is no way to purify the gold, but to burn it. TALMAGE.

JOB xxiii. 12. *I have esteemed the words of his mouth more than my necessary food.*

Every growing Christian is a ruminating animal; he chews Bible truths and nutritious sermons and wholesome books and other such provender, as the cow cheweth her cud. One strong Bible text lodged in the memory, and turned over and over and well digested, will be a breakfast for your soul, and in the strength of it you go through the whole day. CUYLER.

JOB xxxiii. 27, 28. *If any say, I have sinned . . . he will deliver his soul from going into the pit.*

A Turkish allegory says every man has two angels, one on the right shoulder and another on the left. When he does anything good, the angel on the right shoulder writes it down and seals it, because what is done is done forever. When he does evil, the angel on the left shoulder writes it down. Then he waits till midnight. If before that time the man bows his head, and exclaims, "Gracious Allah; I have sinned: forgive me!" the angel rubs it out; if not, he seals it, and the angel upon the right shoulder weeps.

JOB xxxv. 10. *God . . . who giveth songs in the night.*

It is often in sorrow that our lives are taught their sweetest songs. There is a story of a German baron who stretched wires from tower to tower of his castle, to make a great Æolian harp. Then he waited and listened to hear the music from it. For a time the air was still and no sound was heard. The wires hung silent in the air. After a while came gentle breezes, and the harp sang softly. At length came the stern winter winds, strong and storm-like in their forces. Then the wires gave forth majestic music which was heard far and near. There are human lives that never, in the calm of quiet days, yield the music that is in them. When the breezes of common care sweep over them they give out soft murmurings of song. But it is only when the storms of adversity blow upon them that they answer in notes of noble victoriousness. It takes some trouble to bring out the best that is in them.   J. R. MILLER.

He openeth also their ear to discipline.   JOB

Sorrow is apt to be selfish. The soul, occupied xxxvi. with its own griefs, and refusing to be comforted, be- 10. comes presently a Dead Sea, full of brine and salt, over which the birds do not fly, and beside which no green thing grows. And thus we miss the very lesson that God would teach us. His constant war is against the self-life, and every pain He inflicts is to lessen its hold upon us. But we may thwart His purpose and extract poison from His gifts, as men get opium and alcohol from innocent plants.

He saith to the snow, Be thou on the earth; likewise JOB
to the small rain, and to the great rain of his xxxvii.
strength.   6.

A dewdrop does the will of God as much as a thunderstorm.

JOB
xxxviii
28, 29.

Hath the rain a father? or who hath begotten the drops of dew? out of whose womb came the ice? and the hoary frost of heaven, who hath gendered it?

Who could go to a picture gallery and while admiring the beautiful blending of the colors, and the perfect outline of the various pictures, could ever believe the pictures came by chance, and that no mind conceived them and no hand painted them? Who then can look out upon this glorious earth, with all its wondrous form and color, which seem to defy all the best attempts of our greatest geniuses, and then disbelieve in the great Artist of the universe, the God who painted the sunset and gave to the lily its sweet fragrance, its delicate texture and its lovely hue? No, there is a God Who made us all, and He is the King of all the earth. Away, then, with treason and rebellion; be loyal to God. F. S. WEBSTER.

JOB
xlii. 12.

The Lord blessed the latter end of Job more than his beginning.

All the afflictions of the righteous open out into something glorious. The prisoner is not merely delivered, but he finds an angel waiting for him at the door. And with every deliverance comes a specific blessing. One angel is named faith; another, love; another, joy; another, long-suffering; another, gentleness; another, goodness; another, meekness; another, temperance; another, peace. Each of these graces says, "We have come out of great tribulation." BOWEN.

PS.
iii. 3.

Thou, O Lord, art a shield for me.

In the battle of this world, the Christian is seen without a shield. And just where he is, is the thickest of the fight. The adversary hurls his best forces against that spot, evidently supposing that there is only this impediment between him and victory. It is wonderful then that the Christian should pass scathless through this shower of fiery darts. Those that are in the secret know that—while apparently unprotected—he is in reality defended by an invisible shield. While he abides in faith, God encompasses him round about and nothing can by any means harm him. BOWEN.

I will both lay me down in peace and sleep: for thou, PS.
Lord, only makest me dwell in safety. iv. 8.

Sweet Evening Hymn! I shall not sit up to watch through fear, but I will *lie down;* and then I will not lie awake listening to every rustling sound, but I will lie down *in peace and sleep,* for I have naught to fear. He that hath the wings of God above him needs no other curtain. Better than bolts or bars is the protection of the Lord. Armed men kept the bed of Solomon, but we do not believe that he slept more soundly than his father, whose bed was the hard ground, and who was haunted by bloodthirsty foes. Note the word *"only,"* which means that God alone was his keeper, and that though alone, without man's help, he was even then in good keeping, for he was "alone with God. . . ." They slumber sweetly whom faith rocks to sleep. No pillow so soft as a promise; no coverlet so warm as an assured interest in Christ. SPURGEON.

My voice shalt thou hear in the morning, O Lord; PS.
in the morning will I direct my prayer unto thee. V. 3.

On the first of May in the olden times, according to

71

annual custom, many inhabitants of London went into the fields to bathe their faces with the early dew upon the grass, under the idea that it would render them beautiful. Some writers call the custom superstitious; it may have been so, but this we know, that to bathe one's face every morning in the dew of heaven by prayer and communion, is the sure way to obtain true beauty of life and character.

SPURGEON.

PS.
v. 3.
I . . . will look up.

Those that have searched into the monuments of Jerusalem write that our Lord was crucified with His face to the west; which, however spitefully meant of the Jews (as not allowing Him worthy to look on the holy city and temple), yet was not without a mystery. "His eyes looked to the Gentiles," etc., saith the Psalmist. As Christ, therefore, on His cross, looked toward us, sinners of the Gentiles, so let us look up to Him.   BISHOP HALL.

PS.
vi. 8.
The Lord hath heard the voice of my weeping.

What a fine Hebraism, and what grand poetry it is in English! "He hath heard the voice of my weeping." Is there a voice in weeping? Does weeping speak? In what language doth it utter its meaning? Why, in that universal tongue which is known and understood in all the earth, and even in heaven above. When a man weeps, whether he be a Jew or Gentile, Barbarian, Scythian, bond or free, it has the same meaning in it. Weeping is the eloquence of sorrow. It is an unstammering orator, needing no interpreter, but understood of all. Is it not sweet to believe that our tears are understood even when words fail? Let us learn to think of tears as liquid prayers, and of weeping as a constant dropping of importunate intercession which will wear its way right surely into the very heart of mercy, despite the stony difficulties which obstruct the way. My God, I will "weep" when I cannot plead, for Thou hearest the voice of my weeping. SPURGEON.

When I consider thy heavens, the work of thy fingers PS.
. . . what is man that thou art mindful of him? viii. 3, 4.

Just as the mountain supports the tiny blade of grass and the modest floweret, as well as the giant pine or cedar; just as that ocean bears up in safety the sea-bird seated on its crested waves, as well as the leviathan vessel: so, while the great Keeper of Israel can listen to the archangels' song and the seraphs' burning devotions, He can carry in His bosom the feeblest lamb of the fold, and lead gently the most sorrowing spirit. MACDUFF.

The Lord . . . will be a refuge for the oppressed, PS.
a refuge in times of trouble. ix. 9.

It is reported of the Egyptians that living in fens, and being vexed with gnats, they used to sleep in high towers, whereby those creatures, not being able to soar so high, they were delivered from the biting of them; so would it be with us when bitten with cares and fears, did we but run to God for refuge, and rest confident of His help. TRAPP.

Because he is at my right hand, I shall not be moved. PS.
The nearer the soul is to God, the less its perturba- xvi. 8
tions; as the point nearest the centre of a circle is subject to the least motion.

PS.
xvi.
11.

Thou wilt show me the path of life.

There is a path in which every child of God is to walk, and in which alone God can accompany him.

DENHAM SMITH.

PS.
xviii.
32.

God . . . maketh my way perfect.

I heard a gentleman assert that he could walk almost any number of miles when the scenery was good; but, he added, "When it is flat and uninteresting, how one tires!"

What scenery enchants the Christian pilgrim; the towering mountains of predestination, the great sea of providence, the rocks of sure promise, the green fields of revelation, the river that makes glad the city of God, all these compose the scenery which surrounds the Christian, and at every step fresh sublimities meet his view! SPURGEON.

PS.
xix. 4.

Their line is gone out through all the earth and their words to the end of the world.

Sun, moon, and stars are God's travelling preachers: apostles on their journeys, confirming those who fear the Lord; judges on circuit, condemning those who worship idols. SPURGEON.

PS.
xix.12.

Cleanse thou me from secret faults.

The world wants men who are saved from secret faults. The world can put on an outside goodness and go very far in uprightness and morality, and it expects that a Christian shall go beyond it, and be free from secret faults. A little crack will spoil the ring of the coin. . . . The world expects, and rightly, that the Christian should be more gentle, and patient, and generous, than he who does not profess to be a

74

disciple of the Lord Jesus. For the sake of those who take their notion of religion from our lives we need to put up this prayer earnestly, "Cleanse thou me from secret faults." MARK GUY PEARSE.

He asked life of thee, and thou gavest it him, even PS.
length of days forever and ever. xxi. 4.

When poor men make requests to us, we usually answer them as the echo does the voice: the answer cuts off half the petition. We shall seldom find among men Jael's courtesy, giving milk to those that ask water, except it be as this was, an entangling benefit, the.better to introduce a mischief. There are not many Naamans among us, that, when you beg of them one talent, will force you to take two; but God's answer to our prayers is like a multiplying glass, which renders the request much greater in the answer than it was in the prayer. BISHOP REYNOLDS.

Beneath me: green pastures. PS.
Beside me: still waters. xxiii.
With me: my Shepherd.
Before me: a table.
Around me: mine enemies.
After me: goodness and mercy.
Beyond me: the house of the Lord.

"The Lord is my shepherd; I shall not want."
I shall not want rest. "He maketh me to lie down in green pastures."
I shall not want drink. "He leadeth me beside the still waters."
I shall not want forgiveness. "He restoreth my soul."

I shall not want guidance. "He leadeth me in the paths of righteousness for his name's sake."

I shall not want companionship. "Yea, though I walk through the valley of the shadow of death, I will fear no evil; for thou art with me."

I shall not want comfort. "Thy rod and thy staff they comfort me."

I shall not want food. "Thou preparest a table before me in the presence of mine enemies."

I shall not want joy. "Thou hast anointed my head with oil."

I shall not want anything. "My cup runneth over."

I shall not want anything in this life. "Surely goodness and mercy shall follow me all the days of my life."

I shall not want anything in eternity. "And I will dwell in the house of the Lord forever."

That is what David said he would find in the Good Shepherd. And one day it occurred to me to see how this twenty-third Psalm was fulfilled in Christ. This is what I found in Christ's own words:

"I am the Good Shepherd."

Thou shalt not want rest. "Come unto me all ye that labor and are heavy laden, and I will give you rest."

Thou shalt not want drink. "If any man thirst let him come unto me and drink."

Thou shalt not want forgiveness. "The Son of man hath power on earth to forgive sins."

Thou shalt not want guidance. "I am the way, and the truth, and the life."

Thou shalt not want companionship. "Lo, I am with you 'all the days.'"

Thoughts from My Library

Thou shalt not want comfort. "The Father shall give you another Comforter."

Thou shalt not want food. "I am the bread of life; he that cometh to me shall not hunger."

Thou shalt not want joy. "That my joy may be in you and that your joy may be filled full."

Thou shalt not want anything. "If ye shall ask anything of the Father in my name He will give it you."

Thou shalt not want anything in this life. "Seek ye first the kingdom of God and his righteousness and all these things shall be added unto you."

Thou shalt not want anything in eternity. "I go to prepare a place for you that where I am there ye may be also." MRS. J. R. MOTT.

Thy rod and thy staff. PS. xxiii.4.

In 1849 Dr. Duff was travelling near Simla, under the shadow of the great Himalaya mountains. One day his way led up to a narrow bridle-path cut out on the face of a steep ridge. Along this narrow path, that ran so near a great precipice, he saw a shepherd leading on his flock, the shepherd going first, and the flock following him. But now and then the shepherd stopped and looked back. If he saw a sheep creeping up too far on the one hand, or going too near the edge of the dangerous precipice on the other, he would at once turn back, and go to it, gently pulling it back. He had a long rod, as tall as himself, around the lower half of which was twisted a *band of iron*. There was a crook at one end of the rod, and it was with this the shepherd took hold of one of the hind legs of the wandering sheep to pull it back. The thick band of iron at the other end of the rod was really a staff, and was ready for use whenever he saw a hyena, or wolf, or some other troublesome animal, come near the sheep; for, especially at night, these creatures prowled about the flock. With the iron part of the rod he could give a good blow when any attack was threatened. In Psalm xxiii. 4, we have mention made of " *Thy rod and Thy staff.*" There is meaning in both, and distinct meaning. *God's rod* draws us back kindly and lovingly if we go astray from His path ; *God's staff* protects us against the onset, open or secret, whether it be men or devils, that are the enemies watching an opportunity for attack. In this we find unspeakable comfort. The young, inexperienced believer may reckon on having the *crook* of that blessed *rod* put forth to draw him back from danger and wandering; and also may expect that the *staff* of it shall not fail to come down upon those that "seek his soul to destroy it."

PS.
xxiii.6. *Surely goodness and mercy shall follow me all the days of my life.*

They say in England if a man walks he must be poor, if he sometimes calls a cab he is better off, if one footman rides behind him he is rich, but if two are on the back of his carriage he must have a great inheritance. God has no poor children; they all have a great inheritance; two footmen are always behind, "Goodness and mercy shall follow me all the days of my life." Or, goodness and mercy may be called God's watchdogs, following in the rear. MOODY.

PS.
XXV. 1. *Unto thee, O Lord, do I lift up my soul.*

In waiting upon God we must often speak to Him,

Thoughts from My Library

must take all occasions to speak to Him; and when we have not opportunity for a solemn address to Him, He will accept of a sudden address if it comes from an honest heart. David waited on God all day: "Unto Thee, O Lord, do I lift up my soul"; to Thee do I dart it, and all its gracious breathings are after Thee. We should, in a holy ejaculation, ask pardon for this sin, strength against this corruption, victory over this temptation, and it shall not be in vain. This is to pray always, and without ceasing.   MATTHEW HENRY.

Lead me in thy truth, and teach me.

PS. XXV. 5.

Truth shines like light from heaven; but the mind and conscience within the man constitute the reflector that receives it.   ARNOT.

The secret of the Lord is with them that fear him.

PS. XXV. 14.

Trust the Lord much while He is with you. Keep no secrets from Him. His secrets are with you; let your secrets be with Him.   SPURGEON.

Mine eyes are ever toward the Lord.

PS. XXV. 15.

Rev. Charles Simeon kept the picture of Henry Martyn in his study. Move where he would through the apartment, it seemed to keep its eyes upon him, and ever to say to him, "Be earnest, be earnest! don't trifle, don't trifle!" And the good Simeon would gently bow to the speaking picture, and, with a smile, reply, "Yes: I will be in earnest; I will, I will be in earnest; I will not trifle; for souls are perishing, and Jesus is to be glorified." O Christian! look away to Martyn's Master, to Simeon's Saviour, to the omniscient One. Ever realize the inspection of His eye, and hear His voice.

S. J. MOORE.

One Thousand and One

Look up and not down; look forward and not back; look out and not in; and lend a hand.   E. E. HALE.

PS.
xxvii.
I.
The Lord is . . . my salvation.

The arithmetic of full Salvation may be stated thus: (1) Sin subtracted. (2) Grace added. (3) Gifts divided. (4) Peace multiplied.

PS.
xxvii.
I.
The Lord is the strength of my life.

Perhaps thou findest the duty of thy calling too heavy for thy weak shoulders.   Make bold by faith to lay the heaviest end of thy burden on God's shoulder, which is thine, if a believer, as sure as God can make it by promise.   When at any time thou art sick of thy work, and ready to think with Jonas to run from it, encourage thyself with that of God to Gideon, whom He called from the flail to thresh the mountains: ''Go in this thy might.''   Hath not God called thee ?   Fall to the work God sets thee about, and thou engagest His strength for thee.   ''The way of the Lord is strength.'' Run from thy work, and thou engagest God's strength against thee; He will send some storm or other after thee to bring home His runaway servant.   How oft hath the coward been killed in a ditch, or under some hedge, when the valiant soldier that stood his ground and kept his place got off with safety and honor!

GURNALL.

PS.
xxx. 5.
Weeping may endure for a night, but joy cometh in the morning.

Lo! there comes hitherward, as though making for the door of our house, a dark form.   She is slightly bent, but not with age.   She has a pale face; her step is languid, like one who has travelled far and is weary;

80

and her tears flow so fast that she cannot wipe them away. Our hearts beat as we watch her coming. Will she pass or will she stay? "I am a pilgrim," quoth she; "will you lodge me for the night? I am sad, I am weary, for I go round all the world. There are few houses I do not enter, and in some I make a long stay. You ask me for my name. I bear it on my countenance; my name is "Weeping." You wish to see my credentials? It is sufficient that none have been able to keep me outside a door inside of which I wished to be; and I know that notwithstanding your beating hearts, you will not be inhospitable; you will take me in?" "Yes, for a little, to refresh you, to dry your tears if we can, and then to bid you farewell." "Nay, I can make no stipulation; I go where I am sent; I depart at the appointed time!" And now "Weeping" has her chamber in the house. And the blinds are drawn down, and hearts are hushed, and feet tread lightly, and listening all night through, we hear sighs, and sometimes almost sobs, from the chamber where "Weeping" lies sleepless. And we too are sleepless and anxious, and one and another find the tears flowing down their own cheeks as the night goes on; and the house is all full of pain and fear, as the dark thought begins to take shape that she may have come to make a long stay. We are up betimes, for now we are amongst those that "watch for the morning." Some flush of it is in the eastern sky. "And see," we say to each other, "it is beginning to gild yon mountain-peaks, and to flow down into the valleys"; when hearing some footsteps approaching, lo! there comes one whose step is elastic, whose form is graceful, who bears the dawn

81

on his countenance, who sheds light around him as he walks. Again our hearts begin to beat, but this time it is with fear that he will not have a long stay. "I am a pilgrim," quoth he; "I have long been on the road. I can walk through the darkest night and not stumble; I have come to you this morning with the dawn, and I wish to stay." Ah! welcome indeed! If we knew where to give thee room; we have but one guest-chamber, and it is occupied. There came to us last night about sundown a poor pilgrim named "Weeping," who for the first hours of night sighed and wept so sorely that it seemed as if she were breathing her life away. For the last two hours she seems to have fallen asleep, for her chamber is silent and it would be cruel to awake her. "Weeping." Ah! I know her well. My name is Joy. Weeping and Joy have had the world between them since the world was made. But now, look in your room. You will find it empty. I met her an hour ago on the other side of the hill. She told me she had slipped silently away, and that I would just be in time to smile good-morning to you from my bright face, while she went on her way toward the Valley of Baca, and the deeper darker Valley of the Shadow of Death. Weeping will not come here again to-night, and I shall stay, or I shall leave some of the light of my presence to fill your home. Weeping goes westward, and I go east-ward, and we often meet, and always part. Some-times my heart is sorry for her, even as her heart longs after me. But—a word in your ear—I have heard it in the Land of Light from which I come, and she knows it too: There is a time approaching, steadily if not quickly, when even she will not know how to weep.

Thoughts from My Library

"For the Lord God will wipe away tears from all faces." This weary world shall obtain joy and gladness at last, and sorrow and sighing shall flee away. "Wherefore comfort one another with these words."

RALEIGH.

How great is thy goodness, which thou hast laid up for them that fear thee.

PS. xxxi. 19.

God's promises are ever on the ascending scale. One leads up to another, fuller and more blessed than itself. In Mesopotamia, God said, "I will show thee the land." At Bethel, "This is the land." In Canaan, "I will give thee all the land, and children innumerable as the grains of sand. . . ." It is thus that God allures us to saintliness. Not giving us anything till we have dared to act—that He may test us. Not giving everything at first—that He may not overwhelm us. And always keeping in hand an infinite reserve of blessing. Oh! the unexplored remainders of God! Who ever saw His last star?

F. B. MEYER.

I acknowledged my sin unto thee . . . and thou forgavest the iniquity of my sin.

PS. xxxii. 5.

The same moment which brings the consciousness of sin ought to bring also the confession and the consciousness of forgiveness.

H. W. SMITH.

I will instruct thee, and teach thee in the way which thou shalt go.

PS. xxxii. 8.

When God does the directing, our life is useful and full of promise, whatever it is doing, and discipline has its perfecting work.

H. E. COBB.

I will guide thee with mine eye.

PS. xxxii. 8.

How can the Lord guide us thus unless we walk

83

near enough to catch the glance, and take the direction of His eye? Alas! that so many of us are "as the horse, or as the mule, which have no understanding; whose mouth must be held in with bit and bridle."

PS.
xxxiv.
1.

His praise shall continually be in my mouth.

Let not thy praises be transient,—a fit of music, and then the instrument hung by the wall till another gaudy day of some remarkable providence makes thee take it down. God comes not guest-wise to His saints' house, but to dwell with them. David took this up for a life-work: "As long as I live, I will praise Thee."

GURNALL.

PS.
xxxiv.
19.

Many are the afflictions of the righteous; but the Lord delivereth him out of them all.

Faith is the Christian's foundation, and hope is his anchor, and death is his harbor, and Christ is his pilot, and heaven is his country; and all the evils of poverty, or affronts of tribunals and evil judges, of fears and sad apprehensions, are but like the loud winds blowing from the right point,—they make a noise, but drive faster to the harbor. And if we do not leave the ship, and jump into the sea; quit the interest of religion, and run to the securities of the world; cut our cables, and dissolve our hopes; grow impatient; hug a wave and die in its embraces,—we are safe at sea, safer in the storm which God sends us, than in a calm when we are befriended by the world. JEREMY TAYLOR.

PS.
xxxvii.
7.

Rest in the Lord; wait patiently for him.

In Hebrew, "Be silent unto God and let Him mould thee." Keep still, and He will mould thee to the right shape. LUTHER.

Thoughts from My Library

The steps of a good man are ordered by the Lord, and PS.
he delighteth in his way. xxxvii.
Teach me thy way, O Lord.—Ps. xxvii. 11. 23.

God has a book in which is written the ideal history
of every man, the biography as it would have been
had the man's steps been ordered by the Lord; and
another in which is written the actual history of every
man. The books are open side by side, and what a
contrast do they present. "Oh! that they had heark-
ened to my commandments!" saith the Lord; nor is it
possible for any one to look upon these two records
without taking up the lamentation. What a hallowed
and beautiful path is traced in the one; what honorable conflicts and glorious victories; what nobleness
of enterprise, what steadfastness under difficulties,
what beneficence, what usefulness! . . . In comparison with this divine romance, behold the actual
life portrayed in the other book. How mean! how
contemptible! how disordered! What fearful confusion! . . . Suppose the book of your ideal biography should drop from heaven upon your path. You,
with your worldly and gross heart, take it up and look
into it. At first, seeing a good deal about tribulation,
privation, persecution, bonds, defamation, poverty, and
tears, you are ready to throw it away. But stay, my
friend; it is from heaven, see if there be not something coupled with these expressions. At one end of
a sentence you find, "they that mourn," "poor in
spirit," "they that are persecuted," "through much
tribulation"; but what at the other end? "Joy,"
"blessedness," "kingdom of heaven." Remember
the disordered steps of your past life. See how much
misery you have experienced, even in the path of your

own gratification. How unsatisfactory is the retrospect. Are you not willing to live the life that God has sketched for you? Take this book, and live this life; and your biography will be a valuable contribution to the libraries of heaven.   BOWEN.

PS.
xxxix.
6.

Surely every man walketh in a vain shew.

Did you ever stand upon the shore on some day of that uncertain weather when gloom and glory meet together, and notice how swiftly there went racing over miles of billows a darkening that quenched all the play of color in the waves, as if all suddenly the angel of the waters had spread his broad wings between sun and sea, and then how, in another moment, as swiftly it flits away, and with a burst the light blazes out again, and leagues of ocean flash into green and violet and blue? So fleeting, so utterly perishable are our lives, for all their seeming show of solid permanency.   McLAREN.

PS.
xxxix.
12.

I am a stranger with thee.

"A stranger with thee,"—then we are the guests of the King. The Lord of the land charges Himself with our protection and provision; we journey under His safe conduct. It is for His honor and faithfulness that no harm shall come to us travelling in His territory, and relying on His word. Like Abraham with the sons of Heth, we may claim the help and protection which a stranger needs. He recognizes the bond and will fulfill it. We have eaten of His salt, and He will answer for our safety. "He that toucheth you toucheth the apple of His eye."   McLAREN.

Thoughts from My Library

I delight to do thy will, O my God. PS. xl. 8.

We need to watch against a "grudging service." The enemy is always trying to get in the word "duty" instead of the word "delight"; he says a stern "you must" instead of the loving "you may." There is no slavery like the slavery of love, but its chains are sweet. It knows nothing of "sacrifice," no matter what may be given up. It delights to do the will of the beloved one. SMITH.

Thy law is within my heart. PS. xl. 8.

Fill your memory with "words of eternal life." You will need them in the dark and lonely hours of life. Then they will shine out like stars. They will speak in the solitudes with infinite sweetness and power.

How beautifully is the office of conscience set forth in the ring, which according to the fable, a magician presented to his prince! The gift was of inestimable value, not for the diamonds and rubies and pearls that gemmed it, but for a rare and mystic property in the metal. It sat easily enough in ordinary circumstances; but so soon as its wearer formed a bad thought or wish, designed or concocted a bad action, the ring became a monitor. Suddenly contracting, it pressed painfully on the finger, warning him of sin. The ring of that fable is just that conscience which is the voice of God within us, which is His law written on the fleshly tablets of the heart. GUTHRIE.

As the hart panteth after the water-brooks, so panteth my soul after thee, O God. PS. xlii. 1.

Once, a king, in crossing the desert in a lone caravan, was parched with thirst. Dreadful is that dry and thirsty land where no water is! The sands were strewn with the wrecks of caravans, the skeletons of men who had died of thirst lying in that dread cemetery; and then the cry arose, "Water, water! there is no water!" It was a fearful moment. Parched throats and eyes hopelessly looked up to the all-too-cloudy sky along the plain; overhead, the red-hot copper sun. Then said one, "We must *let loose the harts,*—the light, fleet harts." They bounded in all directions. Keen in their instinctive scent of water, the spring was found; and then, when they sat to rest beside the beautiful and blessed pool,—then said the king, as he took forth his tablets and wrote, "*As the hart panteth after the water-brooks, so panteth my soul after thee, O God.*"   E. P. HOOD.

PS. *He is thy Lord; and worship thou him.*
xlv. 11.

The Jews, and the Mahometans also, have curious legends about Abraham's conversion. They say that, when he was forty years of age, his mind took a religious turn. At that time, observing a star when night overshadowed him, he said, "This is my Lord!" but, keeping his eye on the luminary, and observing it sink ere long, he abandoned all faith in it, wisely remarking, "I like not gods which set." As the night wore on and left him in painful perplexity, the moon rose up in silver splendor. He turned to her with the delighted exclamation, "This is my Lord!" But following in the wake of the star, she also set; and when her bright rim dipped below the horizon, with her set his faith in her divinity. By and by, from the purple east, the sun leaped up, illuminating the heavens with splendor and bathing the world in light. All his dark

doubts now scattered with the morning mists before
its beams. " *This,*" exclaimed Abraham, throwing
himself down to worship, " *This* is my Lord!" But
when hours had rolled on, the sun also began to sink;
and when, following star and moon, it vanished from
his gaze, old legends tell how Abraham rose from his
knees to cast aside the faith of his fathers, and worship Him Who alone rules both in heaven and in earth.

GUTHRIE.

There is a river, the streams whereof shall make glad
the city of God, the holy place of the tabernacles of
the Most High.

PS.
xlvi. 4.

They tell us these words were written when Sennacherib's great army besieged Jerusalem, and the first
thing he did was to cut off the aqueduct that supplied
Jerusalem with water, saying to himself, "I will soon
bring them to surrender; I will starve them by cutting
off their water supply." But Sennacherib knew nothing of the pool of Siloam that was at the foundation
stone of the temple of God, a supply unfailing, which
might have stood them for years and years, although this
other was cut off, so that he could not starve Jerusalem
for lack of water; for there was " a river, the streams
whereof shall make glad the city of God." We may
take this " city of God" to mean the church of Christ.
The church of Christ is besieged to-day. Is it not besieged by enemies all around? Yet we, who are in the
church of our God, can look round calmly, and seeing
the attack, say, " There is a river, the streams whereof
shall make glad the city of God."

Be still, and know that I am God.

PS.
xlvi.
10.

There is a *restlessness* and a fretfulness in these

89

days, which stand like two granite walls against godliness. Contentment is almost necessary to godliness, and godliness is absolutely necessary to contentment. A very restless man will never be a very godly, and a very godly man will never be a very restless man.

PS.
xlviii.
14.

He will be our guide even unto death.

He is the guide of those who feel their need of an all-wise, all-powerful, all-condescending guide, and who are willing to yield their own preferences and ideas to His in travelling over the glaciers of life. His Word is a lamp unto their feet, a light unto their path. He will hold their hand till they reach the gate of death, and passing through it they will see that it is the gate of paradise. Death confesses itself vanquished when it sees them walking on the battlements clothed in white. BOWEN.

PS.
xlix.
17.

For when he dieth he shall carry nothing away; his glory shall not descend after him.

I remember an Eastern legend which I have always thought furnished a remarkable, though unconscious, commentary on these words of the Psalmist. Alexander the Great, we are told, being upon his death-bed, commanded that when he was carried forth to the grave, his hands should not be wrapped as usual in the cere cloth, but should be left outside the bier, so that all might see them, and might see that they were empty, that there was nothing in them; that he, born to one empire, and the conqueror of another, the possessor while he lived of two worlds—of the East and of the West—and of the treasures of both, yet now when he was dead could retain no smallest portions of

these treasures; that in this matter the poorest beggar
and he were at length on equal terms.

ARCHBISHOP TRENCH.

My sin is ever before me.   PS.
li. 3.

Poisons may be made medicinal.   Let the thoughts
of old sins stir up a commotion of anger and hatred.

CHARNOCK.

Against thee, thee only have I sinned, and done this   PS.
evil in thy sight.   .   .   .   Wash me and I shall be   li. 4, 7.
whiter than snow.
For Herod had laid hold on John and   .   .   .   put
him in prison for Herodias' sake.—Matt. xiv. 3.

When the ungodly and the godly fall into the same
sin, how can we distinguish between them? By a
simple test,—a test by which you may know a sheep
from a swine, when both have fallen into the same
slough, and are, in fact, so bemired, that you can hardly
tell the one from the other.   The unclean animal, in circumstances agreeable to its nature, wallows in the
mire; but the sheep (type of the godly) fills the air
with its bleatings, nor ceases to struggle to get out.

GUTHRIE.

Restore unto me the joy of thy salvation.   PS.
li. 12.

A man is gazing intently down a deep, still well,
where he sees the moon reflected, and thus remarks to
a friend standing by: "How beautifully fair and round
she is to-night! how quietly and majestically she rides
along!" He has just finished speaking, when suddenly
his friend drops a small pebble into the well.   Now he
exclaims, "Why, the moon is all broken to shivers,
and the fragments are shaking together in the greatest

disorder!" "What gross absurdity!" is the astonished rejoinder of his companion. "Look up, man! the moon hasn't changed one jot or tittle, it is the condition of the well that reflects her that has changed." Your heart is the well. When there is no allowance of evil the Spirit of God takes of the preciousness of Christ, and reveals them to you for your comfort and joy. But the moment a wrong motive is cherished in the heart, or an idle word escapes the lips unjudged, the Holy Ghost begins to disturb the well, your happy experiences are smashed to pieces, and you are all restless and disturbed within, until in brokenness of spirit before God you confess your sin (the disturbing thing), and thus get restored once more to the calm, sweet joy of communion. W. KELLY.

PS. lv. 17. *Evening . . . will I pray.*

Sleep is Death's younger brother, and so like him, that I never dare trust him without my prayers.

T. BROWN.

PS. lv. 22. *Cast thy burden upon the Lord, and he shall sustain thee.*

What an immense lot of overloaded people there are in this world! We can see it in their careworn faces; and each one thinks his burden is the heaviest. There is a certain kind of care that is wise; a man who has no forethought for the future is a sluggard or a fool. The apostle had no reference to a wise thoughtfulness for the future when he said, "Cast all your care upon Him, for He careth for you." That much perverted verse is accurately translated in the Revised Version— "casting all your anxiety on Him because He careth for you." Now just what our almighty and all-loving

92

Thoughts from My Library

Father offers is—to help carry our loads. He who watched over the infant deliverer of Israel in his cradle of rushes, who sent His ravens to feed Elijah by the brookside, who protected Daniel in the den, and kept Paul calm and cheerful in the hurricane, is the very One who says to us—Roll your anxieties over on Me, for I have you in My heart! CUYLER.

What time I am afraid, I will trust in thee. PS. lvi. 3.

Faith and fear do blend, thank God. They are as oil and water in a man's soul, and the oil will float above, and quiet the waves. "What time I am afraid"—there speaks nature and the heart. "I will trust in Thee"—there speaks the better man within, lifting himself above nature and circumstances, and casting himself into the extended arms of God, Who catches him and keeps him safe. McLAREN.

Thou hast been a shelter for me. PS. lxi. 3.

Somewhere in the East, there is said to be a tree which is a non-conductor of electricity. The people know it; and, when a storm comes, they flee toward it for safety. Beautiful picture of the Saviour!—beautiful emblem of the tree on Calvary! It is a non-conductor of wrath. THOMAS JONES.

Trust in him at all times. PS. lxii. 8.

A parable says that there was a great king who employed his people to weave for him. The silk, and woof, and patterns were all given by the king, and he looked for diligent working people. He was very indulgent, and told them when any difficulty arose to send to him, and he would help them; and never to fear troubling him, but to ask for help and instruction.

93

One Thousand and One

Among many men and women busy at their looms was one little child whom the king did not think too young to work. Often alone at her work, cheerfully and patiently she labored. One day, when the men and women were distressed at the sight of their failures—the silks were tangled, and the weaving unlike the pattern—they gathered round the child and said, "Tell us how it is that you are so happy in your work. We are always in difficulties." "Then why do you not send to the king?" said the little weaver; "he told us that we might do so." "So we do, night and morning." "Ah," said the child, "but I send as often as I have a little tangle."

PS. lxiii. 1. *My soul thirsteth for thee, my flesh longeth for thee.*

What epic can equal those *unwritten* words which pour into the ear of God out of the heart's fullness! still more, those *unspoken* words which never find the lip, but go up to heaven in unutterable longings and aspirations! Words are but the bannerets of a great army, a few bits of waving color here and there: thoughts are the main body of the footmen that march unseen below. BEECHER.

PS. lxxii. 15. *Daily shall he be praised.*

See yon starry host! see the mighty cohorts of cherubs and seraphs! Let men begone, and they shall praise Him; let the troops of the glorified cease their notes, and let no sweet melodies ever come from the lips of sainted men and women,—yet the chariots of God are twenty thousand, even many thousands of angels, who always in their motion chant His praise. There is an orchestra on high, the music of which shall never cease, even were mortals extinct, and all the human race swept from existence. Again: if angels were departed, still daily would He be praised; for are there not worlds on worlds, and suns on suns, and systems on systems, that could forever sing His praise? Yes! The ocean—that house of storms—would howl out His glories; the winds would swell the notes of His praise with their ceaseless gales; the thunders would roll like drums in the march of the God of armies; the illimitable void of ether would become vocal with song; and space itself would burst forth into one universal chorus, "Hallelujah, hallelujah, hallelujah! still the Lord God omnipotent reigneth." And if these were gone, if creatures ceased to exist, He who ever liveth and reigneth, in whom all the fullness of the Godhead bodily dwells, would still be praised, praised in Himself, and glorious in Himself; for the Father would praise the Son, and the Spirit would praise Him: and mutually blessing one another, and rendering each other beatified, still "daily would He be praised."

SPURGEON.

I will meditate also of all thy work.

PS. lxxvii. 12.

In the works of God I know nothing more beautiful than the perfect skill with which He suits His creatures to their conditions. He gives wings to birds, fins to the fish, sails to the thistle-seed, a lamp to light the glowworm, great roots to moor the majestic cedar, and to the aspiring ivy a thousand hands to climb the wall. Nor is the wisdom thus conspicuous in nature less remarkable and adorable as exhibited in the arrangements of the Kingdom of Grace. He forms a holy people for a holy state. He fits heaven for the redeemed and the redeemed for heaven. GUTHRIE.

One Thousand and One

PS.
lxxviii.
53. *He led them on safely.*

What a God is ours! He overthrows our foes in the sea, and disciplines His people in the desert. He leads us over the burning sand, and rests us in luxuriant glades. He permits disappointment at Marah, and surprises us at Elim. He leads us by a cloud; but He speaks to us by a human voice. He counts the number of the stars; but He feeds His flock like a shepherd, and gently leads those that give suck. He chooses a thundercloud as the canvas on which He paints His promise in rainbow hues. He proves by Marah, and at Elim recruits us.   F. B. MEYER.

PS.
lxxxiv.
4. *Blessed are they that dwell in thy house: they will be still praising thee.*

As God turns His thoughts of us into promises, so let us turn our thoughts of Him into prayers; and since His regards for us are darted in beams upon us, let them be reflected back upon Him in thankfulness for the gift, and earnestness both for the continuance and increase of such impressions.   CHARNOCK.

PS.
lxxxiv.
7. *They go from strength to strength.*

High hearts are never long without hearing some new call, some distant clarion of God, even in their dreams; and soon they are observed to break up the camp of ease and start on some fresh march of faithful service.   J. MARTINEAU.

PS.
lxxxiv.
11. *No good thing will he withhold from them that walk uprightly.*

Spiritual mercies are good things, and not only good things, but the best things, so that you may well ask for them; for if no good things will be withholden, much more will none of the best things.

SPURGEON.

I will hear what God the Lord will speak.
PS.
lxxxv.
8.

Wilt thou indeed? Art thou really purposed to ascertain what revelation there is of thy Creator's will concerning thee? . . . But this determination of thine will amount to nothing, just nothing, if there be not in thee a willingness to hear *all* that the Lord will speak. If out of a hundred words of God, thou fix upon one and resolve to honor it while the rest lie all dishonored, that word which thou hearest will turn against thee, and in the last day bring on thee additional condemnation. How many fancy that they are hearkening to God's word, while all the time they are only hearkening to their own heart's lusts. Half a dozen pages would contain all their Bible—theirs truly, not God's. It is impossible to hear what God the Lord will speak, while a thousand vain voices are allowed to have thy attention. There is too much noise in thine own heart for thee to hear. Thou art too much busied about thine own will, to become acquainted with the will of God. The Lord will not lead thee by the right hand, while another leads thee by the left.

BOWEN.

Unto thee, O Lord, do I lift up my soul.
PS.
lxxxvi.
4.

Lift up your heart to God, and lay out your talents for the world.

ARNOT.

Glorious things are spoken of thee, O city of God.
PS.
lxxxvii
3.

A city never built with hands, nor hoary with the years of time—a city, whose inhabitants no census has

97

numbered—a city through whose streets rush no tides of business, nor nodding hearse creeps slowly with its burden to the tomb—a city, without griefs or graves, without sins or sorrows, without births or burials, without marriages or mournings—a city, which glories in having Jesus for its King, angels for its guards, saints for its citizens; whose walls are salvation, and whose gates are praise.   GUTHRIE.

PS. lxxxvii 7.   *All my springs are in thee.*

It is observed of the spider that in the morning, before she seeks her prey, she mends her broken web, and in doing this she always begins in the middle. And shall those who call themselves Christians rise and pursue the callings and profits of the world, and yet be unconcerned about the broken webs of their lives, and especially of their hearts? Those who would have the cocks run with wholesome water should look well to the springs that supply them. The heart is the presence-chamber where the King of glory takes up His residence. That which is most worthy in us should be resigned to Him Who is most worthy of us.   SECKER.

PS. XC. 12.   *So teach us to number our days, that we may apply our hearts unto wisdom.*

Coming hastily into a chamber, I had almost thrown down a crystal hour-glass: fear lest I had, made me grieve as if I had broken it. But, alas! how much more precious time have I cast away without any regret? The hour-glass was but crystal, each hour a pearl: that, but like to be broken—this, lost outright: that, but casually—this, done willfully. A better hour-glass might be bought; but time once lost is lost for-

Thoughts from My Library

ever. Thus we grieve more for toys than for treasures. Lord, give me an hour-glass, not to be by me, but in me. Teach me the number of my days—an hour-glass to turn me—that I may apply my heart unto wisdom. FULLER.

Every day is a little life; and our whole life is but a day repeated: whence it is that old Jacob numbers his life by days; and Moses desires to be taught this point of holy arithmetic, to number not his years, but his days. Those, therefore, that dare lose a day, are dangerously prodigal; those that dare misspend it, desperate. BISHOP HALL.

Ignorance and inoperative knowledge divide mankind between them, and but a small remnant have let the truth plough deep into their inmost being and plant therein a holy fear of God. Therefore, the Psalmist prays for himself and his people, as knowing the temptations to inconsiderate disregard and to inadequate feeling of God's opposition to sin, that His power would take untaught hearts in hand and teach them this—to count their days. Then we shall bring home as from a ripened harvest field, the best fruit which life can yield, "a heart of wisdom," which, having learned the power of God's anger, and the number of our days, turns itself to the eternal dwelling-place and no more is sad, when it sees life ebbing away, or the generations moving in unbroken succession into the darkness. McLAREN.

Thou shalt tread upon the lion and adder: the young lion and the dragon shalt thou trample under feet. PS. xci. 13.

Let us not be afraid of Satan. We may be but as atoms in the feet of Christ, but even then we are above the devil, for it is written that God has put all things under His feet.   Let us not look up at Satan from below, but descend on him from above.   He matched his power against Christ and failed, and he will fare similarly in conflict with all those in whom Christ dwells.   F. B. MEYER.

PS.
xcii. 2.   *To shew forth thy loving-kindness in the morning and thy faithfulness every night.*

Prayer is the key of the morning and the bolt of the evening.

PS.
xcv. 7.   *To-day, if ye will hear his voice.*

A sculptor once showed a visitor his studio.   It was full of gods.   One was very curious.   The face was concealed by being covered with hair, and there were wings on each foot.

"What is his name ? " said the spectator.

"Opportunity," was the reply.

"Why is his face hidden ? "

" Because men seldom know him when he comes to them."

"Why has he wings on his feet ? "

" Because he is soon gone, and once gone can never be overtaken."

PS.
xcv.
7, 8.   *To-day if ye will hear his voice, harden not your heart.*

It is a solemn thing to say *to-morrow* when God says *to-day ;* for man's to-morrow and God's to-day never meet.   The word that comes from the eternal throne is " *now,*" and it is a man's own choice that fixes his doom.   DUNCAN MATHIESON.

On a winter evening, when the frost is setting in

with growing intensity, and when the sun is now far past the meridian, and gradually sinking in the western sky, there is a double reason why the ground grows every moment harder and more impenetrable to the plough. On the one hand, the frost of evening, with ever increasing intensity, is indurating the stiffening clods: on the other hand, the genial rays which alone can soften them are every moment withdrawing and losing their enlivening power. Take heed that it be not so with you. As long as you are unconverted, you are under a double process of hardening. The frosts of an eternal night are settling down upon your souls; and the Sun of Righteousness, with westering wheel, is hastening to set upon you forevermore. If, then, the plough of grace cannot force its way into your *ice-bound heart* to-day, what likelihood is there that it will enter *to-morrow?*   McCHEYNE.

He cometh to judge the earth.   PS.

You may dim the surface of the glass, so that it XCVI. shall no longer be painfully bright, like a little sun 13. lying on the ground; but your puny operation does not extinguish the great light that glows in heaven. Thus to trample conscience in the mire, so that it shall no longer reflect God's holiness, does not discharge holiness from the character of God. He will come to judge the world, although the world madly silence the witnesses who tell of His coming.   ARNOT.

Moses and Aaron . . . called upon the Lord and PS. *he answered them.*   xcix.6.

Ejaculatory prayer is like the rope of a belfry—the bell is in one room, and the handle or the end of the rope which sets it ringing in another. Perhaps the bell will not be heard in the apartment where the rope is, but it is heard in its own apartment. Moses laid hold of the rope and pulled it hard on the shore of the Red Sea, and though no one heard or knew anything of it in the lower chamber, the bell rang loudly in the upper one till the whole place was moved, and the Lord said: "Wherefore criest thou unto me?" And "the Lord saved Israel that day out of the hand of the Egyptians." WILLIAMS.

PS. c. 2. *Serve the Lord with gladness.*

God wants our life to be a song. He has written the music for us in His Word and in the duties that come to us in our places and relations in life. The things we ought to do are the notes set upon the staff. To make our life beautiful music we must be obedient and submissive. Any disobedience is the singing of a false note and yields discord. J. R. MILLER.

PS. ci. 1. *I will sing of mercy and judgment.*

Like two streams which unite their separate waters to form a common river, justice and mercy are combined in the work of redemption. Like the two cherubim whose wings met above the ark; like the two devout and holy men who drew the nails from Christ's body, and bore it to the grave; like the two angels who received it in charge, and, seated like mourners within the sepulchre (the one at the head, the other at the feet), kept silent watch over the precious treasure,—justice and mercy are associated in the work of Christ. They are the supporters of the shield on which the cross is emblazoned; they sustain the arms of our heavenly Advocate; they form the two solid and eternal pillars of the Mediator's throne. On Calvary, mercy and truth meet together, righteousness and peace embrace each other. GUTHRIE.

Bless the Lord, O my soul, and forget not all his PS.
benefits. ciii. 2.

All eyes see God's benefits, but few see God.

MARK GUY PEARSE.

It is said that once when Sir Michael Costa was having a rehearsal, with a vast array of performers and hundreds of voices, as the mighty chorus rang out with thunder of the organ, and roll of drums, and ringing horns, and cymbals clashing, some one man who played the piccolo far away up in some corner, said within himself, "In all this din it matters not what I do"; and so he ceased to play. Suddenly the great conductor stopped, flung up his hands, and all was still—and then he cried aloud, "Where is the piccolo!" The quick ear missed it, and all was spoiled because it failed to take its part. O my soul, do thy part with all thy might! Little thou mayest be, insignificant and hidden, and yet God seeks thy praise. He listens for it, and all the music of His great universe is made richer and sweeter because thou givest Him thanks. Bless the Lord, O my soul. MARK GUY PEARSE.

Who forgiveth all thine iniquities=the Guilt of Sin. PS.
Who healeth all thy diseases=the Stain of Sin. ciii.
Who redeemeth thy life from destruction=the Power 3, 4.
of Sin. DRUMMOND.

As far as the east is from the west, so far hath he re- PS.
moved our transgressions from us. ciii. 12.

If God has buried my sins, there let them lie, in that sepulchre with a great stone upon the mouth of it which none can roll away, sealed with God's own seal whereon is graven a cross encircled with the blessed words: *Thy sins are forgiven thee.*

MARK GUY PEARSE.

PS. cvii. 7.
He led them forth by the right way that they might go to a city of habitation.

Each of us has his Gilgal, and his Bethel, and then his Jordan. His Gilgal, where at the beginning of life God summons him to His work, crowns and endows him for it, tries him; and if he fails, takes it from him, and gives it to a better. His Bethel, when God visits the young soul, and gives it His assurance of provision, His smile of welcome, His sense of protection, His promise of fatherly love, and then sends it on. His Jordan, the end of life, whether long or short, bright or dull, defeat or victory, shame or glory, whether approached suddenly or seen from afar, whether recognized with a shudder of fear or welcomed as the thought of home. BISHOP THOROLD.

PS. cvii. 9.
He satisfieth the longing soul.

You may as soon fill a bag with wisdom, a chest with virtue, or a circle with a triangle, as the heart of man with anything here below. A man may have enough of the world to sink him, but he can never have enough to satisfy him. T. BROOKS.

PS. cvii. 23, 24.
They that go down to the sea in ships, that do business in great waters ; these see the works of the Lord and his wonders in the deep.

How true is this! and yet our coward hearts do so shrink from those "great waters"! We prefer carrying on our traffic in the shallows, and, as a result, we

Thoughts from My Library

fail to see "the works" and "wonders" of our God; for these can only be seen and known "in the deep."

C. H. McINTOSH.

Thy mercy is great above the heavens.

PS. cviii. 4.

O this mercy of God! I am told it is like an ocean. Then I place on it four swift-sailing craft, with compass, and charts, and choice rigging, and skillful navigators, and I tell them to launch away, and discover for me the extent of this ocean. That craft puts out in one direction, and sails to the north; this to the south; this to the east; this to the west. They crowd on all their canvas, and sail ten thousand years, and one day come up the harbor of heaven, and I shout to them from the beach, "Have you found the shore?" and they answer, "No shore to God's mercy!" Swift angels, dispatched from the throne, attempt to go across it. For a million years they fly and fly, but then come back and fold their wings at the foot of the throne, and cry, "No shore! no shore to God's mercy!"

TALMAGE.

I give myself unto prayer.

PS. cix. 4.

The godly man's prayers are his best biography, his most exact portrait.

It is better to trust in the Lord than to put confidence in man.

PS. cxviii. 8.

The Scripture is the sun; the church is the clock. The sun we know to be sure and regularly constant in his motions; the clock, as it may fall out, may go too fast or too slow. As then, we should condemn him of folly that should profess to trust the clock rather than the sun, so we cannot but justly tax the credulity

of those who would rather trust to the church than to
the Scripture.   BISHOP HALL.

PS. *With my whole heart have I sought thee.*
cxix.
10.   Be wholly given to God, then you too shall live in
the light, as He is in the light. The warmth of His
love shall fill your emotions with its glow, and teach
you the art of love; the light of His truth shall banish
obscurity and ignorance from your mind, and endow
it with direct and certain knowledge; the ray of His
presence shall inspire you with strength, vigor, elas-
ticity, immortal youth. Where sunshine is, there is
life, health, gladness, vigorous strength.

                                          F. B. MEYER.

PS. *Open thou mine eyes, that I may behold wondrous*
cxix.   *things out of thy law.*
18.
        Let me suppose a person to have a curious cabinet,
which is opened at his pleasure, and not exposed to
common view. He invites all to come and see it, and
offers to show it to any one who asks him. It is hid,
because he keeps the key, but none can complain, because he is ready to open it whenever he is desired.
Some, perhaps, disdain the offer, and say, "Why is
it locked at all?" Some think it is not worth seeing,
or amuse themselves with guessing at the contents.
But those who are simply desirous for themselves,
leave others disputing, go according to appointment,
and are gratified. These have reason to be thankful
for the favor, and the others have no just cause to find
fault. Thus the riches of Divine grace may be compared to a richly-furnished cabinet to which "Christ
is the door." The Word of God likewise is a cabinet
generally locked up, but the key of prayer will open

it. The Lord invites all, but He keeps the dispensation in His own hand. They cannot see these things, except He shows them; but then He refuses none that sincerely ask Him. The wise men of the world can go no further than the outside of this cabinet; they may amuse themselves and surprise others with their ingenius guesses at what is within; but a child that has seen it opened can give us satisfaction, without studying or guessing at all. If men will presume to aim at the knowledge of God, without the knowledge of Christ, Who is the way and the door; if they have such a high opinion of their own wisdom and penetration as to suppose they can understand the Scriptures without the assistance of His Spirit; or, if their worldly wisdom teaches them that those things are not worth their inquiring, what wonder is it that they should continue to be hid from their eyes?

NEWTON.

Thy testimonies . . . are . . . my counsellors. PS. cxix. 24.

Boleslaus, one of the kings of Poland, carried about him the picture of his father; and when he was to do any great work, or set about any extraordinary design, he would look on the picture, and pray that he might do nothing unworthy of such a father's name. The Scriptures are the picture of God's will. Before a man engages in any business whatsoever, let him look there, and read what is to be done, and what to be omitted.

Give me understanding. PS. cxix. 34.

Prayer is a proper means for the increase of knowledge. Prayer is the golden key that unlocks that treasure. When Daniel was to expound the secret contained in the king's dream, about which the Chaldean magicians had racked their brains to no purpose; what course did Daniel take? "He went to his house," Dan. ii. 17, 18, "and made the thing known to Hananiah, Michael, and Azariah, his companions; that they would desire mercies of the God of heaven concerning his secret." And then was the secret revealed to Daniel.   FLAVEL.

PS. cxix. 35. *Make me to go in the path of thy commandments.*

The path of fellowship—*with* God.

The path of holiness—*before* God.

The path of obedience—*after* God.

PS. cxix. 67. *Before I was afflicted I went astray; but now have I kept thy word.*

An old Puritan said, "God's people are like birds; they sing best in cages, they sing best when in the deepest trouble." Said old Master Brooks, "The deeper the flood was, the higher the ark went up to heaven." So it is with the child of God: the deeper his troubles the nearer to heaven he goeth, if he lives close to his Master. Troubles are called weights; and a weight, you know, generally cloggeth and keepeth down to the earth; but there are ways, by the use of the laws of mechanics, by which you can make a weight lift you; and so it is possible to make your troubles lift you nearer heaven instead of making them sink you. Ah! we thank our God, He has sometimes opened our mouth when we were dumb; when we were ungrateful, and did not praise Him, He has opened our mouth by a trial; and though when we had a thousand mercies we did not bless Him, when He sent a sharp affliction, then we began to bless Him.
                                    SPURGEON.

Often our trials act as a thorn-hedge to keep us in the good pasture; but our prosperity is a gap through which we go astray. SPURGEON.

It is good for me that I have been afflicted. PS. cxix. 71.

The air from the sea of affliction is extremely beneficial to invalid Christians. Continued prosperity, like a warm atmosphere, has a tendency to unbind the sinews and soften the bones; but the cold winds of trouble make us sturdy, hardy, and well-braced in every part. Unbroken success often leads to an undervaluing of mercies, and forgetfulness of the giver; but the withdrawal of the sunshine leads us to look for the sun. SPURGEON.

Forever, O Lord, thy word is settled in heaven. PS. cxix. 89.

The balances of God never lose their adjustment. With them, a pound is a pound, and right is right, and wrong is wrong, and a soul is a soul, and eternity is eternity. TALMAGE.

I have more understanding than all my teachers; for thy testimonies are my meditation. PS. cxix. 99.

O young man! build thy studio on Calvary; there raise thine observatory, and scan by faith the lofty things of Nature. Take thee a hermit's cell in the garden of Gethsemane, and lave thy brow with the waters of Siloa. Let the Bible be thy standard classic, thy last appeal in matters of contention; let its light be thine illumination: and thou shalt become more wise than Plato, more truly learned than the seven sages of antiquity. SPURGEON.

Thy testimonies are my meditation. PS. cxix. 99.

Meditation is prayer's handmaid, to wait on it both

before and after the performance. It is as the plough before the sower to prepare the heart for the duty of prayer, and the harrow to cover the seed when 'tis sown. As the hopper feeds the mill with grist, so does meditation supply the heart with matter for prayer.   GURNALL.

PS. cxix. 105.

Thy word is a lamp unto my feet, and a light unto my path.

In joy and sorrow, in health and in sickness, in poverty and in riches, in every condition of life, God has a promise stored up in His Word for you. If you are impatient, sit down quietly and commune with Job. If you are strong-headed, read of Moses and Peter. If you are weak-kneed, look at Elijah. If there is no song in your heart, listen to David. If you are a politician, read Daniel. If you are getting sordid, read Isaiah. If you are chilly, read of the beloved disciple. If your faith is low, read Paul. If you are getting lazy, watch James. If you are losing sight of the future, read in Revelation of the promised land.   MOODY.

PS. cxix. 111.

Thy testimonies have I taken as an heritage forever.

It is said of some mines of Cornwall, that the deeper they are sunk the richer they prove; and though some lodes have been followed a thousand and even fifteen hundred feet, they have not come to an end. Such is the Book of God. It is a mine of wealth which can never be exhausted. The deeper we sink into it the richer it becomes.   C. GRAHAM.

PS. cxix. 117.

Hold thou me up, and I shall be safe.

Do not spoil the chime of this morning's bells by ringing only half a peal! Do not say, "Hold thou me up," and stop there, or add, "But all the same, I shall stumble and fall!" Finish the peal with God's own music, the bright words of faith that He puts into your mouth, "Hold thou me up, *and I shall be safe!*"

FRANCES RIDLEY HAVERGAL.

Thy testimonies are wonderful.
PS. cxix. 129.

Some look upon the Bible as a garden of spices, in which you may walk, and at your leisure pluck the flowers and gather the fruits of the Eden of God. But this does not accord with my experience. I have found it more like a mine, in which you must dig and labor, the wealth of which is not to be obtained without labor,—a mine rich in gold and precious things, but it must be wrought day and night in order to produce them.
J. TODD.

Unto thee lift I up mine eyes.
PS. cxxiii. 1.

If you want to be wretched, look *within.* If you want to be distracted and fearful, look *around.* If you want to be peaceful and happy, look *up.*

*Him which divided the Red sea into parts . . .
and made Israel to pass through the midst of it
. . . but overthrew Pharaoh and his hosts.*
PS. cxxxvi 13, 14, 15.

The way through the Red Sea was safe enough for Israel, but not for Pharaoh; he had no business to go that way, it was a private road that God had opened up for His own family.
THOMAS RHYS DAVIES.

Such knowledge is too wonderful for me.
PS. cxxxix 6.

There is a tradition that the descendants of Seth lived on the summit of so lofty a mountain as to be able to hear and join in the song of the heavenly host.

The Bible is that mountain. Its peak pierces beyond the clouds into the sublimest elevations and atmospheres. Where the Word of God ends, Heaven begins. The conceptions of things, human and divine, found herein surpass in grandeur and magnificence all the dreams of the ages and of the sages.

A. T. PIERSON.

PS. cxxxix 17. *How precious . . . are thy thoughts unto me, O God.*

The book of Nature is an expression of the thoughts of God. We have God's terrible thoughts in the thunder and lightning; God's loving thoughts in the sunshine and the breeze; God's bounteous, prudent, careful thoughts in the waving harvest. We have God's brilliant thoughts, which are beheld from mountaintop and valley; and we have God's most sweet and pleasant thoughts of beauty in the little flowers that blossom at our feet. SPURGEON.

When a holy thought lights suddenly upon you, which hath no connection with any antecedent business in your mind, receive it as a messenger from heaven, and the rather because it is a stranger. You know not but you may entertain an angel—yea, even the Holy Spirit. CHARNOCK.

PS. cxxxix 23. *Search me, O God, and know my heart.*

If thou desirest Christ for a perpetual guest, give Him all the keys of thine heart; let not one cabinet be locked up from Him; give Him the range of every room, and the key of every chamber; thus you will constrain Him to remain. SPURGEON.

PS. cxlii.5. *I said, Thou art my . . . portion.*

You will never possess any more of Christ than you claim as your own. WEBB–PEPLOE.

Thoughts from My Library

I am thy servant.

PS. cxliii. 12.

Every day let us renew the consecration to God's service; every day let us in His strength, pledge ourselves afresh to do His will, even in the veriest trifle, and to turn aside from anything that may displease Him. . . . He does not bid us bear the burdens of to-morrow, next week, or next year. Every day we are to come to Him in simple obedience and faith, asking help to keep us, and aid us through that day's work; and to-morrow, and to-morrow, and to-morrow, through years of long to-morrows, it will be but the same thing to do; leaving the future always in God's hands, sure that He can care for it better than we. Blessed trust! that can thus confidingly say: "This hour is mine with its present duty, the rest is God's, and when it comes, His presence will come with it." MADAM GUYON.

Happy is that people whose God is the Lord.

PS. cxliv. 15.

There is no man so happy as the Christian. When he looks up unto heaven, he thinks, "That is my home; the God that made it and owns it is my Father; the angels, more glorious in nature than myself, are my attendants; mine enemies are my vassals." Yea, those things which are the terriblest of all to the wicked are most pleasant to him. When he hears God thunder above his head, he thinks, "This is the voice of my Father." When he remembereth the tribunal of the last judgment, he thinks, "It is my Saviour that sits in it"; when death, he esteems it but as the angel set before Paradise, which, with one blow, admits him to eternal joy. And (which is most of all) nothing in earth or hell can make him miserable. There is nothing in the world worth envying, but a Christian. BISHOP HALL.

PS. cxlv. 13. *Thy kingdom is an everlasting kingdom.*

The old Britons whom we English conquered and drove out of the land fifteen hundred years ago—they had their fable for a long time which gave them hope —how their great King Arthur was not really dead, but slept a charmed sleep in the Isle of Avalon—and how he should awake at last to set them free and rule righteously over the land. That was but a fable, and has come to nought; but still it was true to the best instincts of human nature, true to the image of God, Whose kingdom shall one day come, and His will be done on earth as it is in heaven. KINGSLEY.

PS. cxlvii. 6. *The Lord lifteth up the meek.*

Oh! how few, how rare are those meek ones! Am I one of them, O Lord? Am I quite content to be overlooked in the day when Thou distributest honors on the earth? Am I willing to be made of no account? Is my chief ambition to be useful, eminently but not ostensibly useful? And if I get this spirit one day, does it abide with me? Do I not find myself coming into new circumstances where my mean estate troubles me? And through some insidious suggestion does there arise impatience of God's depressing providence? Thou Who art meek and lowly of heart, teach me to be meek, give me a meekness that shall pass through every ordeal. BOWEN.

PS. cxlvii. 8. *Who covereth the heaven with clouds.*

The most wonderful of God's visible creations are still wrought out in cloud; what landscapes, cities,

Thoughts from My Library

temples, forests, minarets of snow, and palaces fit for
heavenly kings, are to be found in the clouds!

JOSEPH PARKER.

The Lord taketh pleasure in them that fear him.

If this world should resolve to send an embassy to
the most high God, whom would it choose? The
princes of this world would be represented by the
brother of some czar, or the nephew of some emperor.
The bishops and high clergy would be represented by
some legate of ample wealth. The literary world
would send some Goethe, or Confucius, or Plato. The
merchants would send a Rothschild. The artists a
Raphael. There would be an ermined judge and a dec-
orated physician. The military would send a Hannibal, the transcendentalists a Kant. All orders would
be represented. But if, as the servant of some one of
this company, a meek and lowly Christian might obtain permission to go, this one alone of all the company would be permitted to enter the audience-cham-
ber of God. He taketh pleasure in such, not in the
wise, the noble, the wealthy, the mitred. "The Lord
taketh pleasure in *His* people."

BOWEN.

Stormy wind fulfilling his word.

PS. cxlviii. 8.

One day by God's great mercy, we shall stand upon
the sea of glass, having the harps of God, and having
gotten victory: then shall we sing the song of Moses, the
servant of God, and the song of the Lamb: "Just and
true are Thy ways, Thou King of saints." We shall
know then how the stormy winds have wrought out
our deliverance. Now you see only the mystery of
this great sorrow; then you shall see how the threatening enemy was swept away in the wild night of fear

115

and grief. Now you look only at the loss; then you shall see how it struck at the evil that had begun to rivet its fetters upon you. Now you shrink from the howling winds and muttering thunders; then you shall see how they beat back the waters of destruction and opened up your way to the goodly land of promise.   MARK GUY PEARSE.

PROV.
i. 32.
The prosperity of fools shall destroy them.
Prosperity is like salt water: the more you drink of it the thirstier you are.   TALMAGE.

PROV.
iii. 6.
In all thy ways acknowledge him and he shall direct thy paths.

An artist painted a picture of a little child in the dress of a pilgrim. He is walking slowly along a narrow path. This path has on each side of it a dreadful precipice. The edges of these precipices are hidden from view by means of beautiful flowers that are growing there. Behind the child is an angel. His face is full of tenderness and love. His hands are resting lightly on the shoulders of the child, to keep him in the centre of the path. The child has closed his eyes, that the sight of the flowers may not tempt him into danger. He is walking carefully along, feeling, and yielding to the gentle touch of the angel that is leading him. He acknowledges the angel by following his touch, and while he does this the angel "directs his paths."   R. NEWTON.

In all thy ways. In thy worship. In thy study of His word. In thy intercourse with His people. In thy traffic with the world. In thy business and in thy recreation. At thy meals. In thy correspondence. In thy reading. In thy dress. What! In all these petty matters? Yes! In *all* thy ways. Thinkest thou that God will have no word for thee on such topics? Be undeceived. Thou shalt find a revelation of the will of God for every one of thy paths. There is no need for thee to ever let go His hand. Not a single hair of thy head receives its aliment without Him. Why then should a single step be taken without Him?

BOWEN.

The merchandise of (wisdom) is better than silver, and the gain thereof than fine gold.   PROV. iii. 14.

Capital is not what a man *has*, but what he *is*. Character is capital; honor is capital.   MACDUFF.

The Lord shall be thy confidence.   PROV. iii. 26.

Though the mariner sees not the pole-star, yet the needle of the compass which points to it tells him which way he sails; thus the heart that is touched with the loadstone of divine love, trembling with godly fear, and yet still looking toward God by fixed believing, interprets the fear by the love in the fear, and tells the soul that its course is heavenward, toward the haven of eternal rest.   LEIGHTON.

The path of the just is as the shining light, that shineth more and more unto the perfect day.   PROV. iv. 18.

Have I begun this path of heavenly love and knowledge now? Am I progressing in it? Do I feel some dawnings of the heavenly light,—earnests and antepasts of the full day of glory? Let all God's dealings serve to quicken me in my way. Let every affliction it may please Him to send, be as the moving pillar-cloud of old, beckoning me to move my tent onward, saying, " Arise ye, and depart, for this is not your rest." Let me be often standing now on faith's lofty eminences, looking for "the day of God"—the rising sun which is to set no more in weeping clouds. Wondrous progression! How will all earth's learning,—its boasted acquirements and eagle-eyed philosophy,—sink into the lispings of very infancy in comparison with this manhood of knowledge! Heaven will be the true "*Excelsior.*" Its song, "*A song of degrees*"; Jesus. leading His people from height to height of glory, and saying, as He said to Nathaniel, "*Thou shalt see greater things than these.*"

MACDUFF.

To-day it is fair, the next day there may be the thundering storm: to-day I may want for nothing; tomorrow I may be like Jacob, with nothing but a stone for my pillow and the heavens for my curtains. But what a happy thought it is!—though we know not where the road winds, we know where it ends. It is the straightest way to heaven to go round about. Israel's forty years' wanderings were, after all, the nearest path to Canaan. We may have to go through trial and affliction; the pilgrimage may be a tiresome one, but it is safe. We cannot trace the river upon which we are sailing; but we know it ends in floods of bliss at last. We cannot track the roads; but we know that they all meet in the great metropolis of heaven, in the centre of God's universe. God help us to pursue the true pilgrimage of a pious life! SPURGEON.

PROV. iv. 23. *Keep thy heart with all diligence; for out of it are the issues of life.*

The heart of man is a furnace continually burning.

If thou wilt nourish it with meditations of the love of God, there will appear a bright flame of love to God and man; but if thou maintain it with thoughts of self-love, then it will be full of vile smoke, stench, and darkness. CAWDRAY.

You have seen the great reservoirs provided by our water companies, in which the water which is to supply hundreds of streets and thousands of houses is kept. Now, the heart is just the reservoir of man, and our life is allowed to flow in its proper season. That life may flow through different pipes—the mouth, the hand, the eye; but still all the issues of hand, of eye, of lip, derive their source from the great fountain and central reservoir, the heart; and hence there is no difficulty in showing the great necessity for keeping this reservoir, the heart, in a proper state and condition, since otherwise, that which flows through the pipes must be tainted and corrupt. SPURGEON.

Pride . . . do I hate. PROV. viii. 13.
The difference between pride and vanity is that we have one and other people have the other.

The fear of the Lord is the beginning of wisdom: and PROV. ix. 10.
the knowledge of the holy is understanding.
He is the best grammarian who has learned to speak the truth from his heart; the best astronomer who has conversation in heaven; the best musician who has learned to sing the praise of his God; the best arithmetician who so numbers his days as to apply his heart to wisdom. He is knowing in ethics who trains up his family in the fear of the Lord; he is the best economist who is wise to salvation, prudent in giving

and taking good counsel; he is the best politician and he is a good linguist, that speaks the language of Canaan.　　　　　　　　　　　　　　SPENCER.

PROV. xi. 21. *Though hand join in hand, the wicked shall not be unpunished.*

He that is not afraid of sinning has good need to be afraid of damning.　　　　　　　　　SPURGEON.

PROV. xi. 25. *The liberal soul shall be made fat.*

Such was Hannah's experience. She gave away one child, and God paid her back with five.

　　　　　　　　　　　　　　　　GUTHRIE.

PROV. xi. 25. *He that watereth shall be watered also himself.*

The effective life and the receptive life are one. No sweep of arm that does some work for God, but harvests also some more of the truth of God, and sweeps it into the treasury of life.　　PHILLIPS BROOKS.

PROV. xiii. 20. *He that walketh with wise men shall be wise.*

The tree-frog acquires the color of whatever it adheres to for a short time. If it be found on the oak, it is a brown color; on the sycamore or cedar it is of a whitish-brown color; but, when found on the growing corn, it is sure to be green. So a man is sure to be influenced by those with whom he associates.

PROV. xiv. 8. *The wisdom of the prudent is to understand his way.*

My daily task whate'er it be,
That is what mainly educates me.

PROV. xv. 8. *The prayer of the upright is his delight.*

The bank-note without a signature at the bottom, is nothing but a worthless piece of paper. The stroke of a pen confers on it all its value. The prayer of a poor child of Adam is a feeble thing in itself, but once endorsed by the hand of the Lord Jesus, it availeth much. There was an officer in the city of Rome who was appointed to have his doors always open, in order to receive any Roman citizen who applied to him for help. Just so the ear of the Lord Jesus is ever open to the cry of all who want mercy and grace. It is His office to help them. Their prayer is His delight. Reader, think of this. Is not this encouragement? RYLE.

Every one that is proud in heart is an abomination to the Lord. PROV. xvi. 5.

Naturalists find it much less easy to teach a mountain-flower to accommodate itself to a low locality than to get one which by birth belongs to the valleys to live and thrive at a lofty elevation. So there seems nothing more difficult to men than to descend gracefully. How few who have been accustomed to a high position in society are able to reconcile themselves to a humble one! . . . So it is with us in our low and lost estate. Spiritually poor, we are spiritually proud, saying, " I am rich, and increased in goods, and have need of nothing;" while we are "wretched and miserable and poor and blind and naked." Even when we are in some degree sensible of our poverty, and know we cannot pay, like the unjust steward, we are ashamed to beg. Indulging a pride out of all keeping "with filthy rags," we will not stoop to stand at God's door, poor mendicants, who ask for mercy.

GUTHRIE.

He that ruleth his spirit (is better) than he that taketh a city. PROV. xvi. 32.

Men are always wanting to do some great thing.

121

One Thousand and One

Let them overcome themselves, for that is the greatest conquest. DRUMMOND.

PROV. xviii. 16. *A man's gift maketh room for him.*

Nothing hides a blemish so completely as cloth of gold. HARE.

PROV. xxii. 6. *Train up a child in the way he should go.*

The heathen mother takes her babe to the idol temple, and teaches it to clasp its little hands before its forehead, in the attitude of prayer, long before it can utter a word. As soon as it can walk, it is taught to gather a few flowers or fruits, or put a little rice upon a banana-leaf, and lay them upon the altar before the idol god. As soon as it can utter the names of its parents, so soon it is taught to offer up its petitions before the images. Who ever saw a heathen child that could speak, and not pray? Christian mothers, why is it that so many children grow up in this enlightened land without learning to pray?

PROV. xxiii. 7. *As he thinketh in his heart, so is he.*

What you love, what you desire, what you think about, you are photographing, printing, on the walls of your immortal nature. And just as to-day, thousands of years after the artists have been gathered to the dust, we may go into Egyptian temples and see the figures on their walls, in all the freshness of their first coloring, as if the painter had but laid down his pencil a moment ago, so, on your hearts, youthful evils, the sins of your childhood, the misdeeds of your earliest days, may live ugly shapes, that no tears and no repentance will ever wipe out. Nothing can do away with "the marks of that which once hath been."

Thoughts from My Library

What are you painting on the chambers of imagery in your hearts? . . . Everything which you do leaves its effect with you forever, just as long-forgotten meals are in your blood and bones to-day. Every act that a man performs has printed itself upon his soul; it has become a part of himself; and, though, like a newly-painted picture, after a little while the colors go in, why is that? Only because they have entered into the very fibre of the canvas, and have left the surface because they are incorporated with the substance, and they want but a touch of varnish to flash out again.

MACLAREN.

See that each hour's feelings and thoughts and actions are pure and true; then will your life be such. The wide pasture is but separate spears of grass; the sheeted bloom of the prairies but isolated flowers.

BEECHER.

Holy thoughts in the heart have also a transfiguring influence on the life.

J. R. MILLER.

Buy the truth, and sell it not.

Buy the truth whatever it may cost; sell it not whatever may be offered. ARNOT.

PROV. xxiii. 23.

Give me thine heart.

Give your heart to God and your life to earnest work and loving purpose, and you can never live in vain. PUNSHON.

PROV. xxiii. 26.

Boast not thyself of to-morrow, for thou knowest not what a day may bring forth.

Life's uncertainties give us a new hold upon the everlasting. MARK GUY PEARSE.

PROV. xxvii. 1.

123

One Thousand and One

The only preparation for the morrow is the right use of to-day. . . . The morrow comes for nought, if to-day is not heeded.   BOWEN.

PROV.
xxix.
25.

The fear of man bringeth a snare: but whoso putteth his trust in the Lord shall be safe.

We fear men so much because we fear God so little.

GURNALL.

ECCL.
ii. 14.

One event happeneth to them all.

When Severus, Emperor of Rome, found his end approaching, he cried out, "I have been everything; and everything is nothing." Then, ordering the urn to be brought to him in which his ashes were to be enclosed on his body being burned, he said, "Little urn, thou shalt contain one for whom the world was too little."

ECCL.
iii. 1.

To everything there is a season, and a time to every purpose under the sun.

Real duties never interfere with each other.

FINNEY.

ECCL.
iii. 11.

He hath made everything beautiful.

When men travel in stage coaches in grand mountain countries, some ride in the inside with the curtains fastened down. They see nothing of the beauty of the scenes through which they pass. Others ride outside, and see every grand thing by the way. This illustrates the way different persons go through God's world. Many pass through shut up inside a dark, dismal coach, with all the curtains drawn tight, themselves shut in, and all of God's joy and beauty shut out; others ride outside, and catch a glimpse of every fair and lovely thing by the way. They breathe the

124

Thoughts from My Library

fresh air, hear the joyous songs of the birds, see the fields, brooks, rivers, mountains and skies, and quaff delight everywhere.   J. R. MILLER.

Everything in the world must be in its true place and time, or it is not beautiful. . . . You lay your own stumbling-block in your own way. God made the block indeed, but He made it for a part of the strength and beauty of the walls. It was you who dragged it down to the floor and insisted upon laying it where you could stumble over it.

         PHILLIPS BROOKS.

I know that there is no good in them, but for a man   ECCL.
   . . . to do good in his life.   iii. 12.

See that well on the mountain-side,—a small, rude, rocky cup full of crystal water, and that tiny rill flowing through a breach in its brim. The vessel is so diminutive, that it could not contain a supply of water for a single family a single day. But ever getting through secret channels, and ever giving by an open overflow, day and night, summer and winter, from year to year, it discharges in the aggregate a volume to which its own capacity bears no appreciable proportion. The flow from that diminutive cup might, in a drought or war, become life to all the inhabitants of a city. It is thus that a Christian, if he is full of mercy and good fruits, is a greater blessing to the world than either himself or his neighbors deem.

         ARNOT.

I saw the wicked buried, who had come and gone from   ECCL.
   the place of the holy.   viii. 10.

The saddest road to hell is that which runs under

the pulpit, past the Bible, and through the midst of warnings and invitations. RYLE.

ECCL. viii. 12. *It shall be well with them that fear God.*

A quiet modest word, but full of significance. The fear of God took Abraham to Mount Moriah, and it was well with him there. It was *not* the fear of God that took Lot to Sodom; it went not well with him there. The fear of God took Daniel into the lion's den, and the three Hebrews into the seven times heated furnace; they feared Him Who had the power to cast both soul and body into hell; and it was well with them. The Spirit of glory and of God resteth as a dove upon them that fear God; invisible to the world; telling of the new Jerusalem that cometh down from God out of heaven. BOWEN.

ECCL. ix. 11. *The race is not to the swift, nor the battle to the strong.*

There is more chance for a cripple on the right road than for a racer on the wrong.

ECCL. ix. 11. *Time . . . happeneth to them all.*

Time wasted is existence, used, is life. YOUNG.

ECCL. xi. 1. *Cast thy bread upon the waters.*

Sometimes the Nile overflows its banks, and the people throw the seed upon the water. As the water subsides, the seed strikes into the ground and comes up. Hence the allusion, "Cast thy bread upon the waters, and it will come back after many days." What you sow you will reap. TALMAGE.

Thoughts from My Library

Remember now thy Creator in the days of thy youth. ECCL. xii. 1.

I saw once, lying side by side in a great workshop, two heads made of metal. The one was perfect; all the features of a noble, manly face came out clear and distinct in their lines of strength and beauty; in the other, scarcely a single feature could be recognized; it was all marred and spoiled. "The metal had been let grow a little too cool, sir," said the man who was showing it to me. I could not help thinking how true that was of many a form more precious than metal. Many a young soul that might be stamped with the image and superscription of the King, while it is warm with the love and glow of early youth, is allowed to grow too cold, and the writing is blurred and the image is marred. CANON TEIGNMOUTH SHORE.

Fear God and keep his commandments: for this is the whole duty of man. ECCL. xii. 13.

Duties are ours, events are God's. This removes an infinite burden from the shoulders of a miserable, tempted, dying creature. On this consideration only, can he securely lay down his head, and close his eyes. CECIL.

God shall bring every work into judgment. ECCL. xii. 14.

Just as the tiny shells make up the chalk hills, and the chalk hills together make up the range, so the trifling actions make up the whole account, and each of these must be pulled asunder separately. You had an hour to spare the other day—what did you do? You had a voice—how did you use it? You had a pen—you could use that—how did you employ it? Each particular shall be brought out, and there shall be demanded an account for each one. SPURGEON.

One Thousand and One

The little foxes, that spoil the vines.

When Pompey could not prevail with a city to billet his army with them, he persuaded them to admit of a few weak, maimed soldiers; but those soon recovered their strength, and opened the gates to the whole army. And thus is it that the devil courts us only to lodge some small sin—a sin of infirmity or two— which, being admitted, soon gathers strength and sinews, and so subdues us. PRICE.

The science of chemistry teaches us that a single grain of iodine will impart color to seven thousand times its weight of water. So one sin may affect the whole life, one false brick may cause the fall of the whole building. J. HARRIS.

There are two ways of coming down from the top of a church-steeple: one is to jump down, and the other is to come down by the steps; but both will lead you to the bottom. So, also, there are two ways of going to hell: one is to walk into it with your eyes open (few people do that), the other is to go down by the steps of *little sins;* and that way, I fear, is only too common. Put up with a few little sins, and you will soon want a few more, (even a heathen could say, "Whoever was content with only one sin?") and then your course will be regularly worse and worse every year. The devil only wants to get the wedge of a little allowed sin into your hearts, and you will soon be all his own. Never play with fire; never trifle with little sins! RYLE.

The smell of thy garments is like the smell of Lebanon.

In the days when the Mosque of Omar was first

built, over that spot of Moriah where the worshipper could touch a piece of the unhewn original rock of the hill, it was customary to bring loads of incense and all aromatic shrubs into the shrine, which was called Sakhrah. As a consequence, if any one from the city had been worshipping there, he carried away with him so much of the fragrance of the place, that when people passed him in the market-place of Jerusalem, or in the streets, they used to say to each other, "He has been in the Sakhrah to-day!" Would to God we thus lived, coming forth daily with our "garments" smelling of the "myrrh, and aloes, and cassia, from the ivory palaces." With fresh holiness every day drawn out of Christ, what witnesses for Him should we be! How joyfully should we listen to the loving voice that is ever calling, "Be ye holy, for I am holy"; and He Who speaks thus would hasten to give us more and more when we repair to Him.   BONAR.

Though your sins be as scarlet, they shall be as white as snow.   IS. i. 18.

I have heard of a certain divine, that he used always to carry with him a little book. This tiny volume had only three leaves in it; and truth to tell, it contained not a single word. The first was a leaf of black paper, black as jet; the next was a leaf of red-scarlet; and the last was a leaf of white, without spot. Day by day he would look upon this singular book, and at last he told the secret of what it meant. He said, "Here is the black leaf, that is my sin, and the wrath of God which my sin deserves; I look and look, and think it is not half black enough to represent my guilt, though it is as black as black can be. The red leaf reminds me of the atoning sacrifice and the precious blood; and I delight to look at it, and weep, and look again. The white leaf represents my soul, as it is washed in Jesus' blood and made white as snow." SPURGEON.

IS.
vi. 5,
6, 7.

Woe is me! for I am undone, because I am a man of unclean lips . . . Then flew one of the seraphim unto me . . . and said . . . Thine iniquity is taken away.

Soon as the word is uttered, "I have sinned," that very moment flies the seraph. God "is faithful and just to forgive us our sins." When we confess them in the name of Jesus, justice, having been satisfied by the blood of Christ, is swift to pardon.

IS.
vi. 8.

Here am I.

I am only one, but I am one. I cannot do everything, but I can do something. What I can do, I ought to do, and what I ought to do, by the grace of God I will do.

IS.
xxvi.
I.

Salvation will God appoint for walls and bulwarks.

Men appoint walls and bulwarks for salvation; but God appoints salvation for walls and bulwarks. Salvation is often without walls and bulwarks, and walls and bulwarks without salvation. Salvation is the safer safeguard. VENNING.

IS.
xxvi.
3.

Thou wilt keep him in perfect peace whose mind is stayed on thee.

The habit of reckoning on Christ is the key to a restful life. F. B. MEYER.

IS.
xxx. 7.

Their strength is to sit still.

The still and quiet soul is like a ship that lies quiet

in the harbor: you may take in what goods you please whilst the ship lies still. So, when the soul lies quiet under the hand of God, it is most fitted to take in much of God, of Christ, of heaven, of the promises, and of ordinances; but, when souls are unquiet, they are like a ship in a storm: they can take in nothing.

BROOKS.

In quietness and in confidence shall be your strength. IS. XXX. 15.

In all the departments of life it is the quiet forces that effect most. The sunbeams fall all day long, silently, unheard by human ear; yet there is in them a wondrous energy and a great power for blessing and good. Gravitation is a silent force, with no rattle of machinery, no noise of engines, no clanking of chains, and yet it holds all the stars and worlds in their orbits and swings them through space with unvarying precision. The dew falls silently at night when men sleep and yet it touches every plant and leaf and flower with new life and beauty. It is in the lightning, not in the thunder-peal, that the electric energy resides. Thus even in nature, strength lies in quietness and the mightiest energies work noiselessly. J. R. MILLER.

God often encourages the weak in faith by giving speedy answers to prayer; but the strong in faith will be tested by God's delays.

Sow beside all waters. IS. XXXii. 20.

Never mind whereabouts your work is. Never mind whether it be visible or no. Never mind whether your name is associated with it. You may never see the issues of your toils. You are working for eternity. . . . If you cannot see results here in the hot working day, the cool evening hours are drawing near, when you may rest from your labors, and then they will follow you. So do your duty, and trust God to give the seed you sow "a body as it hath pleased Him." McLAREN.

IS. xxxiii. 16.

He shall dwell on high: his place of defense shall be the munitions of rocks.

I remember a story in Alexander's wars, that when he came to besiege the Sogdians, a people who dwelt upon a rock, or had the literal munition of rocks for their defence, they jeered him and asked him whether his soldiers had wings or no. "Unless your soldiers can fly in the air, we fear you not." It is a most certain truth, when God exalts a people, He can set them upon a rock so high that, unless their adversaries have wings, and those more than eagles' wings, to soar higher than God himself, they are beyond annoyance. He carries His own upon eagles' wings; what wings, then, must they have who get above His people.

CARYL.

IS. xxxiv. 16.

Seek ye out of the book of the Lord, and read.

Do not think you are getting no good from the Bible, merely because you do not see that good day by day. The greatest effects are by no means those which make the most noise and are most easily observed. The greatest effects are often silent, quiet, and hard to detect at the time they are being produced. Think of the influence of the moon upon the earth, and of the air upon the human lungs. Remember how silently the dew falls, and how imperceptibly the grass grows. There may be far more doing than you think in your soul by your Bible-reading. RYLE.

Thoughts from My Library

The word of our God shall stand forever.   IS.

The word of God is the water of life; the more ye xl. 8.
lave it forth, the fresher it runneth: it is the fire of
God's glory; the more ye blow it, the clearer it burn-
eth: it is the corn of the Lord's field; the better ye
grind it, the more it yieldeth: it is the bread of heaven;
the more it is broken and given forth, the more it remaineth: it is the sword of the Spirit; the more it is
scoured, the brighter it shineth.   BISHOP JEWEL.

They that wait upon the Lord shall . . . mount IS.
    up with wings as eagles.   xl. 31.

Yes, "they shall mount up with wings as eagles."
You know what eagles' wings mean. The eagle is
the king of birds, it soars the highest into the heavens.
Believers are to live a heavenly life, in the very Presence and Love and Joy of God. They are to live where
God lives; they need God's strength to rise there. To
them that wait on Him it shall be given.

You know how the eagle wings are obtained. Only
in one way—by the eagle birth. You are born of God.
You have the eagles' wings. You may not have
known it: you may not have used them; but God can
and will teach you to use them.   ANDREW MURRAY.

Fear thou not for I am with thee; be not dismayed, IS.
    for I am thy God.   xli. 10.

Fear in all its forms is a kind of atheism. The man
who is afraid has lost faith; he no longer believes in
God.

That which justifies courage in facing the possibilities of life is the conviction that its master is our Lord
as well; that it is so framed that "all things work together for good" to those who are obedient to the

laws of life; that our little plans are embraced in a greater and wiser plan; that "light is sown for the righteous."

Many a man looks backward and thanks God for the events in his life which once seemed disastrous, but which, in the clearer light of time, disclose the beauty of noble opportunity.

IS.
xli. 10. *I will uphold thee with the right hand of my righteousness.*

If God bear us in His arms when we are children, yet when we are well grown He looks we should go on our own feet; it is enough that He upholds us, though He carry us not.   BISHOP HALL.

IS.
xli. 13. *I the Lord thy God will hold thy right hand.*

Don't try to hold God's hand; let Him hold yours. Let Him do the *holding,* and you do the *trusting.*

WEBB-PEPLOE.

IS.
xlii. 3. *A bruised reed shall he not break, and the smoking flax shall he not quench.*

He dost not wait until we are at our fairest and best. He stoops to help us at our deadest and dullest, our poorest and worst, when life is almost gone out and the fire is at its last spark. He can help us and keep us in the most trying circumstances, however bleak winds blow, whatever biting frosts come. A most gracious, gentle, pitiful Saviour is He, and as mighty as He is gentle. Press up to Him; go on your way communing with Him. Cleave to Him, your Life; rest in Him, your loving Lord; exult in Him, your Almighty Saviour.   MARK GUY PEARSE.

Thoughts from My Library

I have created him for my glory.   IS.

God made you for an end. Find out what that end xliii. 7.
is; find out your niche, and fill it. If it be ever so little, if it is only to be a hewer of wood and drawer of
water, do something in this great battle for God and
truth.   SPURGEON.

This people have I formed for myself; they shall show IS.
*   forth my praise.*   xliii.
                                                        21.
I have read of an author, who, whilst he was writing a book he was about to publish, would every now
and then look back to the title to see if his work cor-
responded thereto, and if it answered the expectation
raised thereby. Now, the use I would make hereof,
and would recommend to you, is for thee, O sinner,
to look back every now and then, and consider for
what thou wast created; and for thee, O saint, to look
back every now and then, and consider for what thou
wast redeemed.   ASHBURNER.

Thou shalt not be forgotten of me.   IS.

He may leave you long without succor. He may xliv.
allow you to toil against a tempestuous sea until the 21.
fourth watch of the night. He may seem silent and
austere, tarrying two days still in the same place, as if
careless of the dying Lazarus. He may allow your
prayers to accumulate like unopened letters on the
table of an absent friend. But at last He will say:
"O man, O woman, great is thy faith: be it unto thee
even as thou wilt."   F. B. MEYER.

I will give thee the treasures of darkness.   IS.

If you can find no bright side in your trouble to look xlv. 3.
upon, polish up the dark one.

IS.
xlv.21.

A just God and a Saviour.

When the Son of God was made of a woman, and made under the law, there was heard the most awful voice that ever was heard in the universe yet: "Awake, O sword! against the Man that is my fellow, and smite the shepherd,"—smite him! When there was a man in the world that was Jehovah's fellow, there was some one who could magnify the law, in smiting whom justice could obtain its demands. The sword of justice smote him, struck him, cut him. The sword of justice had a commission to smite the Man that was Jehovah's fellow: it smote Him in Bethlehem; it smote Him all along the highway of His life, even to Calvary. On Calvary, the strokes of the sword fell heavy; the glances of that sword then darkened the sun; the strokes of the sword shook earth, shook hell; it kept smiting and smiting the Man that was God's fellow, till at last He cried, "It is finished!" Then the sword fell down at the foot of the cross, hushed, lulled, pacified: and it lay there till the third hallowed morning, when it was found changed into a sceptre of mercy; and that sceptre of mercy has been waving among mankind ever since.

BEAUMONT.

IS.
xlv.24.

In the Lord have I . . . strength.

A believer's watchfulness is like that of a soldier. A sentinel posted on the walls, when he discerns a hostile party advancing, does not attempt to make head against them himself, but informs his commanding officer of the enemy's approach, and leaves him to take the proper measures against the foe. So the Christian does not attempt to fight temptation in his own strength; his watchfulness lies in observing its approach, and in telling God of it by prayer.

W. MASON.

Thoughts from My Library

I have chosen thee in the furnace of affliction.

It is a great help when passing through the fire to know that we are there because there is gold to be extracted or silver to be refined as well as dross to purge away.   EL NATHAN.

IS. xlviii. 10.

There is no peace, saith the Lord, unto the wicked.

As the ant-hill, when stirred, sets in motion its living insects in every direction, so the conscience of the sinner, disturbed by the Spirit or judgments of God, calls up before its vision thousands of deeds which fill the soul with agony and woe.   M'COSH.

IS. xlviii. 22.

My God shall be my strength.

Give what Thou commandest, and then command what Thou wilt.   AUGUSTINE.

IS. xlix. 5.

Zion said, The Lord, hath forsaken me, and my Lord hath forgotten me. Can a woman forget her sucking child, that she should not have compassion on the son of her womb? yea, they may forget, yet will I not forget thee.

God's promises are dated, but with a mysterious character; and, for want of skill in God's chronology, we are prone to think God forgets us, when, indeed, we forget ourselves in being so bold to set God a time of our own, and in being angry that He comes not just then to us.   GURNALL.

IS. xlix. 14, 15.

They shall not be ashamed that wait for me.

These waiting seasons, trying though they are to flesh and blood, are nevertheless precious ones for the soul. Ah, how much do we learn in them that will pass on with us into eternity, and draw from our lips

IS. xlix. 23.

there the loudest praises! Yes, it will be then seen
that our waiting time here has been the most precious
part of our heavenward journey. How will the joy of
that world of unbroken rest be enhanced by the trials
and struggles of life's pilgrimage, where not one wave
of sorrow shall ever break over the soul! Each shall
look back and exclaim, "He hath done all things well!"

F. WHITFIELD.

IS.
l. 10. *Who is among you that . . . walketh in darkness
and hath no light? let him trust in the name of the
Lord and stay upon his God.*

This is God's way. In the darkest hours of the
night His tread draws near across the billows. As the
day of execution is breaking, the angel comes to Peter's
cell. When the scaffold for Mordecai is complete, the
royal sleeplessness leads to a reaction in favor of the
threatened race. Ah! soul, it may have to come to the
worst with thee ere thou art delivered; but thou wilt
be! God may keep thee waiting; but He will ever be
mindful of His covenant, and will appear to fulfill His
inviolable word.

F. B. MEYER.

IS.
li. 1. *Look unto the rock whence ye are hewn, and to the hole
of the pit whence ye are digged.*

God would build for Himself a palace in heaven of
living stones. Where did He get them? Did He go
to the quarries of Paros? Hath He brought forth the
richest and the purest marble from the quarries of perfection? No, ye saints: look to "the hole of the pit
whence ye were digged, and to the rock whence ye
were hewn!" Ye were full of sin: so far from being
stones that were white with purity, ye were black with
defilement, seemingly utterly unfit to be stones in the

spiritual temple, which should be the dwelling-place of the Most High. Goldsmiths make exquisite forms from precious material; they fashion the bracelet and the ring from gold: God maketh His precious things out of base material; and from the black pebbles of the defiling brooks He hath taken up stones, which He hath set in the golden ring of His immutable love, to make them gems to sparkle on His finger forever. He hath not selected the best, but apparently the worst of men to be the monuments of His grace; and, when He would have a choir in heaven, He sent Mercy to earth to find out the dumb, and teach them to sing.

SPURGEON.

He was wounded for our transgressions, he was bruised for our iniquities: the chastisement of our peace was upon him; and with his stripes we are healed. IS. liii. 5.

Two friends are said to come into Vulcan's shop, and to beg a boon of him: it was granted. What was it ? that he would either beat them on his anvil, or melt them in his furnace, both into one. But without fiction, here is a far greater love in Christ; for He would be melted in the furnace of wrath, and beaten on the anvil of death, to be made one with us. And to declare the exceeding love, here were not both to be beaten on the anvil, or melted in the furnace; but without us He alone would be beaten on the anvil, He alone melted that we might be spared. THOMAS ADAMS.

My thoughts are not your thoughts, neither are your ways my ways, saith the Lord. IS. lv. 8.

Take a straight stick, and put it into the water, and it will seem crooked. Why ? Because we look upon it through two mediums,—air and water. Thus the proceedings of God in His justice, which in themselves are straight, without the least obliquity, seem unto us crooked. That wicked men should prosper, and good men be afflicted; that the Israelites should make the bricks, and the Egyptians dwell in the houses; that servants should ride on horseback, and princes go on foot,—these are things that make the best Christians stagger in their judgments. And why? But because they look upon God's proceedings through a double medium,—of flesh and spirit; that so all things seem to go cross, though, indeed, they are right enough. And hence it is that God's proceedings in His justice are not so well discerned; the eyes of man alone being not competent judges thereof.

A child might say to a geographer, "You talk about the earth being round! Look on this great crag; look on that deep dell; look on yonder great mountain, and the valley at its feet, and yet you talk about the earth being round." The geographer would have an instant answer for the child; his view is comprehensive; he does not look at the surface of the world in mere detail; he does not deal with inches and feet and yards; he sees a larger world than the child has had time to grasp. He explains what he means by the expression, "The earth is a globe," and justifies his strange statement. And so it is with God's wonderful dealings with us: there are great rocks and barren deserts, deep, dank, dark pits and defiles, and glens and dells, rugged places that we cannot smooth over at all; and yet when He comes to say to us at the end of the journey, "Now, look back; there is the way that I have brought you," we shall be enabled to say,

Thoughts from My Library

"Thou hast gone before us, and made our way
straight."   JOSEPH PARKER.

For as the heavens are higher than the earth, so are IS.
my ways higher than your ways, and my thoughts lv. 9.
than your thoughts.

You will notice that in the placid waters of a lake
everything which is highest in reality is lowest in
the reflection. The higher the trees, the lower their
image. That is the picture of this world; what is
highest in this world is lowest in the other, and what
is highest in that world is lowest in this. Gold is on
top here; they pave the streets with it there. To serve
is looked upon as ignoble here; there those that serve
reign, and the last are first. Any girl is willing to
fling away paste diamonds for the real stones; when a
man understands what God can be to the soul, he
loses his taste for things he used to care for most.

                                             F. B. MEYER.

The high and lofty One . . . *inhabiteth eternity.* IS.
Eternity hath neither beginning nor end. Time hath lvii. 15.
both. Eternity comprehends in itself all years, all
ages, all periods of ages, and differs from time as the
sea and the rivers; the sea never changes place, and is
always one water, but the rivers glide along and are
swallowed up in the sea; so is time by eternity.

                                             CHARNOCK.

The Lord shall guide thee continually. IS.
The bells of Westminster Abbey chime hourly a lviii.
sweet, simple melody. The words allied to the tune 11.
are these:

> All through this hour,
> Lord, be my guide,
> And through Thy power
> No foot shall slide.

141

IS.
lix. 2.

Your iniquities have separated between you and your God, and your sins have hid his face from you.

At a rehearsal for a Sabbath-school entertainment, some time since, a little girl, five years old, was placed upon the platform to recite a short poem. She commenced very bravely, but her eyes wandered all round the church, gathering more and more of disappointment in her face. Soon the lips began to quiver, and the little form shook with sobs. Her father stepped from behind a pillar, from whence he had been watching her, and taking her in his arms, said, "Why, darling, what is the matter? I thought my little girl knew the verses so well." "So I do, papa; but I couldn't see you. Let me stand where I can look right into your face, and then I won't be afraid." Is it not so with our heavenly Father's children? We stand too often where we cannot look into His face. Darling sins and our pride, like pillars, rise up between us and God, and disappointment and tears are ours, until, casting these behind us, we stand in the light of the Father's face.

IS.
lx. 20.

The Lord shall be thine everlasting light.

God is Light. God is a Sun. Paul says: "God hath shined in our hearts to give the light." What light? "The light of the glory of God, in the face of Jesus Christ." Just as the sun shines its beautiful, life-giving light on and into our earth, so God shines into our hearts the light of His glory, of His love, in Christ His Son. Our heart is meant to have that light filling and gladdening it all the day. It can have it, because God is our sun, and it is written, "Thy sun shall no more go down forever." God's love shines on us without ceasing.   ANDREW MURRAY.

Thoughts from My Library

All our righteousnesses are as filthy rags. IS. lxiv. 6.

Day by day, are you busy, and even painstaking, in the attempt to weave and work out a righteousness of your own. Leave that loom! Your vows and promises are gossamer threads; ever snapping in your hands and breaking at each throw of the shuttle. The "fine linen" that robes the saints, the only raiment meet for thy soul and approved of God, was woven on the cross; and dyed there, with color more enduring than Tyrian purple, in the blood of the Son of God.

GUTHRIE.

What will ye do in the end thereof? JER. v. 31.

Better it is, toward the right conduct of life, to consider what will be the end of a thing, than what is the beginning of it; for what promises fair at first may prove ill, and what seems at first a disadvantage, may prove very advantageous. WELLS.

Shall iron break the northern iron and the steel? JER. xv. 12.

I know not, but probably the Bible here alludes to the superior excellence of a Damascus blade. I once happened to see this steel put to the test. It was in France, and in the chemistry class of the Sorbonne. In the course of a lecture on iron, Thenard, the professor, produced a Damascus blade, stating that he believed that these swords owed their remarkable temper to the iron of which they were made being smelted by the charcoal of a thorn-bush that grew in the desert. To put it to the trial, he placed the sword in the hand of a very powerful man, his assistant; desiring him to strike it with all his might against a bar of iron. With the arm of a giant the assistant sent the blade flashing around his head, and then down on the iron block, into which, when I expected to see it shivered like glass, it embedded itself, quivering but uninjured; giving, besides a remarkable proof of the trustworthiness of the sword, new force to the proverb, *True as steel.*

GUTHRIE.

JER.
XV. 16. *Thy word was unto me the joy and rejoicing of mine heart.*

The Bible is a rock of diamonds, a chain of pearls, the sword of the Spirit; a chart by which the Christian sails to eternity; the map by which he daily walks; the sun-dial by which he sets his life; the balance in which he weighs his actions. T. WATSON.

JER.
xvii. 9. *The heart is deceitful above all things.*

The dank mossy sward is deceitful: its fresh and glossy carpet invites the traveller to leave the rough moorland tract; and, at the first step, horse and rider are buried in the morass. The sea is deceitful; what rage, what stormy passions sleep in that placid bosom! and how often, as vice serves her used-up victims, does she cast the bark that she received into her arms with sunny smiles a wreck upon the shore. The morning is oft deceitful; with bright promise of a brilliant day, it lures us from home; the sky ere noon begins to thicken; the sun looks sickly; the sluggish, heavily-laden clouds gather upon the hilltops; the landscape closes in all around; the lark drops songless into her nest; the wind rises, moaning and chill; and at length, like adversities gathering round the grey head of age, tempest, storm, and rain, thicken on the dying day. The desert is deceitful; it mocks the traveller with its mirage. How life kindles in his drooping eye, as he sees the playful waves chase each other to the shore, and the plumes of the palm waving in the watery mirror! Faint, weary, parched, perishing with thirst, he turns to bathe and drink; and exhausting what little strength remains in pursuit of a phantom, unhappy man! he has turned to die. Deceitful above sward or sea, sky or enchanting desert, is the heart of man; nor do I know a more marked or melancholy proof of this than that afforded by our light treatment of such weighty matters as sin and judgment. There is no exaggeration in the prophet's language, "The heart is deceitful above all things, and desperately wicked." GUTHRIE.

I the Lord search the heart.

Before men we stand as opaque beehives. They can see the thoughts go in and out of us; but what work they do inside of a man, they cannot tell. Before God we are as *glass* beehives, and all that our thoughts are doing within us He perfectly sees and understands. BEECHER.

JER. xvii. 10.

Behold, as the clay is in the potter's hand, so are ye in mine hand, O house of Israel.
God is love.—1 John iv. 8.

I am clay in the hands of *God*, I tremble; I am clay in the hands of *Love*, I trust. G. GAMPBELL MORGAN.

JER. xviii. 6.

I spake unto thee in thy prosperity.

We shade our eyes with the hand to shut out the glare of the strong daylight, when we want to see far away. God thus puts, as it were, His hand upon our brows, and tempers the glow of prosperity, that we may take in the wider phases of His goodness. It is a common experience that, looking out from the gloom

JER. xxii. 21.

of some personal affliction, men have seen for the first time beyond the earth plane, and caught glimpses of the Beulah Land. Let us not shrink from the Hand which we know is heavy only with blessing.

LUDLOW.

JER. XXVI. 14.

I am in your hand; do with me as seemeth good . . . unto you.

Here is the crest for the Lord's worker: An arrow, polished and feathered—content to lie in the quiver until the Master uses it. Lying on the string for His unerring fingers to send it forth: then going, strong, swift, sure, smiting through the heart of the king's enemies. And with this for the motto: *I fly where I am sent.* MARK GUY PEARSE.

JER. XXXI. 3.

I have loved thee with an everlasting love.

Get up into the high mountains, believing children of God, and view the everlasting love of your Father toward you in Jesus! Recount all that that love has brought for you before you had any being! Is it likely to drop you now because of any unworthiness it perceives? Can anything appear in us which was not anticipated by One Who before taking us for His own possession sat down and counted the cost? Is there not comfort in knowing that your keel is caught by a current which emanated from the purpose of Him Who worketh all things after the counsel of His own will, and is bearing you toward His heart? "Oh, the depth of the riches both of the wisdom and the knowledge of God! How unsearchable are His judgments, and His ways past finding out! For of Him, and through Him, and to Him are all things! To Him be the glory forever. Amen." F. B. MEYER.

Thoughts from My Library

I will put my law in their inward parts, and write it in their hearts. JER. xxxi. 33.

Lycurgus would allow none of his laws to be written. He would have the principles of government interwoven in the lives and manners of the people, as most conducive to their happiness. Their education would be such as to imprint these laws upon their minds, that they might remain perpetually before them. He will most faithfully abide by the king's commandment who has the word of God so engraven upon his heart that nothing can erase it. The multiplication of Bibles that stand upon book-shelves or lie upon tables is an easy matter; but to multiply copies of walking Scriptures, in the form of holy men who can say, "Thy word have I hid in my heart," is much more difficult.

Thus saith the Lord, Behold, they whose judgment was not to drink of the cup have assuredly drunken; and art thou he that shall altogether go unpunished? thou shalt not go unpunished. JER. xlix. 12.

The tale of the goblet which the genius of a heathen fashioned was true, and taught a moral of which many a deathbed furnishes the melancholy illustration. Having made the model of a serpent, he fixed it in the bottom of the cup. Coiled for the spring, a pair of gleaming eyes in its head, and in its open mouth fangs raised to strike, it lay beneath the ruby wine. Nor did he who raised that golden cup to quench his thirst, and quaff the delicious draught, suspect what lay below, till, as he reached the dregs, that dreadful head rose up, and glistened before his eyes. So, when life's cup is nearly emptied, and sin's last pleasure quaffed, and

unwilling lips are draining the bitter dregs, shall rise
the ghastly terrors of remorse and death and judgment
upon the despairing soul. Be assured, a serpent lurks
at the bottom of guilt's sweetest pleasure.   GUTHRIE.

JER.
li. 34.
An empty vessel.

We must be emptied of self before we can be filled
with grace; we must be stripped of our rags before
we can be clothed with righteousness; we must be
unclothed that we may be clothed; wounded, that we
may be healed; killed, that we may be made alive;
buried in disgrace, that we may rise in holy glory.
These words, "sown in corruption, that we may be
raised in incorruption; sown in dishonor, that we may
be raised in glory; sown in weakness, that we may be
raised in power," are as true of the soul as the body.
To borrow an illustration from the surgeon's art, the
bone that is set wrong must be broken again, in order
that it may be set aright. I press this truth on your
attention. It is certain, that a soul filled with self has
no room for God; and, like the inn of Bethlehem,
given to lodge, crowded with meaner guests, a heart
preoccupied by pride and her godless train has no
chamber within which Christ may be born "in us the
hope of glory."   GUTHRIE.

JER.
li. 58.
The people shall labor in vain.

A man may stop his chronometer in the night, but
he cannot arrest the sunrise.   JOHN KER.

LAM.
iii.
22, 23.
*His compassions fail not. They are new every morn-
ing; great is thy faithfulness.*

It is the glory of God's love that it is always fresh
and new. It is never the same in its expression any

148

two days. We have to patch up our old things and keep using them over and over again; but God never does. He never gives us the old leaves a second time; each spring every tree gets new foliage, new garments of beauty. He does not revive last year's withered flowers, and give them to us again for this year; He gives us new flowers for each summer.

So He does with His messages of love—they are not repeated over and over again, always the same old ones. Every time the reverent heart reads the Bible, its words come fresh from the lips of God, always new. They never get old. They are like the water that bubbles up in living streams from the depths in the wayside spring, always fresh, sweet, and new.

So it is with the blessings of prayer. Morning by morning we kneel before God, seeking His benediction and favor. He does not give us always the same blessing, but has a new one ready for each new day. Our needs are not the same any two mornings when we bow before Him, and He always suits the blessing to the need. We are taught to live day by day. God's goodness comes to us new every morning.

J. R. MILLER.

So thick do Heaven's mercies fly that the arrow of prayer can never be shot aright without bringing down some blessing. If it bring not that which we seek, it shall bring us that which we need.

MARK GUY PEARSE.

He doth not afflict willingly, nor grieve the children of LAM.
men. iii. 33.

It is the rough work that polishes. Look at the pebbles on the shore! Far inland, where some arm of the sea thrusts itself deep into the bosom of the land, and expanding into a salt loch, lies girdled by the mountains, sheltered from the storms that agitate the deep, the pebbles on the beach are rough, not beautiful; angular, not rounded. It is where long white lines of breakers roar, and the rattling shingle is rolled about the strand, that its pebbles are rounded and polished. As in nature, as in the arts, so in grace; it is rough treatment that gives souls as well as stones their lustre; the more the diamond is cut the brighter it sparkles; and in what seems hard dealing, their God has no end in view but to perfect His people's graces. Our Father, and kindest of fathers. He afflicts not willingly; He sends tribulations, but hear Paul tell their purpose: "Tribulation worketh patience, patience experience, experience hope."   GUTHRIE.

O ye children of poverty and toil, of misfortune and sorrow! God is better to you than ye know. Ye see but one side of the veil now; and that is fretted with troubles, and dark with adversity. But it has another side. On that side are angel faces and the smile of God. Your worldly plans are thwarted, and you are tempted to think the Lord unkind. Your business becomes entangled in events, which shift, ye see not how. A sudden blast sweeps all your goods away: ye think it hard, and ye sigh. O weeping followers of Jesus, look! Faithful amid misfortune, gaze! Your crowns are gathering lustre. Your harps are being attuned to sweeter notes and deeper melodies of joy. Your trials project their shadows upon the walls of your heavenly mansion; and, lo! they are transformed into images of seraphic loveliness that shall gleam in beauty there forever.   J. ATKINSON.

Thoughts from My Library

Thy beauty . . . was perfect through my comeliness which I had put upon thee, saith the Lord God. EZEK. xvi. 14.

At heaven's gate there stands an angel, with charge to admit none but those who in their countenances bear the same features as the Lord of the place. Here comes a monarch with a crown upon his head. The angel pays him no respect, but reminds him that the diadems of earth have no value in heaven. A company of eminent men advance dressed in robes of state, and others adorned with the gowns of learning, but to these no deference is rendered, for their faces are very unlike the Crucified. A maiden comes forward, fair and comely, but the celestial watcher sees not in that sparkling eye and ruddy cheek the beauty for which he is looking. A man of renown cometh up heralded by fame, and preceded by the admiring clamor of mankind; but the angel saith, "Such applause may please the sons of men, but thou hast no right to enter here." But free admittance is always given to those who in holiness are made like their Lord. Poor they may have been; illiterate they may have been; but the angel as he looks at them smiles a welcome as he says, "It is Christ again; a transcript of the holy child Jesus. Come in, come in; eternal glory thou shalt win. Thou shalt sit in heaven with Christ, for thou art like Him." SPURGEON.

I will cause you to pass under the rod. EZEK. xx. 37.

It was the custom of the Jews to select the tenth of their sheep after this manner: the lambs were separated from the dams, and enclosed in a sheepcote, with only one narrow way out; the dams were at the entrance. On opening the gate, the lambs hastened to

151

join the dams; and a man placed at the entrance, with a rod dipped in ochre, touched every tenth lamb, and so marked it with his rod, saying, "Let this be holy." Hence, saith the Lord by the prophet Ezekiel, "I will cause you to pass under the rod."

EZEK. xlvii.9. *And everything shall live whither the river cometh.*

Away among the Alleghanies there is a spring, so small that a single ox could drain it dry on a summer's day. It steals its unobtrusive way among the hills, till it spreads out into the beautiful Ohio; thence it stretches away a thousand miles, leaving on its banks more than a hundred villages and cities, and many thousand cultivated farms, and bearing on its bosom more than half a thousand steamboats; then, joining the Mississippi, it stretches away some twelve hundred miles or more, until it falls into the great emblem of eternity. It is one of the great tributaries of the ocean, which, obedient only to God, shall roll and roar till the angel, with one foot on the sea, and the other on the land, shall lift up his hand to heaven, and swear that time shall be no longer. So with moral influence. It is a rivulet, an ocean, boundless and fathomless as eternity.

DAN. i. 8. *Daniel purposed in his heart.*

The longer I live, the more I am certain that the great difference between men, between the feeble and the powerful, the great and the insignificant, is energy, invincible determination—a purpose once fixed, and then death or victory!   FOWELL BUXTON.

DAN. vi. 10. *Daniel . . . kneeled upon his knees three times a day, and prayed.*

Constantine the Great was one day looking at some

statues of noted persons, who were represented *standing*. "I shall have mine taken *kneeling*," said he; "for that is how I have risen to eminence." Thus it is with the Christian: if he would obtain any real eminence in the Christian life, he must be often kneeling in prayer to God.

To the Lord our God belong mercies and forgivenesses. DAN.
ix. 9.

As a spring-lock closes of itself, but cannot be unlocked without a key; so we of ourselves may run into sin, but cannot return without the key of God's grace.
CAWDRAY.

I was left alone, and saw this great vision. DAN.
x. 8.

When you are most alone you will have most of God. JOSEPH PARKER.

Solitude is the ante-chamber of God; only one step more and you can be in His immediate presence.
LANDOR.

O Daniel, a man greatly beloved . . . unto thee DAN.
am I now sent. x. 11.

To be known in heaven is the best fame.
JOSEPH PARKER.

The people that do know their God shall be strong and DAN.
do. xi. 32.

The old archers took the bow, put one end of it down beside the foot, elevated the other end, and it was the rule that the bow should be just the size of the archer. If it were just his size, then he would go into the battle with confidence. Your power to project good in the world will correspond exactly to your own spiritual stature. TALMAGE.

One Thousand and One

A silver egg was once presented to a Saxon princess. On opening the silver by a secret spring, there was found a yolk of gold. The spring of the gold being found, it flew open and disclosed a beautiful bird. On pressing the wings of the bird, in its breast was found a crown, jewelled and radiant. And even within the crown, upheld by a spring like the rest, was a ring of diamonds which fitted the finger of the princess herself. Oh, how many a promise there is within a promise in the Scripture, the silver around the gold, the gold around the jewels; yet how few of God's children ever find their way far enough among the springs to discover the crown of His rejoicing or the ring of His covenant of peace!

DAN. xii. 10. *Many shall be purified, and made white, and tried.*

There is a mountain in Scotland called Cairngorm—literally, "the blue mountain"—and on it are found valuable rock crystals. The way in which the Highlanders gather the stones called Cairngorms is this: when there is a sunburst after a violent shower, they go and look along the whole brow of the mountain for certain sparkling spots; the shower has washed away the loose earth, the sunbeams light upon and are reflected from the stones, and thus they are detected. It is just God's way of bringing forth His own—His "jewels." Affliction lays them bare.   CUMMING.

HOS. vi. 3. *Then shall we know, if we follow on to know the Lord.*

The Lord has brought us into the pathway of the knowledge of Him, and bids us pursue that path through all its strange meanderings till it opens out upon the plain where God's throne is. Our life is a following on to know the Lord. We marvel at some

154

of the experiences through which we are called to pass: but afterward we see that they afforded us some new knowledge of our Lord. Our path suddenly disappeared in some hideous cavern where we seemed to hear the roaring of wild beasts; and we could not at all conceive what benefit would arise from our entering; but we entered; and when by a favoring passage we emerged from that obscurity and danger, we felt that we had obtained some new and valuable insight into the divine character. Again, our path shot right down into the impenetrable darkness of some deep pit; it was some time before our eyes got accustomed to that darkness; then we discovered a little door, and soon found ourselves in a gallery of hidden treasures, several of which we gathered and still retain. Pursuing thus the knowledge of God we found ourselves like Joseph in Egypt, alone in the midst of a nation that knew not God; and found that there was something here to be learned concerning the divine perfection that could not be learned elsewhere. We have not then to wait for some future brighter opportunity; but by improvement of the present are to build for ourselves a bridge to that future.   BOWEN.

They have sown the wind, and they shall reap the whirlwind.   HOS. viii. 7.

The story runs, that, as Abdallah lingered over his morning repast, a little fly alighted on his goblet, took a sip, and was gone. It came again and again; increased its charms; became bolder and bolder; grew in size till it presented the likeness of a man; consumed Abdallah's meat, so that he grew thin and weak while his guest became great and strong. Then contention arose between them, and the youth smote the demon, so that he departed; and the youth rejoiced at his deliverance. But the demon soon came again, charmingly arrayed, and was restored to favor. On the morrow, the youth came not to his teacher. The mufti, searching, found him in his chamber lying dead upon his divan. His visage was black and swollen; and on his throat was the pressure of a finger, broader than the palm of a mighty man. His treasures were gone. In the garden, the mufti discovered the footprints of a giant, one of which measured six cubits. Such is the Oriental portrayal of the growth and power of habit.

HOS.
xiv. 5. *I will be as the dew unto Israel.*

The dew does not fall on rude or stormy nights; there must be stillness and repose. And it does not fall on cloudy nights; there must be nothing of cloud between our souls and God if we would have His dews. The dew does not fall on the world's beaten highways, but on the green grass, on the least and lowliest blade of life; for God cherishes all He plants. Grace always attracts dew. C. A. FOX.

AMOS
i. 3. *Thus saith the Lord.*

Everything we believe as doctrine, everything we do as duty, and everything we observe as worship, must have this authority—"The Master saith it." All tampering with Scripture as the sole and sufficient rule of faith and practice, and all tampering with conscience as bound by that rule, is a guilty resistance of the authority of Christ, and a perilous thing to our own welfare. JOHN ANGELL JAMES.

156

Thoughts from My Library

Arise, go to Nineveh. . . . But Jonah rose up to JONAH
  flee unto Tarshish.   i. 2, 3.

Ruminating upon trouble is bitter work. Children
fill their mouths with bitterness when they rebelliously
chew the pill which they ought obediently to have
taken at once.   SPURGEON.

The word of the Lord came unto Jonah the second time JONAH
  saying, Arise, go to Nineveh. . . . So Jonah   iii. 1,
  arose and went to Nineveh.   2, 3.

Come, take that task of yours which you have been
hesitating before, and shirking, and walking around,
and on this very day lift it up and do it.
                              PHILLIPS BROOKS.

Arise ye, and depart; for this is not your rest.   MIC.
  " As an eagle stirreth up her nest." This illustration ii. 10.
is one of the most beautiful and appropriate that could
be conceived. It is taken from the habits of the eagle,
which, when her young ones are well-fledged and
would prefer to linger in downy ease, disturbs their
nest, that they may be taught how to fly. Look at
that parent bird picking at the nest which she hath
built for her tender offspring: see how she breaks off
one twig after another, exciting her brood to leave
their nest and soar on high amid the sunshine of
heaven. And if they will not leave it, she will break
it further and further, until it is utterly broken up, and
they are forced to fly or fall. Thus God deals with
us. He knows our tendency to make this earth our
rest, and He disturbs our nest to teach us to rise on
the wings of faith toward the enduring realities of
heaven. How often does God take away our earthly
comforts when He sees that we cling too fondly **to**

them! How often, in this world of vicissitude and change, do riches make themselves wings and fly away! By some unfortunate speculation, or in some way we know not how, lands and possessions are swept away at a stroke, and stranger feet now tread that abode which was once the home of competence and ease. The hopes of a rising family are blighted, and those who were fostered in the downy softness of luxury are turned out into a cold and pitiless world to work for their daily bread. Perhaps something upon which we placed the utmost reliance, upon which seemed to rest our only stay, is suddenly and mysteriously taken from us, and when we attempt to grasp it we find it gone. A gale at sea may destroy the hopes of the merchant; depression in trade may bring want to your door; the bankruptcy of some large mercantile firm, or the failure of a bank, may involve numbers in ruin, and plunge many families in misery hitherto unknown. How many have had occasion, from these and similar causes, and how many more will yet have occasion, to mourn over altered circumstances! Marvel not if it be thus with you; it is God stirring up your nest to teach you to wing your flight to heaven. All these things have a voice if ye will but hear, and seem to say, "Arise ye, and depart; for this is not your rest." BROCK.

MIC. *Walk humbly with thy God.*
vi. 8.
In A. D. 59, not many years after Paul's conversion, he was "the least of the apostles . . . not meet to be called an apostle." Five years later in A. D. 64, he speaks of himself as being "less than the least of all saints," and in A. D. 65, he calls himself "the chief" of "sinners."

Thoughts from My Library

Lightly laden vessels float high in the water, heavy cargoes sink the barques to the water's edge. The more grace the soul has the humbler it will be.

I will look unto the Lord; I will wait for the God of MIC.
my salvation; my God will hear me. vii. 7.

There is no sense in always telegraphing to heaven for God to send a cargo of blessing, unless we are at the wharf to unload the vessel when it comes.

F. B. MEYER.

When I sit in darkness, the Lord shall be a light unto MIC.
me. vii. 8.

When God gives faith He gives the opportunity of proving it. "Thou shalt sit in darkness," He says to His trusting servant. But first He leads him along some flowery walk and accustoms him to a high measure of spiritual prosperity. Then suddenly an unexpected tempest gathers about him, and he finds himself in deepest, strangest night. Darkness is come; but it is different in some of its elements from what the believer had contemplated in the day of his declared faith. Yes, designedly different. It was needful that his darkness should be something never anticipated in order that his faith might have its full proof. The darkness seems to say: "God is not in me; I am sent in wrath. Thy faith is presumption. . . . Despair is the only thing that harmonizes with me." The shadow thus speaks and frowns. But faith comes nobly out of this conflict. . . . It seizes the Word of God with a compulsory grasp, and immediately the believer is compassed about with light. BOWEN.

MIC. *Thou will cast all their sins into the depths of the sea.*
vii. 19.
    A Welsh minister speaking of the burial of Moses, said: "In that burial not only was the body buried, but the grave and the graveyard. This is an illustration of the way in which God's mercy buries sins."

NAH. *Slow to anger.*
i. 3. *Make haste to help me.—Psalm xl. 13.*

    Though the Lord often spares reproof, He never spares commendation. He is slow to anger; He makes haste to be gracious.

HAB. *The just shall live by his faith.*
ii. 4.
    Faith is the grand principle of the divine life from first to last. By faith we are justified, and by faith we live; by faith we stand, and by faith we walk. From the starting-post to the goal of the Christian course it is all by faith.   C. H. McINTOSH.

HAB. *Although the fig-tree shall not blossom, neither shall*
iii. *fruit be in the vines; the labor of the olive shall fail,*
17, 18. *and the fields yield no meat; the flock shall be cut off from the fold, and there shall be no herd in the stalls; yet I will rejoice in the Lord, I will joy in the God of my salvation.*

    This is a noble utterance, Habbakuk! Thou hast surely read the book of Job, and art echoing that great word of his—"Though the Lord slay me, yet will I trust in Him." Thou believest that the love which God has toward us rests on some more solid evidence than the temporal benefits which He bestows upon us; upon evidence so satisfactory, so unimpeachable, that even if the greatly-prospered servant of God saw his flocks and herds rapidly perish, his merchandise carried

off by robbers or consumed by fire, his houses and
lands confiscated by unjust power, his gold and silver
fraudulently taken from him, his friends alienated, his
name beclouded, his person imprisoned, his health
impaired, his appetite vitiated, his sight extinguished,
his utterance impeded, he would still have occasions
of undying and fervent gratitude, motives for joy unspeakable, a foundation for peace which passeth all
understanding. Thanks be unto Him that sitteth upon
the throne for the innumerable avenues by which the
expressions of His goodness come to us. But oh,
while we adore Him for these, let us feel that He has
placed the great truth of His love toward us sinners,
once for all, upon an inviolable basis; so that though
the day, as it passes, may or may not have particular
tokens of His goodness to impart, that goodness can
in no wise be questioned. It is most likely, O Habbakuk, that God took thee at thy word; and in some
surprising way, gave thee an opportunity of evincing
thy singleness of heart toward Him; and that thou
now wearest some peculiar crown of honor and fe-
licity in consequence of that proof given.   BOWEN.

Consider your ways.   HAG.
i. 5.

Before proceeding to any work, we should weigh it.
Letters are charged in the post office according to
weight. I have written and sealed a letter containing
several sheets. I desire that it should pass; I think it
will; but I know well that it will not be allowed to
pass because I desire that it should or think that it will.
I know well it will be tested by imperial weights and
measures. Before I plunge it beyond my reach, I place
it on a balance before me, not constructed to please

my desire, but honestly adjusted to the legal standard.
I weigh it there, and check it myself by the very rules
which government will apply. So should we weigh
our purposes in the balance, before we launch them
forth in action. ARNOT.

ZECH. *Who hath despised the day of small things?*
iv. 10.
A tall chimney had been completed; and the scaf-
folding was being removed. One man remained on
the top to superintend the process. A rope should
have been left for him to descend by. His wife was
at home washing, when her little boy burst in with,
"Mother, mother, they've forgotten the rope, and he's
going to throw himself down!" She paused; her lips
moved in the agony of prayer; and she rushed forth.
Crowds stood looking up to the poor man, who was
moving round and round the narrow cornice, terrified
and bewildered. He seemed as if at any moment he
might fall, or throw himself down in despair. His
wife from below cried out, "Wait, John!" The man
became calm. "Take off thy stocking; unravel the
worsted." And he did so. "Now tie the end to a
bit of mortar, and lower gently." Down came the
thread and the bit of mortar, swinging backward and
forward. Lower and lower it descended, eagerly
watched by many eyes: it was now within reach, and
was gently seized by one of the crowd. They fastened
some twine to the thread. "Now pull up." The man
got hold of the twine. The rope was now fastened
on. "Pull away again." He at length seized the
rope, and made it secure. There were a few moments
of suspense, and then, amidst the shouts of the people,
he threw himself into the arms of his wife, sobbing,

Thoughts from My Library

"Thou'st saved me, Mary!" The worsted thread was not despised: it drew after it the twine, the rope, the rescue! Ah! my friend, thou mayest be sunk very low down in sin and woe; but there is a thread of divine love, that comes from the throne of heaven, and touches even thee. Seize that thread. It may be small; but it is golden. Improve what you have, however little, and more shall be given. That thin thread of love, if you will not neglect it, shall lift even you up to God and glory. NEWMAN HALL.

He shall build the temple of the Lord. ZECH. vi. 12.

What a fine emblem of death is that floating of the trees of Lebanon after being sawn into planks and made ready to be fixed as pillars of the temple! Is it not just so with us? Here we grow, and are at length cut down, and made ready to become pillars of the temple. Across the stream of death we are ferried by a loving hand, and brought to the port of Jerusalem, where we are safely landed, to go no more out forever, but to abide as eternal pillars in the temple of our Lord. The Tyrians floated these rafts; but no stranger, no foreigner shall float us across the stream of death; no king of Tyre and Sidon shall do it; Jesus Christ, who is the "death of death and hell's destruction," Himself shall pilot us across the stream, and land us safe on Canaan's side. SPURGEON.

I . . . will refine them as silver is refined, and will try them as gold is tried. ZECH. xiii. 9.

I have read of a fountain that is cold at midday, and warm at midnight. Thus are saints frequently cold in the midday of prosperity, and warm in the midnight of adversity. Afflictions are not a *consuming*,

163

but a *refining* fire to the godly. They are like the thorn at the nightingale's breast, which rouses and puts her upon her delightful notes.   SECKER.

ZECH.
xiii. 9.

They shall call on my name, and I will hear them.

Prayer is the rope in the belfry; we pull it and it rings the bell up in heaven.   CHRISTMAS EVANS.

MAL.
iii. 6.

I am the Lord, I change not.

Our hope is not hung upon such untwisted thread as "I imagine so," or "It is likely"; but the cable, the strong rope of our fastened anchor, is the oath and promise of Him who is eternal verity: our salvation is fastened with God's own hand and Christ's own strength to the strong stake of God's unchanging nature.   RUTHERFORD.

MAL.
iii. 17.

And they shall be mine, saith the Lord of hosts, in that day when I make up my jewels.

"What dirty, dreadful, disgusting stuff," exclaims a man regarding that peculiarly unpleasant compound, the mud of London streets. "Hold, my friend," says Ruskin. "Not so dreadful after all. What are the elements of this mud? First there is sand, but when its particles are crystallized according to the law of its nature, what is nicer than clean white sand? And when that which enters into it is arranged according to a still higher law, we have the matchless opal. What else have we in this mud? Clay. And the materials of clay, when the particles are arranged according to their higher laws, make the brilliant sapphire. What other ingredients enter into the London mud? Soot. And soot in its crystallized perfection forms the diamond. There is but one other—water. And water when distilled according to the higher law of its nature, forms the dewdrop resting in exquisite perfection in the heart of the rose." So in the muddy, lost soul of man is hidden the image of his Creator, and God will do His best to find His opals, His sapphires, His diamonds and dewdrops. RAINSFORD.

Unto you that fear my name shall the Sun of righteousness arise with healing in his wings. MAL. iv. 2.

Let me tell you again my old story of the eagle. For many months it pined and drooped in its cage, and seemed to have forgotten that it was of the lineage of the old plumed kings of the forest and the mountain; and its bright eye faded, and its strong wings drooped, and its kingly crest was bowed, and its plumes were torn and soiled amid the bars and dust of its prison-house. So, in pity of its forlorn life, we carried its cage out into the open air, and broke the iron wire and flung wide the lowly door; and slowly, falteringly, despondingly, it crept forth to the sultry air of that cloudy summer noon and looked listlessly about it. But just then, from a rift in an overhanging cloud, a golden sunbeam flashed upon the scene. And it was enough. Then it lifted its loyal crest, the dim eye blazed again, the soiled plumes unfolded and rustled, the strong wings moved themselves; with a rapturous cry it sprang heavenward. Higher, higher, in broader, braver circles it mounted toward the firmament, and we saw it no more as it rushed through the storm-clouds and soared to the sun. And would, O ye winged spirits! who dream and pine in this poor earthly bondage, that only one ray from the blessed Sun of Righteousness might fall on you this hour! for

then would there be the flash of a glorious eye and a
cry of rapture, and a sway of exulting wings, as another redeemed and risen spirit sprang heavenward
unto God.   C. WADSWORTH.

MATT.
iv. 1.
Then was Jesus led up of the Spirit into the wilderness,
to be tempted of the devil.

Only those temptations which we encounter on the
way of duty, in the path of consecration, only those
has our Lord promised us that we shall conquer.
. . . If you are in temptation for temptation's sake,
with no purpose beyond it, you are lost.

PHILLIPS BROOKS.

MATT.
iv. 5,
6, 11.
The devil . . . saith unto him, If thou be the Son
of God, cast thyself down: for it is written, He shall
give his angels charge concerning thee: and in their
hands they shall bear thee up, lest at any time thou
dash thy foot against a stone. . . . Then the
devil leaveth him.

Faith melts promises into arguments as the soldier
doth lead into bullets, and then helps the Christian to
send them with a force to heaven in fervent prayer;
whereas a promise in an unbeliever's mouth is like a
shot in a gun's mouth without any fire to put to it.

GURNALL.

MATT.
iv. 9.
All these things will I give thee, if thou wilt fall down
and worship me.

Rowland Hill once began his sermon by saying, "My
friends, the other day I was going down the street, and
I saw a drove of pigs following a man. This excited
my curiosity so much that I determined to follow. I
did so; and, to my great surprise, I saw them follow

him to the slaughter-house. I was anxious to know how this was brought about; and I said to the man, 'My friend, how did you manage to induce these pigs to follow you here?'—'Oh! did you not see?' said the man. 'I had a basket of beans under my arm; and I dropped a few as I came along, and so they followed me.' "Yes," said the preacher; "and I thought, so it is the devil has his basket of beans under his arm; and he drops them as he goes along: and what multitudes he induces to follow him to an everlasting slaughter-house! Yes, friends; and all your broad and crowded thoroughfares are strewn with the beans of the devil."

Those of us who have travelled in mountain coun- MATT. tries know how one range of hills rises behind another, V. one ever seeming the highest, till yet a higher appears 3–12. behind it; each has its own beauty, each its own peculiarity. But in mountain countries there is one range, one line of lofty summits, which always conveys a new sense of beauty, of awe, of sublimity, which nothing else can give—the range of eternal snow. High above all the rest, we see the white peaks standing out in the blue sky, catching the first rays of the rising sun, and the last rays of the sun as it departs. So is it with this range of high Christian character which our Lord has set before us in the Sermon on the Mount. High above all earthly lower happiness, the blessedness of those eight beatitudes towers into the heaven itself. They are white with the snows of eternity; they give a space, a meaning, a dignity to all the rest of the earth over which they brood.

STANLEY.

Ye are the salt of the earth. MATT.

The salt in Judea was a native salt mingled with V. 13.

167

various earthy substances. When exposed to the atmosphere and rain, the saline particles in due time wasted away and what was left was an insipid earthy mass, looking like salt, but entirely destitute of a conserving element, and absolutely good for nothing. It was not only good for nothing, but absolutely destructive of all fertility wherever it might be thrown; therefore it was cast into the streets to be trodden under foot of men. The carcass of sheep or bullock might be buried deep in this worthless mass, and the process of corruption not be delayed a moment.

What an illustration is this of the absolute worthlessness of the form of godliness when the power is utterly lacking! "If the salt have lost his savor, wherewith shall it be salted?" How can its salting, conserving property be recovered? What can you do with it? So your savorless religion is not only worthless in its influence on others, but of no good to yourself. It will save neither them nor you from corruption. How sad for one to have lost the power that belongs to the Christian calling, and instead of being the instrument of saving others, becoming a means of their perdition! Well does the Saviour say, in another place, "Have salt in yourselves."

D. D. DEMAREST.

MATT. *Ye are the light of the world.*
V. 14.   Every Christian is placed in a centre, of which the globe is the circumference; and each must fill that circumference, as every star forms a centre, and shines through the whole sphere; and yet all meet and mingle, forming one vast field of light.

SPENCER.

Thoughts from My Library

Let your light so shine before men, that they may see MATT.
your good works, and glorify your Father which is V. 16.
in heaven.

They say the world has an eagle eye for anything
inconsistent; and it has an eagle eye, sharp to discover
the vagaries and inconsistencies in the defaulty and the
unworthy. It has an eagle eye; but the eagle winks
before the sun, and the burning iris of its eye shrinks
abashed before the unsullied purity of noon. Let your
light so shine before men, that others, awed and
charmed by the consistency of your godly life, may
come to inquire, and to say they have been with
Jesus.   PUNSHON.

Think not I am come to destroy the law: I am MATT.
. . . come . . . to fulfill. V. 17.

The ten stones of the arch on which our domestic
happiness, the purity of society, the security of life and
property, and the prosperity of nations stand, the Son
of God came from heaven, our substitute, to obey; with
His blood, not to abrogate, but to enforce; on His cross
to exalt, not in His tomb to bury; and, cementing the
arch with His precious blood, to lend to laws that had
the highest authority of Sinai, the no less solemn and
more affecting sanctions of Calvary.   GUTHRIE.

When thou prayest, enter into thy closet, and, when MATT.
thou hast shut thy door, pray to thy Father which is vi. 6.
in secret.

Secret devotions resemble the rivers which run
under the earth; they steal from the eyes of the world
to seek the eyes of God; and it often happens that
those of whom we speak least on earth, are best
known in heaven.   CAUSSIN.

The closets of God's people are where the roots of the church grow. And if the roots be not nourished, there can be no tree with branches and fruit. In many senses the root of the plant is the most important part of it. Men do not see it. It is hidden away down under the ground. Yet in the dark it works away, and in its secret laboratory it prepares the life which goes up into the plant or tree, and manifests itself in trunk and branches, in leaves and fruits. The beautiful leaf-fabrics are woven down in the looms of that dark earth-factory. The colors that tint the flowers are prepared in that lowly workshop. The little blocks that are piled in silence, one by one, as the fabric of the tree goes up, are hewn out in the secret quarries of the roots. He that would bless a tree must first bless its roots. So it is in the spiritual life. It is not the closet which men see. It is not a man's secret, personal religious life which the world understands and praises. Yet it is in the closet that the roots of his life grow. And if the roots be not nourished, then the tree will soon die.

J. R. MILLER.

MATT.
vi. 9.

Our Father.

There is one thing more pitiable, almost worse than even cold, black, miserable atheism. To kneel down and say, "*Our Father*," and then to get up and live *an orphaned life.* To stand and say, "I believe in God the Father Almighty," and then to go fretting and fearing, saying with a thousand tongues, "I believe in the love of God!—but it is only in heaven. I believe in the power of God!—but it stoppeth short at the stars. I believe in the providence of God!—but it is limited to the saints in Scripture. I believe that 'the Lord reigneth'—only with reference to some far-off time with which we have nothing to do." *That* is more insulting to our heavenly Father, more harmful to the world, more cheating to ourselves, than to have no God at all.   MARK GUY PEARSE.

Thy will be done in earth, as it is in heaven.   MATT. vi. 10.

There is a cathedral in Europe with an organ at each end. Organ answers organ, and the music waves backward and forward with indescribable effect. The time will come when heaven and earth will be but different parts of one great accord. It will be joy here and joy there! Jesus here and Jesus there! Trumpet to trumpet! Organ to organ! Hallelujah to hallelujah.   TALMAGE.

Where your treasure is, there will your heart be also.   MATT. vi. 21.

A friend of mine who had been in Eastern lands told me he saw a shepherd who wanted his flock to cross a river. He went into the water himself and called them; but no, they would not follow him into the water. What did he do? Why, he girded up his loins, and lifted a little lamb under each arm and plunged right into the stream, and crossed it without even looking back. When he lifted the lambs the old sheep looked up into his face and began to bleat for them; but when he plunged into the water the dams plunged after him, and then the whole flock followed. When they got to the other side he put down the lambs, and they were quickly joined by their mothers, and there was a happy meeting. Our great Divine Shepherd does this. Your child which He has taken from the earth is but removed to the green pastures of Canaan, and the Shepherd means to draw your hearts after it, to teach you to "set your affections on things above." MOODY.

MATT. vi. 24.
No man can serve two masters.

When you see a dog following two men, you know not to which of them he belongs while they walk together; but let them come to a parting road, and one go one way, and the other another way, then you will know which is the dog's master. So at times will you and the world go hand in hand. While a man may have the world, and a religious profession too, we cannot tell which is the man's master, God or the world: but stay till the man comes to a parting road; God calls him this way, and the world calls him that way. Well, if God be his master, he follows religion, and lets the world go; but if the world be his master, then he follows the world and the lusts thereof, and lets God, and conscience, and religion go. R. ERSKINE.

MATT. vi. 33.
Seek ye first the kingdom of God and his righteousness.

When some peculiar pressure is upon you, be like Queen Esther, whose first request was the king's company. In each trial "seek first the kingdom of God and His righteousness," and all other things shall be added: your seeking first the removal of the trial shows that you need the continuance of it.

MATT. vi. 34.
Sufficient unto the day is the evil thereof.

Sometimes I compare the troubles we have to undergo in the course of a year to a great bundle of fagots, far too large for us to lift. But God does not require us to carry the whole at once: He mercifully unties the bundle, and gives us, first one stick, which we are to carry to-day; and then another, which we are to carry to-morrow; and so on. This we might easily manage if we would only take the burden appointed for each day; but we choose to increase our trouble by carrying yesterday's stick over again to-day, and adding to-morrow's burden to our load before we are required to bear it.   JOHN NEWTON.

You remember how Leonidas, the Spartan, kept back the Persian hosts. He stood in the narrow pass of Thermopylæ, and as the foe came up, one by one, each man was able to push back his enemy, and they might have kept Greece thus for many a day. But suppose Leonidas and his handful of men had gone out into the wide open plain, and attacked the Persians —why, they must have died at once, though they should have fought like lions. Christian, stand you in the narrow pass of to-day, and as your troubles come, one by one, by faith you shall find out that your strength is sufficient for you; but if you go out into the vast plain of time, and think to meet all the troubles that shall ever come at once, it must be too much for you. Will you please not to borrow misery, for you will have enough of your own.   SPURGEON.

By their fruits ye shall know them.   MATT.
vii. 20.
Some people can talk Christianity by the yard, but they cannot walk it by the inch.   BLAISDELL.

Some church-members have their roots on one side of the church wall and their boughs all hang over and drop the fruit on the world's side. It is not only a question of where your roots are, but where the boughs hang and the apples fall. We want more in these days of clear, distinct, emphatic, Christly religion, so that we do not need to look into the church-roll to find out whether a man is a Christian or not.

CUYLER.

There is a counterfeit olive-tree in Palestine. It is called the wild olive, or the *oleaster*. It is in all points like the genuine tree, *except* that it yields no fruit. Alas! how many wild olives are there in the church! When I see a man taking up large space in Christ's spiritual orchard, and absorbing a vast deal of sunlight and soil, and yielding no real fruit, I say, "Ah! there is an oleaster!"

BOWES.

MATT.
ix. 13.
I am not come to call the righteous, but sinners to repentance.

Among the several wonders of the loadstone, this is not the least, that it will not draw gold nor pearl, but, despising these, it draws the iron to it, one of the most inferior metals: thus Christ leaves the angels, those noble spirits, the gold and the pearl, and He comes to poor sinful man, and draws him into His embraces.

T. WATSON.

MATT.
ix. 29.
According to your faith be it unto you.

Faith never goes home with an empty basket.

ELIJAH P. BROWN.

So it ever is. Christ's mercy, like water in a vase, takes the shape of the vessel that holds it. On the one hand, His grace is infinite and "is given to every one of us according to the measure of the gift of Christ," with no limitation but His own unlimited fullness; on the other hand, the amount we practically receive from

174

that inexhaustible store is determined by the measure and the purity and the intensity of our faith. On His part there is no limit but infinity; on our side the limit is our capacity, and our capacity is settled by our desire. His word to us ever is, "Open thy mouth wide and I will fill it." "Be it unto thee even as thou wilt."   McLAREN.

It shall be given you in that same hour.   MATT. X. 19.

How often hast thou found thyself, at the entrance into a duty, becalmed, as a ship, which, at first setting sail, hath hardly wind to swell its sails while under the shore and shadow of the trees, but meets a fresh gale of wind when got into the open sea! Yea, didst thou never launch out to duty as the apostles to sea, when the wind in thy face, as if the Spirit of God, instead of helping thee on, meant to drive thee back, and yet hast found Christ walking to thee before the duty was done, and a prosperous voyage made of it at last? Abraham saw not the ram which God had provided for his sacrifice till he was in the mount. In the mount of prayer God is seen, even when the Christian does often go up the hill toward duty with a heavy heart because he can as yet have no sight of Him. Turn not, therefore, back, but go on with courage: He may be nearer than thou thinkest. "In that same hour," saith Christ, "it shall be given unto you."
                                                    GURNALL.

He that taketh not his cross, and followeth after me, is   MATT.
not worthy of me.   X. 38.

The cross is easier to him who takes it up than to him who drags it along.   J. E. VAUX.

175

One Thousand and One

MATT.
X. 42. *Whosoever shall give to drink unto one of these little ones a cup of cold water . . . he shall in no-wise lose his reward.*

Life affords but few opportunities of doing great services for others; but there is scarcely an hour of the day that does not afford us an opportunity of performing some little, it may be unnoticed kindness.

BOWES.

MATT.
xi. 28. *Come unto me . . . and I will give you rest.*

The needle in the compass never stands still till it comes right against the north pole. The wise men of the East never stood still till they were right against the star which appeared unto them; and the star itself never stood still till it came right against that other Star, which shone more brightly in the manger than the sun did in the firmament. So the heart of man can find no rest till it comes to Christ.

This is a tired world! Multitudes tired of body or tired of mind or tired of soul! Every one has a burden to carry, if not on one shoulder, then on the other. In the far East, water is so scarce that if a man owns a well, he is rich; and battles have been fought for the possession of a well of water. But every man owns a well, a deep well,—a well of tears. Chemists have tried to analyze a tear, and they say it is made of so much of this and so much of that, but they miss important ingredients. A tear is agony in solution. But by divine power, it may be crystallized into spiritual wealth, and all burdens may be lifted. God is the rest of the soul that comes to Him. He rests us by removing the weight of our sin and by solacing our griefs with the thought that He knows what is best

176

for His children. A wheat sheaf cried out to the farmer, "Why do you smite me with that flail? What have I done that you should so cruelly pound me?" But when the straw had been raked off the wheat and put in the mow, and the wheat had been winnowed by the mill and had been piled in rich and beautiful gold on either side the barn door, then the straw looked down from the mow and saw why the farmer had flailed the wheat sheaf. TALMAGE.

Ye shall find rest unto your souls. MATT. xi. 29.

Rest unto our souls!—'tis all we want, the end of all our wishes and pursuits. Give us a prospect of this, we take the wings of the morning, and fly to the uttermost parts of the earth to have it in possession, till, after many miserable experiments, we have been seeking everywhere for it but where there is a prospect of finding it: that is within ourselves,—in a meek and lowly disposition of heart. STERNE.

Out of the abundance of the heart the mouth speaketh. MATT. xii. 34.

There is so much correspondence betwixt the heart and tongue, that they will move at once. Every man, therefore, speaks of his own pleasure and care. If the heart were full of God, the tongue could not refrain to talk of Him: the rareness of Christian communication argues the common poverty of grace. If Christ be not in our hearts, we are godless; if He be there without our joy, we are senseless; if we rejoice in Him, and speak not of Him, we are shamefully unthankful. I will think of Thee always, O Lord; so it shall be my joy to speak of Thee often; and if I find not opportunity, I will make it. BISHOP HALL.

MATT.
xii. 35.

A good man out of the good treasure of the heart bring-eth forth good things ; and an evil man, out of the evil treasure, bringeth forth evil things.

When the wheels of a clock move within, the hands on the dial will move without. When the heart of a man is sound in conversion, then the life will be fair in profession.

MATT.
xiii. 22.

The cares of this world . . . choke the word, and he becometh unfruitful.

We cannot grow good wheat if we also grow the thorns of the cares of this world, the deceitfulness of riches and the pleasures of this life.

MATT.
xiii. 30.

Let both grow together until the harvest.

It is God's way to let "both grow together." Here are lessons of patience and of charity. If God can wait, His servants can. If the Master of the harvest can bear with the tares, His children need not be anxious about them. The wheat and the tares in their early growth are alike; the best farmer cannot distinguish them. God sees the difference; man cannot, but "the day will declare it." There is no tareless wheat-field, there is no pure Church on earth. The tares will not always be hidden, but when God's sickle is thrust in they will be given to the fire. The wheat will all be gathered in due time,—not one of God's children will be lost. When we see the tares, let us be patient; we would have cast Judas out long before Jesus did. He may try the faith, the charity, and the patience of His people now, by leaving Judas in the Church, as He did then.

Be charitable. What you think to be tares may be God's wheat. What if they walk not with us? They may be for us. Bear with human frailty and sin; you also are frail and sinful. It is safe to leave the results with God.   H. H. JESSUP.

He went up into a mountain apart to pray.   MATT.
                                                  xiv.23.
We may well take the lesson which Christ's prayers teach us, for we all need it—that no life is so high, so holy, so full of habitual communion with God that it can afford to do without the hour of prayer, the secret place, the uttered word. . . . The life that was all one long prayer needed the mountain top, and the nightly converse with God. He who could say, "The Father hath not left me alone, for I do always the things that please Him," felt that He must also have the special communion of spoken prayer. What Christ needed we cannot afford to neglect.

                                                  McLAREN.

Lord, help me.   MATT.
                                                  XV. 25
There is a chain of but three links in this prayer of the poor woman of Canaan, but it reaches a long way. Some of the most beautiful prayers ever uttered are very short prayers. This is a very short prayer—any child can say it. There are three links in the chain, mark you. One link is on the throne of God; it is "Lord." The other link is down here; it is "me." And then there is a great link between that and this; it is "help." "Lord, help me." And the greater your need, the more that middle link in the chain will express.   MARCUS RAINSFORD.

Truth, Lord: yet.   MATT.
                                                  XV. 27.
"Truth, Lord: yet!" is the sum and substance of faith. If we have learned to combine these words, we

have learned to believe. *Truth, Lord:* "sin has abounded unto death"; *yet* "hath Thy grace much more abounded unto life." *Truth, Lord:* "cursed is every one that abideth not in all things which are written in the book of the law to do them"; *yet,* "He who knew no sin was made sin for us, that we might be made the righteousness of God in Him." *Truth, Lord,* is the sea of our sin and guilt, and the righteous anger of God; *yet,* is the rock of Christ's redemption and love. *Truth, Lord,* is a view of self; *yet,* is a view of Jesus. SAPHIR.

MATT. *Be it unto thee even as thou wilt.*
XV. 28.

Oh, the victories of prayer! They are the mountain tops of the Bible. They take us back to the plains of Mamre, to the fords of Peniel, to the prison of Joseph, to the triumphs of Moses, to the transcendent victories of Joshua, to the deliverances of David, to the miracles of Elijah and Elisha, to the whole story of the Master's life, to the secret of Pentecost, to the keynote of Paul's unparalleled ministry, to the lives of saints and the deaths of martyrs, to all that is most sacred and sweet in the history of the Church and the experience of the children of God. And when, for us, the last conflict shall have passed, and the footstool of prayer shall have given place to the harp of praise, the spots of time that shall be gilded with the most celestial and eternal radiance, shall be those, often linked with deepest sorrow and darkest night, over which we have the inscription, "Jehovah-Shammah: The Lord was there!" SIMPSON.

MATT. *How many loaves have ye ?*
XV. 34.

Christ puts that question day by day to each one of

180

us. There be many that say, "I have no work for Christ, and no mission. Mine is no lofty station, mine is no large sphere, mine is no eloquent tongue, or popular manner, or telling influence. It is too late for me—or perhaps, for the heart is versatile in its deceitfulness, it is too soon for me—to undertake anything for Christ; the King of Glory wants chief men, choice gifts, for His ministries: let me live out my little day and go back to the ground from which I was taken." Gravely, sorrowfully, yet earnestly and gently too, does Christ address Himself to you to-day, saying, "Think yet once more—how many loaves have ye?" Nothing? Not a soul? Not a body? Not time? Not one friend, not one neighbor, not one servant, to whom a kind word may be spoken, or a kind deed done, in the name, for the love of Jesus? Bring that— do that, say that—as what thou hast; very small, very trivial, very worthless, if thou wilt: yet remember the saying, "She hath done what she could." VAUGHAN.

Beware of the leaven of the Pharisees. MATT. xvi. 6.

Every variety of character has its own danger, perhaps its own form of Pharisaism. It is easy for us to see the Pharisaism of others. We can stone the Pharisee in an indignant zeal, and what then? When the storm is over, and we have hurled the lightnings, there stands the Master, with eyes that search us through, and He bends over us, and saith *unto His disciples*, first of all, "Beware ye of the leaven of the Pharisees." We, too, may have our own form of Pharisaism eating the life out of us; spoiling all the beauty and blessedness of our religion. To those that are nearest and dearest to Him this word is spoken by the Lord Himself. MARK GUY PEARSE.

MATT.
xvi. 24. *If any man will come after me, let him deny himself,*
and take up his cross, and follow me.

Christ's cross is the sweetest burden that ever I bore;
it is such a burden as wings are to a bird, or sails to a
ship, to carry me forward to my harbor.

RUTHERFORD.

MATT.
xvii.
1, 2. *Jesus taketh Peter, James and John . . . up into*
an high mountain apart, and was transfigured before
them.

Come close to Him. He may take you to-day up
into the mountain top, for where He took Peter with
his blundering, and James and John, those sons of
thunder, who again and again so utterly misunder-
stood their Master and His mission—there is no reason
why He should not take you. You can hardly be
farther back than they were. So don't shut yourself
out of it and say, " Ah, these wonderful visions and
revelations of the Lord are for choice spirits, for an
election within the election!" They may be for you.
The Lord will come to those that are humble and of a
contrite heart and who tremble at His Word.

McNEILL.

MATT.
xvii. 2. *His face did shine as the sun, and his raiment was*
white as the light.

If a thing reflects no light, it is black; if it reflects
part of the rays, it is blue or indigo or red; but, if it
reflects them all, it is white. If we are like Christ, we
shall seek, not to absorb, but to reflect, the light which
falls upon us from heaven upon others: and thus we
shall become pure and spotless; for this is the meaning of the "white robes," which the saints wear in
glory.   BEECHER.

Thoughts from My Library

With God all things are possible. MATT. xix. 26.

Our God does not need noble characters, as the ground-work of His masterpieces. He can raise up stones as children. He can turn thorns into fir-trees, briars into myrtle-trees. He can take fishermen from their nets, and publicans from their toll-booths, making them into evangelists, apostles, and martyrs. We are not much by nature—wild, bad blood may be flowing in our veins; but God will be the more magnified, if from such stones He can raise up children unto Abraham. The miracle of His grace and power will bring more conspicuous glory to His holy name, in proportion to the unpromising character of the materials on which He works. F. B. MEYER.

Behold, we go up to Jerusalem. MATT. xx. 18.

Never had there been such a going up to Jerusalem as that which Jesus here proposes to His disciples. Jesus goes up voluntarily. The act was not enforced by any external compulsion. Jerusalem might at this time have been avoided. It was deliberately sought. Jesus was hereby fulfilling the Father's will, executing the mission on which He had been sent. It was after this journey that He said, "I have finished the work Thou gavest Me to do." His going up was a part of that work. Hence it was right for Him to go up, although He knew that betrayal, arrest, condemnation and crucifixion awaited Him. It was a going up to a triumph to be reached through defeat, a coronation to be attained through ignominy and humiliation.

O believer, in your walk through the world to-day, be strengthened, be comforted, be inspired, by the spectacle of the Captain of your salvation thus going up to Jerusalem! And remember in all those apparently *downward* passages of life, where sorrow and it may be death, lie before you, that all such descents, made or endured in the spirit of Jesus, are really *up-goings*, steps leading you to the mount of God and the resurrection glory.　　　　　JOSEPH B. STRATTON.

MATT.
XXI. 22.

All things whatsoever ye shall ask in prayer, believing, ye shall receive.

Prayer is the bow, the promise is the arrow: faith is the hand which draws the bow, and sends the arrow with the heart's message to heaven. The bow without the arrow is of no use; and the arrow without the bow is of little worth; and both, without the strength of the hand, to no purpose. Neither the promise without prayer, nor prayer without the promise, nor both without faith, avail the Christian anything. What was said of the Israelites, "They could not enter in, because of unbelief," the same may be said of many of our prayers: they cannot enter heaven, because they are not put up in faith.

SALTER.

MATT.
xxiii.
27.

Ye are like unto whited sepulchres, which indeed appear beautiful outward, but are within full of dead men's bones and of all uncleanness.

In the olden times even the best rooms were usually of bare brick or stone, damp and mouldy, but over these in great houses when the family was resident, were hung up arras or hangings of rich materials, between which and the walls persons might conceal themselves, so that literally walls had ears. It is to be feared that many a brave show of godliness is but an arras to conceal rank hypocrisy; and this accounts for

Thoughts from My Library

some men's religion being but occasional, since it is folded up or exposed to view as need may demand. Is there no room for conscience to pry between thy feigned profession and thy real godliness and bear witness against thee? Remember, if conscience do it not, certainly "the Watcher and the Holy One" will make a thorough search within thee. SPURGEON.

The door was shut. MATT. XXV. 10.

The door of mercy has hinges, and it may be shut, and then locked with the adamantine key of justice.
RALEIGH.

After a long time the lord . . . cometh and reckoneth with them. MATT. XXV. 19.

An Eastern allegory runs thus: A merchant, going abroad for a time, gave respectively to two of his friends two sacks of wheat each, to take care of against his return. Years passed: he came back, and applied for them again. The first took him into his storehouse, and showed them him; but they were mildewed and worthless. The other led him out into the open country, and pointed out field after field of waving corn, the produce of the two sacks given him. Said the merchant, "You have been a faithful friend. Give me two sacks of that wheat: the rest shall be thine."

Thou hast been faithful over a few things, I will make thee ruler over many things. MATT. XXV. 21.

Your "few things" may be very few, and very small things, but He expects you to be faithful over them. FRANCES RIDLEY HAVERGAL.

185

One Thousand and One

MATT.
XXV.
23.

Well done, good and faithful servant.

The Hebrews have a saying, that God takes more delight in adverbs than in nouns; 'tis not so much the matter that's done, but the matter how 'tis done, that God minds. *Not how much, but how well!* 'Tis the well-doing that meets with a well-done. Let us, therefore, serve God not nominally or verbally, but adverbially. VENNING.

The master's approval is the servant's best wages.
McLAREN.

MATT.
XXV.
24–26.

He . . . said . . . I . . . hid thy talent in the earth. . . . His Lord answered and said unto him, Thou wicked and slothful servant.

Between the great things we cannot do and the small things we will not do, the danger is that we shall do nothing. MONOD.

MATT.
XXV.
32.

Before him shall be gathered all nations, and he shall separate them one from another.

It is a remarkable fact, that while the baser metals are diffused through the body of the rocks, gold and silver usually lie in veins; collected together in distinct metallic masses. They are in the rocks but not of them. . . . And as by some power in nature God has separated them from the base and common earths, even so by the power of His grace will He separate His chosen from a reprobate and rejected world. GUTHRIE.

MATT.
XXV.
34, 40.

Come, ye blessed of my Father. . . . Inasmuch as ye have done it unto one of the least of these my brethren ye have done it unto me.

Services rendered for Christ never stop. TALMAGE.

Thoughts from My Library

Inasmuch as ye have done it unto one of the least of these my brethren, ye have done it unto me. MATT. XXV. 40.

It is to motives God looks, not results. Fidelity not success regulates the final reward. MACDUFF.

Not as I will, but as thou wilt. MATT. XXVI. 39.

A man's will should be an echo, not a voice; the echo of God, not the voice of self. McLAREN.

Thy will be done. MATT. XXVI. 42.

"Thy will be done" is the keynote to which every prayer must be tuned. A. J. GORDON.

The eleven disciples went . . . into a mountain where Jesus had appointed them. . . . Jesus came and spake unto them saying . . . Go ye and teach all nations. MATT. XXVIII. 16, 18, 19.

The considerable actions in the world have usually very small beginnings. Of a few letters, how many thousand words are made! of ten figures, how many thousand numbers! A point is the beginning of all geometry. A little stone flung into a pond makes a little circle, then a greater, till it enlarges itself to both the sides. So from small beginnings God doth cause an efflux through the whole world. CHARNOCK.

Lo, I am with you alway. MATT. XXVIII. 20.

A mother one morning gave her two little ones books and toys to amuse them, while she went to attend to some work in an upper room. A half hour passed quietly; and then a timid voice at the foot of the stairs called out, "Mamma, are you there?"— "Yes, darling."—"All right, then;" and the child went back to its play. By and by the question was repeated, "Mamma, are you there?"—"Yes."—"All right, then;" and the little ones, reassured of their mother's presence, again returned to their toys. Thus we, God's little ones, in doubt and loneliness, look up and ask, "My Father, art Thou there?" and when there comes, in answer, the assurance of His presence, our hearts are quieted.

The best test of apostolic succession is apostolic success.

MARK i. 1. *The gospel of Jesus Christ, the Son of God.*

See what vitality the Gospel has! Plunge her under the wave, and she rises the purer from her washing; thrust her in the fire, and she comes out the more bright for her burning; cut her in sunder, and each piece shall make another church; behead her, and, like the hydra of old, she shall have a hundred heads for every one you cut away. She cannot die, she must live; for she has the power of God within her.

SPURGEON.

MARK iv. 39. *Peace, be still.*

It was eventide. The setting sun perchance smiled a farewell, flooding the waters with golden light. The sky was cloudless. Gennesaret reposed in quiet loveliness, like Lucerne in Switzerland, or beautiful Loch Lomond among the Scottish hills. The disciples were not afraid as they embarked. Suddenly the storm swept down upon them. The angry waves smote the little ship. Skillful hands plied their oars in vain. They were in jeopardy. Then, in answer to their cry, the Christ arose. It needed but a word: "Peace, be still." "There was a great calm."

And this is life. One hour all is bright and peaceful; the next, the billows break over us, the desire of our hearts dies, human help avails nought. Within the soul itself are all the elements of unrest. When conscience convinces of sin, and memory recalls our selfishness and ingratitude, our own unworthiness is revealed. We are in despair.

Blessed be God, we have a sure refuge! He who calmed the troubled waters speaks peace to human hearts. His blood atones for every sin; His grace supplies every need. Begin my soul, this day with a penitent, trustful prayer to Him, and through its toilsome or suffering hours shall come the cheering refrain, "Peace, be still."   EDWARD A. REED.

(Jesus) . . . looked up to heaven.   MARK vi. 41.

In working for God, first look to heaven. It is a grand plan. Over and over again, our Lord Jesus Christ looked to heaven and said, "Father." Let us imitate Him; although standing on the earth, let us have our conversation in heaven. Before you go out, if you would feed the world, if you would be a blessing in the midst of spiritual dearth and famine, lift up your head to heaven. Then your very face will shine, your very garments will smell of myrrh and aloes and cassia out of the ivory palaces where you have been with your God and Saviour. There will be stamped upon you the dignity and power of the service of the Most High God.   McNEILL.

Looking up to heaven, he sighed.   MARK vii. 34.

Too often we sigh and look within: Jesus sighed and looked without. We sigh, and look down; Jesus sighed, and looked up. We sigh, and look to earth;

Jesus sighed, and looked to heaven. We sigh, and look to man; Jesus sighed, and looked to God!

STORK.

MARK *Whosoever will come after me, let him deny himself*
viii. 34. *and take up his cross and follow me.*

Men will wrangle for religion, write for it, fight for it, die for it; anything but—*live* for it. COLTON.

MARK *What shall it profit a man, if he gain the whole world,*
viii. 36. *and lose his own soul ?*

As you love your soul, beware of the world; it has slain its thousands and ten thousands. What ruined Lot's wife? The world. What ruined Judas? The world. What ruined Simon Magus? The world. And "what shall it profit a man if he gain the whole world, and lose his own soul?"

MARK *Master, it is good for us to be here: and let us make*
ix. 5. *three tabernacles.*

If the contemplation of Christ's glorified manhood so filled the apostle with joy that he was unwilling to be sundered from it, how shall it fare with them who attain to the contemplation of His glorious Godhead? And if it was so good a thing to dwell with two of His saints, how then to come to the "heavenly Jerusalem, to the general assembly and church of the first-born which are written in heaven, and to God, the Judge of all"—these not seen through a glass darkly but face to face? ANSELM.

MARK *Jesus only.*
ix. 8.

The fullness of heaven is Jesus Himself.

The duration of heaven is the eternity of Jesus.

The light of heaven is the face of Jesus.

190

Thoughts from My Library

The joy of heaven is the presence of Jesus.
The melody of heaven is the name of Jesus.
The harmony of heaven is the praise of Jesus.
The theme of heaven is the work of Jesus.
The employment of heaven is the service of Jesus.

If thou canst believe, all things are possible to him that believeth. MARK ix. 23.

What inexhaustible possibilities lie in faith! God Himself is the unseen Author of the visible universe and it was by faith that the worlds were framed, so that things that are seen were not made of things that do appear. In the sublime galaxy woven with divine hand all in and through the eleventh chapter of Hebrews, the light that shines from every star is faith. It was this that carried Noah across the flood. It was this that gave strength to Moses to deliver the people of God from Egypt, to train them in the wilderness, and to transfer them to the Promised Land. It was this that enabled Israel to hold to the hope of the promise until Jesus came. This animated the feeble few of Galilee to carry the Gospel to the perishing world. This is the power by which every sainted Christian has triumphed in life and in death and entered home at last. Our blessed Saviour is Himself the Author and the Finisher of faith. **W. W. PAGE.**

One thing thou lackest. MARK x. 21.

The want of one thing may make void the presence of all things else. Lacking its mainspring—which is but one thing—a watch with jewels, wheels, pinions, and beautiful mechanism, the finest watch, indeed, that was ever made, is of no more use than a stone. A sundial without its gnomen,—as it is called, Time's iron finger that throws its shadow on the circling hours,—but one thing also, is as useless in broad day as in the blackest night. A ship may be built of the strongest oak, with masts of the stoutest pine, and manned by the best officers and crew, but I sail not in her if she lacks one thing—that trembling needle which the child running about the deck might fancy a toy; on that plaything, as it looks, the safety of all on board depends—lacking that, but one thing, the ship shall be their coffin, and the deep sea their grave. It is thus with true piety, with living faith.   GUTHRIE.

MARK *It is easier for a camel to go through the eye of a*
X. 25.   *needle, than for a rich man to enter into the king-*
dom of God.

In Oriental cities there are in the large gates small and very low apertures, called metaphorically "needles' eyes," just as we talk of windows on shipboard as "bulls' eyes." These entrances are too narrow for a camel to pass through them in the ordinary manner, even if unloaded. When a loaded camel has to pass through one of these entrances, it kneels down, its load is removed, and then it shuffles through on its knees. "Yesterday," writes Lady Duff Gordon from Cairo, "I saw a camel go through the eye of a needle, that is, the low, arched door of an enclosure. He must kneel and bow his head to creep through; and thus the rich man must humble himself."

MARK *With God all things are possible.*
X. 27.   Unbelief says, "How can such and such things be?" It is full of "Hows"; but faith has one great answer to ten thousand "Hows," and that answer is, —God.   C. H. McINTOSH.

Thoughts from My Library

Ye know not what ye ask. MARK x. 38.

In every true prayer there are two hearts in exercise. The one is your heart, with its little, dark, human thoughts of what you need and God can do. The other is God's great heart, with its infinite, its divine purposes of blessing. What think you? to which of these two ought the larger place to be given in your approach to Him? Undoubtedly, to the heart of God: everything depends upon knowing and being occupied with that. But how little this is done. This is what waiting on God is meant to teach you. Just think of God's wonderful love and redemption, of the meaning these words must have to Him. Confess how little you understand what God is willing to do for you, and say each time as you pray: "And now what wait I for?" *My* heart cannot say. *God's* heart knows and waits to give. "My hope is in Thee." Wait on God to do for you more than you can ask or think. ANDREW MURRAY.

Beware of the scribes . . . which devour widows' MARK xii. 38, 40.
houses, and for a pretence make long prayers.
One ought to talk only as loud as he lives.

To every man his work. MARK xiii. 34.

In the marts of commerce, in the looms of labor, while the sun is climbing hotly up the sky, and the race of human pursuits and competitions is going vigorously on, there is work enough for the sincere and honest workman. The sphere for personal improvement was never so large. To brace the body for service or for suffering; to bring it into subjection to the control of the master-faculty; to acquaint the mind with all wisdom; to hoard with miser's care every fragment of beneficial knowledge; to twine the beautiful around the true, as the acanthus-leaf around the Corinthian pillar; to quell the sinward propensities of nature; to evolve into the completeness of its moral manhood; to have the passions in harness, and firmly curb them; "to bear the image of the heavenly"; to strive after "that mind which was also in Christ Jesus,"—here is a field of labor wide enough for the most resolute will. PUNSHON.

MARK xiii. 35. *Ye know not when the master of the house cometh.*

Up, and be doing. The heavenly Master is on His journey, and the talents for use or abuse are now in our hands. Oh! let us not have to mourn, when too late, forfeited opportunities. The talents, ours to-day, may be demanded by the Owner to-morrow.

MACDUFF.

MARK xiii. 37. *And what I say unto you, I say unto all, Watch.*

A Christian is always *on duty.* MARK GUY PEARSE.

MARK xiv. 9. *Wheresoever this gospel shall be preached . . . this . . . that she hath done shall be spoken of for a memorial of her.*

That which we do for ourselves is forgotten; that which we do for Christ is immortal. TALMAGE.

MARK xiv. 36. *Not what I will, but what thou wilt.*

The one misery of man is self-will, the one secret of blessedness is the conquest over our own wills.

McLAREN.

LUKE i. 45. *Blessed is she that believed: for there shall be a performance of those things which were told her from the Lord.*

Yes, it is the performance that is so often lacking,

because the faith is not forthcoming on our part. We admire the green pastures of God's word, but fail to lie down and rest our souls upon them. We are caught in the Slough of Despond, and never see the steps of promise, all ready there to guide us out. We are shut up in Doubting Castle, and the key of God's promise lies rusty and unused. We lose heart, and faint, and give up the fight, when one taste of the rich cordial of God's promises would give us fresh life and vigor.

How much simpler our lives would be, how powerful and free from care and worry, if we only believed that in Christ there is all we need to satisfy every longing of our heart, to make us thoroughly happy and useful and holy.   F. S. WEBSTER.

She . . . laid him in a manger.   LUKE
                                                       ii. 7.
Great Prince of Peace, the manger was Thy royal cradle! Therein wast Thou presented to all nations as Prince of our race, before Whose presence there is neither barbarian, Scythian, bond nor free; but Thou art Lord of all. Kings, your gold and silver would have been lavished on Him if ye had known the Lord of Glory; but inasmuch as ye knew Him not, He was declared with demonstration to be a leader and a witness to the people. The things which are not, under Him shall bring to nought the things that are, and the things that are despised, which God hath chosen, shall under His leadership break in pieces the might, and pride, and majesty of human grandeur.

O ye poor, be glad, for Jesus is born in poverty, and cradled in a manger. O ye sons of toil rejoice, for the Saviour is born of a lowly virgin, and a carpenter is His foster-father. O ye people, oftentimes despised and downtrodden, the Prince of the Democracy is born; one chosen out of the people is exalted to the throne. O ye who call yourselves the aristocracy, behold the Prince of the kings of the earth, whose lineage is divine. Behold, O men, the Son of God, who is born of your bone, intimate with all your griefs, who in His after-life hungered as ye hunger, was weary as ye are weary, and wore humble garments like your own; yea, suffered worse poverty than you, for He was without a place whereon to lay His head.

SPURGEON.

LUKE ii. 11. *Unto you is born this day, in the city of David, a Saviour, which is Christ the Lord.*

We esteem every day alike, but still as the season and the general custom suggest thoughts of Jesus, let us joyfully remember our dear Redeemer's *glorious birth.* Every day should be the birthday of the Saviour to a renewed soul. Amid all that is humiliating there is much that is honorable in the circumstances of the birth of our Immanuel. Whose birth was ever ushered in by a long train of prophecy, or longed for by such a multitude of hearts? Who but He can boast of a forerunner who marked Him as the coming Man? When did angels indulge in midnight songs, or did God ever hang a new star in the sky before? To whose cradle did rich and poor make so willing a pilgrimage, and offer such hearty and unsought oblations? Well may earth rejoice, well may all men cease their labor to celebrate " the great birthday " of Jesus. O Bethlehem, house of bread, we see in thee our hopes forever gratified! " 'Tis He, the Saviour, long foretold, to usher in the age of gold." Let gladness rule the hour;

let holy song and sweet heart-music accompany our
soul in its rapture of delight. SPURGEON.

Glory to God in the highest, and on earth peace, good LUKE
will toward men. ii. 14.

How painfully and wearily one thousand years of
the world's existence rolled along, and no Christ.
Two thousand years, and no Christ. Three thousand
years, and no Christ. Four thousand years, and no
Christ. "Give us a Christ," had cried Assyrian, and
Persian, and Chaldean, and Egyptian civilizations, but
the lips of the earth and the lips of the sky made no
answer.

The world had already been affluent of genius.
Among poets had appeared Homer, and Thespis, and
Aristophanes, and Sophocles, and Euripides, and Alexis
Æschylus; yet no Christ to be the most poetic figure
of the centuries. Among historians had appeared
Herodotus, and Xenophon, and Thucydides; but no
Christ from whom all history was to date backward
and forward—B. C. and A. D. Among conquerors
Camillus, and Manlius, and Regulus, and Hannibal, and
Scipio, and Pompey, and Cæsar; yet no Christ, who
was to be conqueror of earth and heaven.

But the slow century, and the slow year, and the
slow month, and the slow hour at last arrived. The
world had had matins or concerts in the morning and
vespers or concerts in the evening, but now it is to
have a concert at midnight. The black window-shut-
ters of night were thrown open, and some of the best
singers of the world stood there, and, putting back the
drapery of cloud, chanted a peace anthem, until all the
echoes of hill and valley applauded and encored the
Hallelujah chorus. TALMAGE.

One Thousand and One

LUKE
ii. 25. *There was a man . . . whose name was Simeon;
and the same man was just and devout, waiting for
the consolation of Israel.*

Some one has written beautifully of Simeon as follows: "What Simeon wanted to see was the Lord's
Christ. Unbelief would suggest to him, 'Simeon, you
are an old man, your day is almost ended, the snow of
age is upon your head, your eyes are growing dim,
your brow is wrinkled, your limbs totter, and death is
almost upon you: and where are the signs of His coming? You are resting, Simeon, upon imagination—it
is all a delusion.' 'No,' replied Simeon, 'I shall not
see death till I have seen the Lord's Christ; I shall see
Him before I die.' I can imagine Simeon walking out
one fine morning along one of the lovely vales of Palestine, meditating upon the great subject that filled his
mind. Presently he meets a friend. 'Peace be with you;
have you heard the strange news?' 'What news?' replies Simeon. 'Do you not know Zacharias the priest?'
'Yes, well.' 'According to the custom of the priest's
office, his lot was to burn incense in the temple of the
Lord, and the whole multitude of the people were
praying without. It was the time of incense, and
there appeared unto him an angel, standing on the
right side of the altar, who told him that he should
have a son, whose name should be called John; one
who should be great in the sight of the Lord, who
should go before the Messiah and make ready a people prepared for the Lord. The angel was Gabriel
who stands in the presence of God, and because Zacharias believed not, he was struck dumb.' 'Oh,' says
Simeon, 'that fulfills the prophecy of Malachi. This is
the forerunner of the Messiah: this is the morning

star: the day dawn is not far off: the Messiah is nigh at hand. Hallelujah! The Lord shall suddenly come to His temple!' Time rolls on. I can imagine Simeon accosted again by one of his neighbors: 'Well, Simeon, have you heard the news?' 'What news?' 'Why there's a singular story in everybody's mouth. A company of shepherds were watching their flocks by night on the plains of Bethlehem. It was the still hour of night, and darkness mantled the world. Suddenly a bright light shone around the shepherds, a light above the brightness of the midday sun. They looked up, and just above them was an angel who said to the terrified shepherds, 'Fear not, I bring you glad tidings of great joy, which shall be to all people!' 'This is the Lord's Christ,' said Simeon, 'and I shall not taste death till I have seen Him.' He said to himself, 'They will bring the child to the Temple to present Him to the Lord.'

"Away went Simeon, morning after morning, to see if he could get a glimpse of Jesus. Perhaps unbelief suggested to Simeon, 'You had better stop at home this wet morning: you have been so often and have missed Him: you may venture to be absent this once.' 'No,' said the Spirit, 'go to the Temple.' Simeon would no doubt select a good point of observation. See how intently he watches the door! He surveys the face of every child as one mother after another brings her infant to be presented. 'No,' he says, 'that is not He.' At length he sees the Virgin appear, and the Spirit tells him it is the long-expected Saviour. He clasps the Child in his arms, presses Him to his heart, blesses God, and says: 'Lord, now lettest Thou Thy servant depart in peace, according to Thy word. For mine eyes have seen Thy salvation, which Thou hast prepared before the face of all people; a light to lighten the Gentiles, and the glory of Thy people Israel.'"

LUKE
iv. 4.

It is written.

"It is written" should be in the heart and on the lips of every Christian. "It is written" should decide every controversy, settle every doubt, and overcome every difficulty. F. WHITFIELD.

LUKE
v. 3.

And he entered into one of the ships which was Simon's.

Do you envy this fisherman who lent his boat to Jesus? He offers us the same honor; He begs us to do Him the same favor; He comes to each of us and asks us to let Him have *our daily occupation* as His preaching place—the office and workshop, the counter, the desk, the mother's work in the home, the servant's work in the house—this is the pulpit He seeks. *Will you let Him have it to-day?* MARK GUY PEARSE.

LUKE
vi. 12.

He . . . continued all night in prayer to God.

We never read that Joshua's hand was weary with wielding the sword, but Moses' hand was weary with holding the rod. The more spiritual the duty, the more apt we are to tire of it. We could stand and preach all day; but we could not pray all day. We could go forth to seek the sick all day, but we could not be in our closets all day one half so easily. To spend a night with God in prayer would be far more difficult than to spend a night with man in preaching. Oh! take care, take care, Church of Christ, that thou dost not cease thy prayers! SPURGEON.

Thoughts from My Library

He loveth our nation and he hath built us a synagogue. LUKE
vii. 5.
Marble and granite are perishable monuments, and
their inscriptions may be seldom read. *Carve your
names on human hearts;* they alone are immortal!

CUYLER.

Thy faith hath saved thee. LUKE
vii. 50.
Whosoever will go to heaven must have a faith of
his own.   In Gideon's camp, every soldier had his own
pitcher; among Solomon's men of valor, every one
wore his own sword: and these were they that got the
victories.   The five wise virgins had every one oil in
her lamp; and only these went in with the bridegroom.
Another's eating of dainty meat makes thee none the
fatter.   T. ADAMS.

Take heed   .   .   .   how ye hear. LUKE
viii. 18.
There are four different kinds of hearers of the word,
—those like a *sponge*, that suck up good and bad together, and let both run out immediately; those like a
sand-glass, that let what enters in at one ear pass out
at the other, hearing without thinking; those like a
strainer, letting go the good, and retaining the bad;
and those like a *sieve*, letting go the chaff, and retaining the good grain.   BOSTON.

If any man will come after me, let him deny himself, LUKE
and take up his cross daily, and follow me. ix. 23.

We are wont to say that Christ died that we might
not die.   We should speak more truly if we affirmed
that He died that we might die.   He died *for* sin that
we might die *to* sin; He bore our guilt in His own
body that we might bear about His dying in our
bodies.   .   .   .

One Thousand and One

Our wills surrender to Christ's, even as His will was surrendered to the Father's; our self-pleasing daily foregone for His sake Who "pleased not Himself"; our ease surrendered day by day in order that we may endure hardness as good soldiers of Jesus Christ,—these are the crucial tests of discipleship. Our souls are saved only by Christ's outward cross of atonement; they are sanctified only by His inward cross of self-abnegation. A. J. GORDON.

LUKE X. 29. *Who is my neighbor?*

"Who is thy neighbor?" It is the sufferer, wherever, whoever, whatsoever he be. Wherever thou hearest the cry of distress, wherever thou seest any one brought across thy path by the chances and changes of life (that is, by the Providence of God), whom it is in thy power to help,—he, stranger or enemy though he be,—*he* is thy neighbor. A. P. STANLEY.

LUKE X. 33, 34. *A . . . Samaritan . . . had compassion on him, and went to him, and bound up his wounds, pouring in oil and wine.*

Thomas Fuller tells of a knight, one Gervase Scroop, who received twenty-six wounds in the battle of Edgehill, and was left for dead amid heaps of slain. The next day his son Adrian sought his corpse to give it a decent burial. When found, the body was not quite cold, and the son began to use the means for restoration, which met with entire success, and the knight lived more than ten years, a monument of his son's affection. There are many souls left as dead, among the slain, along the highways of sin, whom diligent personal effort would rescue. Surprising success often attends this work.

Thoughts from My Library

At Jesus' feet.

At Jesus' feet—that is our place of privilege and of blessing, and here it is that we are to be educated and fitted for the practical duties of life. Here we are to renew our strength while we wait on Him, and to learn how to mount on wings as eagles; and here we are to become possessed of that true knowledge which is power. Here we are to learn how real work is to be done, and to be armed with the true motive-power to do it. Here we are to find solace amidst both the trials of work, and they are not few, and the trials of life in general; and here we are to anticipate something of the blessedness of heaven amidst the days of earth; for to sit at His feet is indeed to be in heavenly places, and to gaze upon His glory is to do what we shall never tire of doing yonder.   AITKEN.

LUKE x. 39.

Martha, Martha, thou art careful and troubled about many things : but one thing is needful.

Hurry is the working of the flesh; faith, like God, works at leisure.

LUKE x. 41, 42.

Thy will be done.

What to others are disappointments, are to believers, intimations of the way and will of God.

                    JOHN NEWTON.

LUKE xi. 2.

Master, speak to my brother, that he divide the inheritance with me.

The requests we make of God *interpret our character*. They show us as we are. God reads our character in our prayers. What we love best, what we covet most, that gives the key to our hearts.

                    CUYLER.

LUKE xii. 13.

One Thousand and One

LUKE
xii. 20. *But God said unto him, Thou fool! this night thy soul shall be required of thee.*

God called him a *fool* in his last hour, and he who dies a fool is a fool forever. TALMAGE.

LUKE
xii. 32. *Fear not, little flock; for it is your Father's good pleasure to give you the kingdom.*

In these words we read the future destinies of the world. When an Alexander arises and hurries through the world, snatching crowns on the right hand and on the left, and threatening to take unto himself all sublunary power, the people of God are told to fear not; the kingdom is for them, not him. So too when a Julius Cæsar grasps at the sceptre of universal dominion. And when a Napoleon appears on the scene, they calmly wait to see him and his kingdom vanish. For they have looked with Daniel on the image that expressed beforehand the vicissitudes of the world from the Babylonian dominion down to the time when dominion is given unto the Son of Man, and by Him to the saints of the Most High. "The meek shall inherit the earth." Not only is there for them an inheritance reserved in heaven; but thrones shall come down from heaven and be set upon the earth; and they shall sit thereon. "For we shall reign on the earth."

Who are these unmanifested kings and priests? They are now a little company of sheep; a little flock; willing to be inglorious, poor, weak, despised, rejected; fitting themselves to be all that is great and excellent and powerful, by their willingness to be nothing. BOWEN.

LUKE
xiv. 18. *I pray thee have me excused.*

A soldier who went to the war took with him some

of the small instruments of his craft—he was a watch-maker and repairer—thinking to make some extra shillings now and then while in camp. He did so. He found plenty of watches to mend, and almost forgot that he was a soldier. One day, when ordered off on some duty, he exclaimed, "Why, how can *I* go? I've got ten watches to mend!" Some Christians are so absorbed in self-seeking that they are ready to say to the Master's call, "I pray thee have me excused!" They are nominally soldiers of Christ, but really only watch-menders.

They all . . . began to make excuse. LUKE xiv. 18.

Excuses are easily made. There is no action so trivial, no crime so great, but the selfish heart can frame an excuse for it. But are these excuses valid? Will our self-vindication absolve us at the judgment-seat of Christ? "He knoweth our hearts." They are not even satisfactory to ourselves,—much less to God. Sinner, if you have a valid excuse for impenitence, write it out; nay, cast it in brass, hang it up in your house; delight in it, for it is your savior; and teach it to others, that they may share your joy. When you come to die, take it with you down into the grave; when the trump of God calls the dead to judgment, convey it to the throne, and show it to the Judge. If it will justify you in life, it will excuse you in eternity.

There is joy in the presence of the angels of God over one sinner that repenteth. LUKE xv. 10.

You remember the occasion when the Lord met with thee. O, little didst thou think what a commotion was in heaven. If the queen had ordered out all her soldiers, the angels of heaven would not have stopped to notice them. If all the princes of earth had marched through the streets, with all their jewelry, and robes, and crowns, and all their regalia, their chariots, and their horsemen; if the pomp of ancient monarchs had risen from the tomb; if all the mighty of Babylon, and Tyre, and Greece had been concentrated in one great parade; yet not an angel would have stopped in his course to smile at these poor, tawdry things; but over you, the vilest of the vile, the poorest of the poor, over you angelic wings were hovering, and concerning you it was said on earth and sung in heaven, "Hallelujah, for a child is born to God to-day!" SPURGEON.

LUKE XV. 17. *How many hired servants of my father's have bread enough and to spare?*

The rabbis report, that, when Joseph gathered much corn in Egypt, he threw the chaff into the Nile, that, flowing to the neighboring cities and nations more remote, they might know what abundance was laid up for them. So God hath thrown some husks to us in this world, that, tasting the sweetness thereof, we might aspire to His bounty above. If there be such glory in God's footstool, what will there be in His throne? If He give us so much in the land of our pilgrimage, what will He not give us in our own country? if so much to His enemies, what will He not give to His friends? SPENCER.

LUKE XVI. 10. *He that is faithful in that which is least, is faithful also in much.*

The least action of life can be as surely done from the loftiest motive as the highest and the noblest. Faithfulness measures acts as God measures

Thoughts from My Library

them. True conscientiousness deals with our duties as God deals with them. Duty is duty, conscience is conscience, right is right, and wrong is wrong, whatever sized type they be printed in. "Large" or "small" are not words for the vocabulary of conscience. It only knows two words,—*right*, and *wrong.*   McLAREN.

When ye shall have done all those things which are LUKE
commanded you, say, We are unprofitable servants. xvii.
Of one thing we may be sure,—if we have all that 10.
we want in any sphere of effort or influence, we have
a lower standard than we ought to have. The best
worker is always behind where he would like to be.
His ideal is ever ahead of him.

The one a Pharisee and the other a publican.   LUKE
One begins by reforming his neighbors and the xviii.
other by reforming himself; the one by looking 10.
around, and the other by looking within; the one by
sweeping the streets of the city, the other by cleansing
the rooms of his own house; the one by attempting
to re-model society, the other by seeking a change
in his own character.

How hardly shall they that have riches enter into the LUKE
kingdom of God.   xviii.
It is not the fact that a man has riches which keeps 24.
him from the kingdom of God—but the fact that
riches have him.

The Son of man is come to seek and to save that which LUKE
was lost.   xix. 10.
Without the Son of Man our daily duties and pleas-

207

ures are the aimless wanderings of men lost in a track-
less existence. Under His guidance they are marches
to a definite end. If that end is not always clear to us
or to others it is to Him. He not only comes to seek,
but to save. We respond to the seeking voice, and at
once the work of salvation begins. A. BROOKS.

LUKE xxi. 19. *In your patience possess ye your souls.*

A glance at our Revised Version, "In your patience
ye shall win your souls," shows us that this text is a
promise, not a command, a blessed hope, not a stern
ordinance. What is the spirit of this promise? "Souls"
is rendered in the margin, "lives"; and the thought
of winning one's life, is of accomplishing the highest
end of life, and of realizing its highest possibility of
power and of peace. Regarded in this light, how
sweet is the promise for those who are compelled to
live in this impetuous, harassing generation! By patience, we shall win our lives! Impatience in our
work; the chafing of the spirit against providential
restrictions; the wild haste to be rich; the intolerant
and consuming ambition, which to satisfy itself will
crush a path over the rights of others,—these are characteristic types of world-life to be seen around us every
day. But the servant of the Lord must not, will not
abandon himself to this impatient, selfish strife. He
will maintain the bright example of the patient Jesus.
He will discern by the light of the Holy Spirit's teaching that the highest end of our life on earth cannot be
won by the selfish and the impatient; he will receive
the strength to remember that impatience is waste and
loss, the strength to live in the hourly atmosphere of
that blessed prayer for every busy and every earnest
life. CHAS. CUTHBERT HALL.

Thoughts from My Library

My blood, which is shed for you.
LUKE xxii. 20.

I dare assert, without fear of successful contradiction, that the inspired writers attribute all the blessings of salvation to the precious blood of Jesus Christ. If we have *redemption*, it is through His blood; if we are *justified*, it is by His blood; if washed from our moral stains, it is by His blood, which cleanseth us from all sin; if we have *victory over the last enemy*, we obtain it not only by the word of the divine testimony, but through the blood of the Lamb; and, if *we gain admittance into heaven*, it is because we "have washed our robes, and made them white in the blood of the Lamb, and therefore are we before the throne of God." Everything depends on the blood of Christ; and "without shedding of blood is no remission." R. NEWTON.

The Lord said, Simon, Simon, behold, Satan hath desired to have you that he may sift you as wheat: but I have prayed for thee, that thy faith fail not.
LUKE xxii. 31, 32.

God's wheat must go through Satan's sieve, but their faith shall not fail.

The Lord turned and looked upon Peter.
LUKE xxii. 61.

We wonder sometimes when God is so great, so terrible in majesty, that He uses so little violence with us, who are so small. But it is not His way. His way is to be gentle. He seldom drives, but draws. He seldom compels, but leads. He remembers we are dust. . . . So God is gentle with us all—molding us and winning us many a time with no more than a silent look. Coarse treatment never wins souls. So God did not drive the chariot of His omnipotence up to Peter and command him to repent. God did not threaten him with the thunderbolts of punishment.

God did not even speak to him. That one look laid a spell upon his soul which was more than voice or language through all his after life.   DRUMMOND.

LUKE
xxiii.
33.

When they were come to the place which is called Calvary, there they crucified him.

Away on the frontier of our country, out on the prairies, where men sometimes go to hunt, or for other purposes, the grass in the dry season sometimes catches fire, and you will see the flames uprise twenty or thirty feet high, and roll over the Western desert faster than any fleet horse can run. Now, what do the men do? They know it is sure death unless they can make some escape. They would try to run away, perhaps, if they had fleet horses. But they can't; that fire goes faster than the fleetest horse can run. What do they do? Why, they just take a match, and they light the grass from it, and away it burns, and then they get into that burnt district. The fire comes on, and there they stand perfectly secure. There they stand perfectly secure—nothing to fear. Why? Because the fire has burned all there is to burn. Such a place is Mount Calvary.   MOODY.

Mount Calvary is lord of the Sacred Mountains, and by its baptism of blood and agony, its moral grandeur, and the intense glory that beams from its summit, is worthy to crown the immortal group. Its moral height no man can measure, for though its base is on the earth, its top is lost in the heaven of heavens. The angels hover around the dazzling summit, struggling in vain to scale its highest point, which has never yet been fanned by even an immortal wing. The divine eye alone embraces its length and breadth, and depth and height. Oh, what associations cluster around it! what mysteries hover there! and what revelations it makes to the awe-struck beholder! Mount Calvary! at the mention of that name the universe thrills with a new emotion, and heaven trembles with a new anthem, in which pity and exultation mingle in strange yet sweet accord! HEADLEY.

He made as though he would have gone further.   LUKE xxiv. 28.

Is not God always acting thus? He comes to us by His Holy Spirit as He did to these two disciples. He speaks to us through the preaching of the gospel, through the Word of God, through the various means of grace, and the providential circumstances of life; and having thus spoken, He makes as though He would go further. If the ear be opened to His voice and the heart to His Spirit, the prayer will go up "Lord, abide with me." But if that voice makes no impression, then He passes on, as He has done thousands of times, leaving the heart at each time harder than before, and the ear more closed to His Spirit's call. F. WHITFIELD.

In him was life.   JOHN i. 4.

A great fable sometimes encloses a great truth. It is an old story of the Empress Helena, how she went to the Holy Land to find the cross. Excavations were made, and they found three crosses; but how were they to know which was the true one? So they took a corpse, and put it upon one and another; and, as soon as the corpse touched the Saviour's cross, it started into life. Now, you are demonstrating the divinity of Christianity, and that is how you test it,— it makes these dead men live. COLEY.

One Thousand and One

JOHN
i. 13. *Born not of blood, nor of the will of the flesh, nor of the will of man, but of God.*

A sculptor may take a piece of rough marble, and work from it the figure of a Madonna; but it is still nothing but marble, and lifeless. A carver may take a piece of wood, and work out of it a scene of conviviality; but it is still wood, and insensible. A watch-cleaner may take a watch, the mainspring of which is broken: he may clean every wheel, cog, pin, hand, the face, and the cases; but, the mainspring not rectified, it will be as useless for going and time-telling as before. A painter may decorate the outside of a pesthouse with the most beautiful colors; but, if he produce no change within, it is still a pesthouse. A poor man may clothe himself in the garb of a monarch; but he is still a poor man. A leper may cover all his spots with his garment; but he is still a leper. So the sinner may reform in all the externals of his life, so that he shall attain to the moral finery of Saul of Tarsus, or Nicodemus, a master in Israel, but, except he be born again FROM ABOVE, he cannot see the kingdom of God. BATE.

JOHN
i. 17. *The law was given by Moses, but grace and truth came by Jesus Christ.*

The Law begins with commands and ends with blessings; but the blessings are fruit upon lofty branches, which fallen man can never reach: he cannot and will not climb the tree. The Gospel, on the contrary, begins with promises, and promises give birth to precepts. The Law demands justice; the Gospel delights in mercy through satisfied justice. Moses blesses the law-doer; Jesus pardons the guilty and saves the lost.

Thoughts from My Library

Whatsoever he saith unto you, do it.　　　　　JOHN
　　Whatsoever God sees fit to require of us is great, be ii. 5.
it of greater or lesser magnitude in appearance.

　　　　　　　　　　　　　　　D. O. MEARS.

　　The fact that God has commanded us to do a thing
proves that we can do it.　　　　GUTHRIE.

Born anew.　　　　　　　　　　　　　JOHN
Nothing will produce a new life but a new nature.　iii. 3
　　　　　　　　　　　　　ARNOT.　(R. V.).

That which is born of the flesh is flesh.　　　JOHN
　　Streams rise no higher than their fountains. The iii. 6.
idea of educing a spiritual nature out of the carnal, is
to reverse an eternal law.

God so loved the world that he gave his only begotten JOHN
　　Son, that whosoever believeth in him should not iii. 16.
　　perish, but have everlasting life.
　　The cross is the stumbling-block against which the
waves of eternal love broke into the silver spray of
speech.　　　　　　　　　　JOSEPH PARKER.

God so loved the world that he gave his only begotten JOHN
　　Son, that whosoever believeth in him should not iii. 16.
　　perish, but have everlasting life.
Whosoever drinketh of the water that I shall give him
　　shall never thirst; but the water that I shall give him
　　shall be in him a well of water springing up into
　　everlasting life.—John iv. 14.
　　God's business is not to be done wholesale. Christ's
greatest utterances were delivered to congregations of
one or two.　　　　　　　　　MOODY.

213

Christ died *for* sin.
Believer dies *to* sin.
Unbeliever dies *in* sin.

JOHN
iii. 27.
A man can receive nothing, except it be given him from heaven.

As the rays come from the sun, and yet are not the sun; even so our love and pity, though they are not God, but merely a poor, weak image and reflection of Him, yet from Him alone they come. If there is mercy in our hearts, it comes from the fountain of mercy. If there is the light of love in us, it is a ray from the full sun of His love. C. KINGSLEY.

JOHN
iii. 30.
He must increase, but I must decrease.

In the part of New England where I spend my summer holiday, I have seen a parable of nature that sets forth union with Christ. It is an example of natural grafting, if you have ever seen such an instance. Two little saplings grew up side by side. Through the action of the wind they crossed each other; by and by the bark of each became wounded and the sap began to mingle, until in some still day they became united together. This process went on more and more, and by and by they were firmly compacted. Then the stronger began to absorb the life of the weaker. It grew larger and larger, while the other grew smaller and smaller; then it began to wither and decline, till it finally dropped away and disappeared, and now there are two trunks at the bottom and only one at the top. Death has taken away the one; life has triumphed in the other.

There was a time when you and Jesus Christ met. The wounds of your penitent heart began to knit up with the wounds of His broken heart, and you were united to Christ. Where are you now? Are the two lives running parallel, or has the word been accomplished in you, "He must increase, but I must decrease"? Has that old life been growing less and less and less? More and more have you been mortifying it, until at last it seems almost to have disappeared? Blessed are ye, if such is the case. Then you can say, "I live; yet not I, but Christ liveth in me; and the life which I now live in the flesh, I live not of myself, but by the faith of the Son of God, who loved me and gave Himself for me." Henceforth "for me to live is Christ"—not two, but one.   A. J. GORDON.

My meat is to do the will of him that sent me.   JOHN
   Seek your life's nourishment in your life's work.   iv. 34.
                              PHILLIPS BROOKS.

   Do what God calls you to do and you are a success.
                              TALMAGE.

Rise, take up thy bed and walk. And immediately the JOHN
   man   .   .   .   took up his bed and walked.   v. 8, 9.
   When Diogenes heard Zeno with subtle arguments endeavoring to prove that there was no motion, he suddenly starts up, and walks. Zeno asking the cause thereof, said Diogenes, "Hereby I confute you, and prove that there is motion." Walking with God is the best way to confute them that think religion to be but a notion: living religion will prove that there is religion.   VENNING.

Making himself equal with God.   JOHN
   It was during the reign of Theodosius the Great, in   v. 18.
the fourth century, that the Arians made their most

215

One Thousand and One

vigorous attempts to undermine the doctrine of the divinity of Jesus Christ. The event, however, of his making his son Arcadius partner with himself on his throne was happily overruled, in the following manner, to his seeing the God-dishonoring character of their creed. Among the bishops who came to congratulate him on the occasion was the famous and esteemed Amphilochus, who, it is said, suffered much under the Arian persecution. He approached the emperor, and, making a very handsome and dutiful address, was going to take his leave. "What!" said Theodosius, "do you take no notice of my son? Do you not know that I have made him a partner with me in the empire?" Upon this the good old bishop went to young Arcadius, then about sixteen years of age, and, putting his hand upon his head, said, "The Lord bless thee, my son!" and immediately drew back. Even this did not satisfy the emperor. "What," said he, "is this all the respect you pay to a prince that I have made of equal dignity with myself?" Upon this the bishop arose, and looking the emperor in the face, with a tone of voice solemnly indignant, said, "Sir, do you so highly resent my apparent neglect of your son because I do not give him equal honor with yourself? What must the eternal God think of you, who have allowed His co-equal and co-eternal Son to be degraded in His proper divinity in every part of your empire?" This was a two-edged sword in the heart of the emperor. He felt the reproof to be just and confounding, and no longer would seem to give the least indulgence to that creed which did not secure the divine glory to the "Prince of peace."

JEFFERS.

Thoughts from My Library

Search the scriptures.

JOHN v. 39.

The truths of the Bible are like gold in the soil. Whole generations walk over it, and know not what treasures are hidden beneath. So centuries of men pass over the Scriptures, and know not what riches lie under the feet of their interpretation. Sometimes, when they discover them, they call them new truths. One might as well call gold newly dug new gold.

BEECHER.

Gather up the fragments that remain, that nothing be lost.

JOHN vi. 12.

Why? Because they all come from Jesus, and nothing that comes from Him must be lost. Your misspent moments, your tardy services, your sluggish energies, your cold affections, your omitted duties— "gather them up." They are lying on the ground, but must not remain there. Gather them up and use them for His glory. Ask the Lord to revive His work in your soul. Ask for a quickened spirit; for more zeal, more devotion, more love to His cause. Awake from slumber! Shake off all earthly, carnal sleep. Thousands are perishing around you! Thousands are dying in sin! The angel of death is on the wing, and the coming of the Lord draweth nigh! Up and warn the world! Be active, diligent, persevering for Christ! "Gather up the fragments that remain, that nothing be lost."

F. WHITFIELD.

I am the living bread which came down from heaven.

JOHN vi. 51.

Christ calls Himself "the living bread"—the manna which came down from heaven. Remember how the manna fell. It lay all round the tents of Israel. The Israelite could not stir from his tent without doing one

217

of two things—he must either *gather* the manna, or *trample* upon it.   Every man living is doing either the one or the other now.   Either the one or the other *you* are doing.   Which is it?   F. WHITFIELD.

He who has the Bread of heaven spends his life in the banqueting house of God.   JOSEPH PARKER.

JOHN *He that eateth me, even he shall live by me.*
vi. 57.
     To feed on Christ is to get His strength into us to be our strength.   You feed on the cornfield, and the strength of the cornfield comes into you, and is your strength.   You feed on Christ, and then go and live your life; and it is Christ in you that lives your life, that helps the poor, that tells the truth, that fights the battles, and that wins the crown.

PHILLIPS BROOKS.

JOHN *The words that I speak unto you, they are spirit and*
vi. 63. *they are life.*
     You cannot read the Bible as you do other books.   I visited Mr. Prang's chromo establishment in Boston and saw the process of printing a picture of some public man.   The first stone made hardly an impression on the paper.   The second stone showed no sign of change.   The third no sign.   The fifth and sixth showed only outlines of a man's head.   The tenth, the man's face, chin, nose and forehead appeared. The fifteenth and twentieth looked like a dim picture. The twenty-eighth impression stood forth as natural as life.   It looked as though it would speak to you.   So, carefully and prayerfully read the Word of God—read the same chapter again and again—and the twenty-eighth time Christ Jesus will shine forth.   MOODY.

Thoughts from My Library

If any man willeth to do his will, he shall know of the   JOHN
teaching whether it be of God.   vii. 17
(R. V.).

It requires a well-kept life to *do* the will of God, and
even a better kept life to *will* to do His will. To be
willing is a rarer grace than to be doing the will of
God. For he who is willing may sometimes have
nothing to do, and must only be willing to wait; and
it is easier far to be doing God's will than to be willing to have nothing to do—it is easier far to be working for Christ than it is to be willing to cease.

DRUMMOND.

Life fellowship with Jesus is the only school for the
science of heavenly things.   ANDREW MURRAY.

He that is without sin among you, let him first cast a   JOHN
stone at her.   viii. 7.

Search thy friend for his virtues, thyself for thy
faults.

I must work the works of him that sent me, while it is   JOHN
day.   ix. 4.

Sins of commission are the usual punishment for
sins of omission. He that leaves a duty, may well
fear that he will be left to commit a crime.

GURNALL.

The night cometh, when no man can work.   JOHN

We are all in this world on divine missions, we are   ix. 4.
all sent from God to take some specific part in blessing the world. To do this we have just a day of time.
A day is a brief time. It is a fixed time. When the
sun comes to his going down, no power in the universe can prolong his stay for one minute.

219

One Thousand and One

Yet the time is long enough for God's plan. The sun never sets too soon for His purpose. Each life is long enough for the little part of the world's work allotted to it. . . . No one can ever offer as an excuse for an unfinished life-work that the time given to him was too short. It is always long enough, if only every moment of it be filled with simple faithfulness.

To have our work completed at the end, we must do it while the day lasts, for there will be no opportunity afterward. If we are living earnestly, we shall live all the time under the pressure of the consciousness that the time is short. We must not waste or lose a moment. Soon it will be night, when we cannot work.   J. R. MILLER.

JOHN
ix. 38.
Lord, I believe.   And he worshipped him.

The life of a doctrine is in its application.

JOHN
x. 5.
A stranger will they not follow.

A traveller asserted to an eastern shepherd, that the sheep knew the dress of their master, not his voice. The shepherd to refute the point changed dresses with the traveller. He went among the sheep with the shepherd's dress, called the sheep, and tried to lead them, but they knew not his voice, and never moved. But when the shepherd called, though in a strange dress, they ran at once to him.   "A stranger will they not follow."

JOHN
x. 9.
I am the door.

The ancient city of Troy had but one gate. Go round and round the city, you would have found no other. If you wanted to get in, there was but one

way.   So to the golden city of heaven there is but one
gate.   Christ says, "I am the door."

My sheep hear my voice, and I know them, and they JOHN
   follow me.   x. 27.

The celebrated W. Jay of Bath was wont to say,
that Christ's sheep were marked in the *ear* and the
foot: "They *hear* My voice, and *follow* Me."

When he heard therefore that he was sick, he abode JOHN
   two days still in the same place where he was.   xi. 6.

And so, the silence of God was itself an answer.
It is not merely said that there was no audible response
to the cry from Bethany; it is distinctly stated that the
absence of an audible response was itself the answer
to the cry—it was *when* the Lord heard that Lazarus
was sick that *therefore* He abode two days still in the
same place where He was.   I have often heard the
outward silence.   A hundred times have I sent up
aspirations whose only answer has seemed to be the
echo of my own voice, and I have cried out in the
night of my despair, "Why art Thou so far from
helping me?"   But I never thought that the seeming
farness was itself the nearness of God—that the very
silence was an answer.   It was a very grand answer
to the household of Bethany.   They had asked not too
much, but too little.   They had asked only the life of
Lazarus; they were to get the life of Lazarus and a
revelation of eternal life as well.

There are some prayers which are followed by a
Divine silence because we are not yet ripe for all we
have asked; there are others which are so followed
because we are ripe for more.   We do not always
know the full strength of our own capacity; we have

to be prepared for receiving greater blessings than we have ever dreamed of. We come to the door of the sepulchre and beg with tears the dead body of Jesus; we are answered by silence because we are to get something better—a living Lord.

My soul, be not afraid of God's silence; it is another form of His voice; God's silence is more than man's speech; God's negative is better than the world's affirmation. Have thy prayers been followed only by a calm stillness? Well, and is not *that* God's voice—a voice that will suffice thee in the meantime till the full disclosure come? Has He moved not from His place to help thee? Well, but His stillness makes *thee* still, and He has something better than help to give thee. Wait for Him in the silence, and ere long it shall become vocal; death shall be swallowed up in victory.

GEORGE MATHESON.

JOHN xi. 9. *Are there not twelve hours in the day?*
The very fact of a Christian being here, and not in heaven, is a proof that some work awaits him.

ARNOT.

JOHN xi. 11. *Our friend Lazarus sleepeth; but I go, that I may awake him out of sleep.*

Jesus called Lazarus His friend,—blessed title, glorious privilege, friend of Jesus! Am I His friend? He gives us the test,—" Ye are My friends if ye do whatsoever I command you." His command is, Trust Me, love Me, serve Me. Do I obey this? Then I am Jesus' friend, and still more, He is my friend. This friendship is a treasure neither time nor chance, men nor devils, life nor death can take away. Let us not imagine Christ is not our friend because we suffer.

Thoughts from My Library

He allowed Lazarus to die, yet we are told, Jesus loved Martha and her sister and Lazarus. Jesus' friends now on earth may all die, may all sleep; but He has not forgotten them. One day He will say to the angels: "My friends sleep, but I go to awake them." Then "the Lord Himself shall descend from Heaven with a shout, with the voice of the archangel and with the trump of God: and the dead in Christ shall rise first; then we which are alive and remain, shall be caught up together with them in the clouds to meet the Lord in the air: and so shall we ever be with the Lord."

E. H. HARDING.

Except a corn of wheat fall into the ground and die, it JOHN
abideth alone: but if it die, it bringeth forth much xii. 24.
fruit.

This is the manner of God's proceedings,—to send good after evil, as He made light after darkness; to turn justice into mercy, as He turned water into wine. For as the beasts must be killed before they could be sacrificed, so men must be killed before they can be sacrificed; that is, the knife of correction must prune and dress them, and lop off their rotten twigs, before they can bring forth fruit. These are the cords which bind the ram unto the altar, lest, when he is brought thither, he should run from thence again; this is the chariot which carrieth our thoughts to heaven, as it did Nebuchadnezzar's; this is the hammer which squareth the rough stones till they be plain and smooth, and fit for the temple. H. SMITH.

I, if I be lifted up from the earth, will draw all men JOHN
unto me. xii. 32.

Archimedes wanted a fulcrum on which to place his

223

lever, and then he said he could move the world.
Calvary is the fulcrum, and the Cross of Christ is the
lever; by that power all nations shall yet be lifted.

TALMAGE.

JOHN *What I do thou knowest not now ; but thou shalt know*
xiii. 7. *hereafter.*

A French artisan questioned much the dispensations
of Providence in the government of the world.   One
day, in visiting a ribbon manufactory, his attention
was attracted by an extraordinary piece of machinery.
Countless wheels and thousands of threads were twirl-
ing in all directions; he could understand nothing of
its movements.   He was informed however, that all
this motion was connected with the centre, where
there was a chest which was kept shut.   Anxious to
understand the principle of the machine, he asked permission to see the interior, "The master has the key,"
was the reply.   The words were like a flash of light.
Here was the answer to all his perplexed thoughts.
Yes; the Master has the key.   He governs and directs
all.   It is enough.

JOHN *He that is washed needeth not save to wash his feet, but*
xiii. 10. *is clean every whit.*

I never understood the full meaning of our Lord's
words in John xiii. 10, until I beheld the better sort of
East Indian natives return home after performing their
customary ablutions.   The passage reads thus, "He
that is washed needeth not save to wash his feet, but
is clean every whit."   Thus as they return to their
habitations barefoot, they necessarily contract in their
progress some portion of dirt on their feet; and this is
universally the case, however nigh their dwellings may

be to the riverside. When, therefore, they return, the first thing they do is to mount a low stool, and pour a small vessel of water to cleanse them from the soil which they may have contracted on their journey homewards; if they are of the higher class of society, a servant performs it for them, and then they are "clean every whit." Does not this in a figure represent to us the defilement which a Christian contracts, although he may have been cleansed by faith in a crucified Saviour; and the necessity of a continual application of the precious blood of atonement, in order that the soul may be "clean every whit"?

STATHAM.

I have given you an example.

JOHN xiii. 15.

A Christian doing good should be like an artist working from a model, looking alternately from the rude material in his hands up to the perfect example which he imitates, and down from that to the rude material again. ARNOT.

Now there was leaning on Jesus' bosom one of his disciples whom Jesus loved.

JOHN xiii. 23.

God is to us what we are to God. JOSEPH PARKER.

A new commandment I give unto you, That ye love one another; as I have loved you.

JOHN xiii. 34.

The love of Christ is a radiating love. The more we love Him, the more we shall love others.

FRANCES RIDLEY HAVERGAL.

I am the way, and the truth, and the life: no man cometh unto the Father but by me.

JOHN xiv. 6.

A carpenter sees by his eye, when he applies the square, whether the wood be straight or not; but yet his eye (without which he could not see) is not the judge to try whether the wood be straight or not: of that, the square alone is the judge. So reason in man, without which, it is true, he could not judge, is not the square to try what is right or wrong in order to salvation. The word of God alone can determine that.

SPENCER.

Whosoever is not in Him as the Way, is out of the way and lost; whosoever is not in Him as the Truth is in fatal error; whosoever is not in Him as the Life is dead in sins.

JOHN HALL.

JOHN xiv.13.

Whatsoever ye shall ask in my name that will I do. Christ . . . maketh intercession for us.—Rom. viii. 34.

As we say "for Jesus' sake" *here*, He says "for my sake" *there*.

G. H. C. MACGREGOR.

JOHN xiv.20.

I am in my Father, and ye in me, and I in you.

In the translucent depths of the southern seas, the voyager is aware of the infinite variety of sponge growth, waving to and fro with the gentle movement of the tide; and the ocean is in the sponge, whilst the sponge is in the ocean, illustrating the reciprocal indwelling of the believer in Christ, and Christ in the believer.

F. B. MEYER.

JOHN xiv.21.

He that loveth me shall be loved of my Father, and I will love him and will manifest myself to him.

That is the great law of manifestation. Have I a clear vision of God? Then am I looking steadily at Him with a heart that longs to be pure. Can I not see Him? Then some secret sins may be holding a veil before my eyes. *I* have changed, not God. When I

seek Him He will be found of me; but if I desire Him
not, He will be a God afar off.   JOSEPH PARKER.

We will . . . make our abode with him.   JOHN
 The abiding presence of God is the heritage of every xiv.23.
child of God. The Father never hides His face from
His child. Sin hides it, and unbelief hides it; but the
Father lets His love shine all the day on the face of His
children. The sun is shining day and night. Your
sun shall never go down. Come and live in the presence of God.   ANDREW MURRAY.

He shall teach you all things.   JOHN
 The Spirit is given to those who ask, for regenera- xiv.26.
tion; to those who obey, for character; to those who
wait, for power.

Every branch that beareth fruit, he purgeth it, that it JOHN
 may bring forth more fruit.   XV. 2.
 I know enough of gardening to understand, that, if
I would have a tree grow upon its south side, I must
cut off the branches there.   Then all its forces go to
repairing the injury; and twenty buds shoot out,
where, otherwise, there would have been but one.
When we reach the garden above, we shall find, that,
out of those very wounds over which we sighed and
groaned on earth, have sprung verdant branches, bearing precious fruit, a thousandfold.   BEECHER.

 When trees grow so that their branches are mostly
on one side, we never restore branches to the deficient
side by cutting the opposite side. We cut the most
barren side, and there nature in seeking to restore
what we cut, drives out new buds and branches. So
the gardener knows that where he puts his knife there

will follow the fruit of the tree.   And blessed are they whom the Heavenly Husbandman prunes, that they may bring forth more fruit, if, when He cuts, there is a bud behind the knife.   But woe to them who, being cut, have no bud to grow, and are more disbranched and barren from being pruned.   BEECHER.

JOHN
XV. 4.
Abide in me, and I in you.

Abiding in Christ does not mean that you must always be thinking about Christ.   You are in a house, abiding in its enclosure or beneath its shelter, though you are not always thinking about the house itself.   But you always know when you leave it.   A man may not be always thinking of his sweet home circle; but he and they may nevertheless be abiding in each other's love.   And he knows instantly when any of them is in danger of passing out of the warm tropic of love into the arctic region of separation.   So we may not always be sensible of the revealed presence of Jesus; we may be occupied with many things of necessary duty—but as soon as the heart is disengaged it will become aware that He has been standing near all the while; and there will be a bright flash of recognition, and a repetition of the Psalmist's cry, "Thou art near, O Lord."   Ah! life of bliss, lived under the thought of His presence; as dwellers in Alpine valleys live beneath the solemn splendor of some grand snow-capped range of mountains!   F. B. MEYER.

The indwelling is reciprocal.   He is in us, and we are in Him.   He is in us as the source of our being; we are in Him as filled with His fullness.   He is in us all-communicative; we are in Him all-receptive.   He is in us as the sunlight in the else darkened chamber; we are in Him as the cold green log cast into the flaming furnace, glows through and through with ruddy and transforming heat. He is in us as the sap in the veins of the tree; we are in Him as the branches.

Without me ye can do nothing. JOHN XV. 5.

There are two kinds of magnets, steel magnets and soft iron magnets. The steel magnet receives its magnetism from the loadstone, and has it permanently; it can get along very well alone in a small way; it can pick up needles and do many other little things to amuse children. There is another kind of magnet which is made of soft iron, with a coil of copper wire round it. When the battery is all ready and the cups are filled with the mercury, and the connection is made with the wires, this magnet is twenty times as strong as the steel magnet. Break the circuit, and its power is all gone instantly. We are soft iron magnets; our whole power must come from the Lord Jesus Christ ; but faith makes the connection, and while it holds we are safe. C. D. FOSS.

Herein is my Father glorified, that ye bear much fruit. JOHN XV. 8.

"Herein is My Father glorified, that ye bear much fruit," said Jesus. What a possibility, what an inspiration, that we can enhance the glory of "our Father"! Our hearts leap at the thought. How can this be done? By bearing "leaves,"—a *profession* of love for Him? No. By bearing *some* fruit? No. "That ye bear *much* fruit." In the abundance of the yield is the joy, the glory, of the husbandman. We should therefore aim to be extraordinary, "hundredfold" Christians, satisfied with none but the largest yield. Our lives should be packed with good deeds. Then at

harvest-time we can say "Father, I have glorified thee
on the earth." This fruitfulness depends on the condition of the heart to receive the seed, the way in
which we hear the Word. Combining the three ver-
sions of the parable of the sower, we find that the
characteristics of a good hearer are,—he understandeth
the Word, he receiveth it, he keepeth it. Apprehen-
sion of the Word, faith in the Word, obedience to the
Word,—these three are indispensable to fruitfulness.
"Take heed, therefore, *how* ye hear." Meditate, believe, obey, "that ye shall neither be barren nor unfruitful in the knowledge of our Lord Jesus Christ."

W. B. JENNINGS.

JOHN *That your joy might be full.*
XV. 11.

Full joy does not exclude sorrow, but it is a joy so
deep that no sorrow can get below it.

G. H. C. MACGREGOR.

JOHN *Ye are my friends.*
XV. 14.

Oh! *Friends of God,* why do you not make more
of your transcendent privileges? Why do you not
talk to Him about all that wearies and worries you, as
freely as Abraham did, telling Him about your Ish-
maels, your Lots, and His dealings? Why do you not
fall on your faces while God talks with you? Life
should be one long talk between God and us. No day
should close without our talking over its history with
our patient, loving Lord: entering into His confes-
sional; relieving our hearts of half their sorrow, and
all their bitterness, in the act of telling Him all. And
if only we get low enough, and be still enough, we
shall hear His accents sweet and thrilling, soft and
low, opening depths which eye hath not seen, nor ear

Thoughts from My Library

heard; but which He has prepared for those who
love and wait for Him.   F. B. MEYER.

Because ye are not of the world . . . therefore the JOHN
world hateth you.   xv. 19.

None of you can be the people of God without pro-
voking envy; and the better you are, the more you
will be hated. The ripest fruit is most pecked by the
birds, and the blossoms that have been longest on the
tree, are the most easily blown down by the wind.
But fear not; you have naught to do with what man
shall say of you. If God loves you, man will hate
you; if God honors you, man will dishonor you. But
recollect, could ye wear chains of iron for Christ's
sake, ye should wear chains of gold in heaven; could ye
have rings of burning iron round your waists, ye
should have your brow rimmed with gold in glory;
for blessed are ye when men shall say all manner of
evil against you falsely, for Christ's name's sake; for
so persecuted they the prophets that were before you.
                                              SPURGEON.

When he is come, he will reprove the world of sin, and JOHN
of righteousness, and of judgment.   xvi. 8.

No human teacher can do it; conscience cannot do
it; law in none of its forms, human or divine, can do
it: nay, the gospel itself cannot do it. Although the
Word of God is the sword of the Spirit, yet, unless
the Spirit of God draws forth that sword, it lies powerless in its sheath. Only when the Spirit of God
wields it, is it quick and powerful, and sharper than a
two-edged sword, piercing to the dividing asunder of
the soul and spirit, a discerner of the thoughts and
purposes of the heart. Therefore, as the work of con-

vincing the world of sin is one which nothing less than the Spirit of God can effect, and which yet must be effected thoroughly, if sin is to be driven out from the world, our Saviour was mercifully pleased to send the Comforter to produce this conviction in mankind.

HARE.

JOHN xvi. 13. *The Spirit of truth . . . will guide you into all truth.*

The Bible is a temple. Unlike that in which Simeon stood, whose holiest courts were open only to a favored few, it is patent to every worshipper. Glorious temple it is! God's own words its living stones; His immutable promises its pillars; His oath and covenant its foundations; its walls salvation; its gates praise; Jesus Christ its corner-stone; prophets, apostles and saints its high priests, giving forth the responses of Deity! But what will all the glories of this temple be to us, unless, like Simeon, we be *led there of the Holy Ghost?* Without His influence we shall find a deserted sanctuary. We may have the name of Jesus on our lips and His praises on our tongue; but without the Spirit of God, there will be "no beauty that we should desire Him." MACDUFF.

Truth may be compared to some cave or grotto with wondrous stalactites hanging from the roof, and others starting from the floor; a cavern glittering with spar and abounding in marvels. Before entering the cavern, you enquire for a guide who comes with his lighted flambeau. He conducts you down to a considerable depth, and you find yourself in the midst of the cave. He leads you through different chambers. Here he points you to a little stream rushing from

amid the rocks, and indicates its rise and progress;
there he points to some peculiar rock, and tells you its
name, then takes you into a large natural hall, and
tells you how many persons once feasted in it, and so
on. Truth is a grand series of caverns, it is our glory
to have so great and wise a conductor as the Holy
Spirit. Imagine that we are coming to the darkness
of it. He is a light shining in the midst of us to guide
us. And by the light He shows us wondrous things.
He teaches us by suggestion, direction and illumination.   SPURGEON.

A little while, and ye shall not see me; and again, a   JOHN
little while, and ye shall see me.   xvi. 16.

Every day is bringing Christ's Advent nearer—less-
ening the span of that arc of promise.   The "little
while, and ye shall not see Me," is widening; the
"little while, and ye shall see Me," is diminishing.
The church is like the shipmen in the Sea of Adria,
who "deemed that they drew near to some country."
The historian of Columbus speaks thus of the great
discoverer's approach to the shores of the unknown
New World: "The admiral gave orders that the sails
should be close reefed and the lead kept going, and
that they should sail closely, being afraid of shoals and
breakers; feeling certain that the first gleam of daybreak would discover land under their bows."   Is this
true in a nobler sense of "the Better Country"?   Are
we thus on the outlook to "see the King in His beauty,
and the land that is very far off"?   MACDUFF.

Whatsoever ye shall ask the Father in my name, he   JOHN
will give it you.   xvi. 23.

It is related of the celebrated scholar, Humboldt,

233

that when he was travelling in tropical America, going chiefly by night to avoid the heat of the day, that his superstitious guides greatly reverenced the constellation of the Southern Cross, and directed their course by it. At that time this constellation reached the mid-heavens just before the break of day, so that its passage over the meridian was an indication that morning was approaching. He says frequently, when he was following after his train, and wearied by a night-long tramp, he could hear the guides shout, "Courage, comrades, the Cross begins to bend." So may the Christian soldier hear and regard this voice in the hour of his trials. In the darkness, and the weariness of lifelong labor, it is enough to know that the cross bends at the earnest pleading of faith and uplifted prayer to God. You know where your strength lies, where you may burnish your weapons, where you may, indeed, stand forth renewed perpetually in the strength of grace. The cross of Christ is with us, and the power of that cross is efficacious to save to the uttermost.   CURRY.

JOHN *In me . . . peace.*
xvi. 33.
There is a plant called samphire, which grows only on cliffs near the sea. But though it grows near the salt waves, yet it is never found on any part of a cliff which is not above the reach of the tide. On one occasion, a party of shipwrecked sailors flung ashore were struggling up the face of precipitous rocks, afraid of the advancing tide overtaking them, when one of their number lighted upon a plant of samphire, growing luxuriantly. Instantly he raised a shout of joy, assuring his companions by this token that they

were now in safety. The sea might come near this spot, and perhaps cast up its spray, but would never be found reaching it. Such is the position of a soul in Christ; justified and united to Him, the person may be in full sight still of the world's threatening and angry waves; but he is perfectly safe, and cannot be overwhelmed.   BONAR.

In the world ye shall have tribulation: but be of good JOHN
cheer: I have overcome the world.   xvi.33.

The very fact that you have troubles is a proof of His faithfulness; for you have got one half of His legacy, and you will have the other half. You know that Christ's last will and testament has two portions in it. "In the world ye shall have tribulation:" you have got that. The next clause is—"In Me ye shall have peace." You have that too. "Be of good cheer; I have overcome the world." That is yours also.
                                         SPURGEON.

With what frankness Christ tells that the vessel of the Church shall not move over smooth seas, with favoring breezes filling her sails till she reaches the desired haven. No, not thus, but on the contrary, wind and wave shall often threaten shipwreck and disaster, though all shall be well at last. Perhaps your desponding heart replies, "This is tantalizing me, not helping. For He may well overcome, but that is not the same as my overcoming!" Is it not? Think again,—think better of the Lord's most gracious words. Did He not say, "Because I live, ye shall live also"? Every branch in the vine is one with the vine. Every believing sinner is a branch in the vine. You were united to Christ the first moment you leaned on Him.

One Thousand and One

The Holy Spirit Who led you to Christ did also unite you to Him; and that union stands fast however great be your trials and tribulations. It was in your feeble nature ("the flesh is weak") that He overcame tribulation,—tribulation ten thousand times more terrible than yours,—and He is following up His victory, when from day to day the feeblest disciple, simply leaning on Him, is shown to be mightier than all hell and stronger than the world. He would lose His fame as Conqueror if you, a member of His body, were to fail.

BONAR.

JOHN xvii. 15. *I pray not that thou shouldest take them out of the world, but that thou shouldest keep them from the evil.*

It is for active service soldiers are drilled, and trained, and fed, and armed. That is why you and I are in the world—not to prepare to go out of it some day, but to serve God in it *now*.

DRUMMOND.

JOHN xvii. 23. *I in them.*

Does the Father find in Jesus no stain of sin? He finds none, believer, in thee, for Jesus is thy righteousness. Does the Father visit Christ no more with judgment because He has fully judged Him as our sin bearer on the cross? Then, believer, He judges thee no more, for "there is now no condemnation to them which are in Christ Jesus." Does the Father look upon the Son with complacency and delight? Then, believer, He rejoices over thee, for thou art "accepted in the Beloved." Dead with Christ, risen with Christ, exalted with Christ to the heavenly places, His righteousness, His life, His glory, all are yours.

Thoughts from My Library

Pilate saith unto him, What is truth?

"What is truth?" In Latin this is "*Quid est veritas?*" The letters can be arranged so as to read, "*Est vir, qui adest,*" meaning, "It is the man who is before you."

They crucified him, and two others with him, on either side one, and Jesus in the midst.

Saved thief.	Jesus.	Unsaved thief.
Sin *in* him not *on* him.	Sin *on* Him not *in* Him.	Sin *in* him and *on* him.

It is finished.

There is intense joy in work when it is done and well done. The humblest mechanic feels this pleasure when he sees the article he has been making passing out of his hands perfect. The poet surely feels it when he writes Finis at the end of the work into which he has poured the full force of his genius. What must it have been to William Wilberforce to hear on his deathbed that the cause to which he had devoted the toil of a lifetime had triumphed, and to know that, when he died, there would not be a single slave breathing in any of the dependencies of Britain. Our Lord drank deeply of this well of pleasure. The work He was doing was done perfectly at every stage; and it was work of the most beneficent and enduring kind. As He saw part after part of it falling accomplished behind Him, as He saw hour after hour receding into the past filled with its God-appointed work, He whispered to Himself, "My meat is to do the will of Him that sent me, and to finish His work." And in the article of death, as He saw the last fold of the grand design unrolled, He passed out of the world with the cry on His lips, "It is finished." He uttered this cry as a soldier might do on a battlefield, who perceives, with the last effort of consciousness, that the struggle in which he has sacrificed his life has been a splendid victory. But the triumph and the reward of *His* work never come to an end; for still, as the results of what He did unfold themselves age after age, as His words sink deeper into the minds of men, as His influence changes the face of the world, and as heaven fills with those whom He has redeemed, "He shall see of the travail of His soul, and shall be satisfied."

STALKER.

JOHN XX. 19. *Peace be unto you.*

The natal song of Christ sung by prophetic angels was "peace" and "glory,"—"glory in the highest, and on earth peace." Yet when Jesus began His ministry, He said: "I came not to send peace, but a sword." Are these statements and others like them contradictions ? No! sweet paradoxes. By nature, man is at peace with the world and at war with God. Christ came to reverse this, and by His atonement to establish a peace between God and man which involves war with the world. The Christian then, is called to fight his way to eternal peace. But has he no peace till the end ? Yes, blessed peace; war without and peace within,—"the peace of God that passeth all understanding." His turbulent passions are stilled; his soul's great anxieties are laid to rest; his sin is forgiven; he is cleansed in the blood of the Lamb; he has promises of final salvation, "a place" in the "house of many mansions," and "a crown of glory that fadeth not away." With a consciousness of

238

Thoughts from My Library

all these in the Christian's soul, time, death and eternity cannot mar his repose.   ROBERT P. KERR.

Believing, ye might have life through his name.   JOHN
xx. 31.

When all around was *life*, God spoke of *death;* now, on the contrary when all around is death, God speaks of life: then the word was, "in the day thou eatest thou shalt *die;*" now the word is, "believe and *live.*"   C. H. McINTOSH.

It is the Lord.   JOHN
xxi. 7.

Did you ever notice how this whole incident might be turned, by a symbolical application, to the hour of death, and the vision which may meet us thither? It admits of the application, and perhaps was intended to receive the application, of such a symbolic reference. The morning is dawning, the grey of night is going away, the lake is still; and yonder, standing on the shore, in the uncertain light, there is one dim figure, and one disciple catches a glimpse of Him, and another casts himself into the water, and they find a fire of coals and fish laid thereon, and bread, and Christ gathers them around His table, and they all know that "It is the Lord." It is what the death of the Christian man, who has gone through life recognizing Christ everywhere, may well become:—the morning dawning, and the finished work, and the figure standing on the quiet beach so that the last plunge into the cold flood that yet separates us, will not be taken with trembling reluctance; but drawn to Him by the love beaming out of His face, and upheld by the power of His beckoning presence, we shall struggle through the latest wave that parts us and scarcely feel its chill or know that we *have* crossed it; till falling blessed at

His feet, we see, by the nearer and clearer visi n of
His face, that this is indeed heaven. And looking
back upon "the sea that brought us thither," we shall
behold its waters flashing in the light of that everlasting morning, and hear them breaking into music upon
the eternal shore. And then, when all the weary
night-watchers on the stormy ocean of life are gathered together around Him Who watched with them
from His throne on the bordering mountains of eternity, where the day shines forever—then He will seat
them at His table in His Kingdom, and none will need
to ask: "Who art Thou?" or "Where am I?" for all
shall know that "It is the Lord," and the full, perfect,
unchangeable vision of His blessed face will be
heaven!   MACLAREN.

ACTS *Wait for the promise of the Father.*
i. 4.
        Tarry at a promise till God meets you there.   He
always returns by way of His promises.

ACTS *Ye shall be baptized with the Holy Ghost.*
i. 5.
        When a lecturer on electricity wants to show an ex-
ample of a human body surcharged with his fire, he
places a person on a stool with glass legs.   The glass
serves to isolate him from the earth, because it will not
conduct the fire,—the electric fluid: were it not for
this, however much might be poured into his frame, it
would be carried away by the earth; but, when thus
isolated from it, he retains all that enters him.   You
see no fire, you hear no fire; but you are told that it is
pouring into him.   Presently, you are challenged to
the proof; asked to come near, and hold your hand
close to his person: when you do so, a spark of fire

shoots out toward you. If thou, then, wouldst have
thy soul surcharged with the fire of God, so that those
who come near thee shall feel some mysterious influence proceeding out from thee, thou must draw nigh
to the source of that fire, to the throne of God and of
the Lamb, and shut thyself out from the world,—that
cold world which so swiftly steals our fire away.
Enter into thy closet, and shut to thy door, and there,
isolated "before the throne," await the baptism: then
the fire shall fill thee; and, when thou comest forth,
holy power will attend thee, and thou shalt labor, not
in thine own strength, but with demonstration of the
Spirit, and with power.   W. ARTHUR.

Ye shall be witnesses unto me.   ACTS
   Christians are the best evidences of Christianity.   i. 8.
                                          ARNOT.

Peter, fastening his eyes upon him, with John.   ACTS
   The apostles "fastened" their eyes on the lame   iii. 4.
man.   Is not this a characteristic of Christianity that it
fastens its eyes on the afflicted and the suffering?
SCIENCE fastens its eyes on inanimate matter! ART
fastens its eyes on beauty! ART going to the temple
to pray, which by the way it seldom does in our day,
would have fixed its gaze on the " gate called Beautiful." But Christianity fixed its eyes on the cripple.
ART standing on the brow of Olivet would have fixed
its gaze on the grandeur of Jerusalem, but Christ fixed
His on its guilty inhabitants and wept over them.
SCIENCE seeks out the secrets of the world.   ART seeks
out its beauties.   Christianity seeks out its sorrows
and ills, and strives to remove them.

One Thousand and One

ACTS iv. 12. *There is none other name under heaven given among men, whereby we must be saved.*

Men who neglect Christ, and try to win heaven through moralities, are like sailors at sea in a storm, who pull, some at the bowsprit, and some at the mainmast, but never touch the helm.　　BEECHER.

ACTS iv. 13. *They . . . perceived that they were unlearned and ignorant men.*

What the Lord blesses everywhere is not great knowledge, but great devotedness of heart to Himself.
R. H. SCHOFIELD.

ACTS iv. 13. *They took knowledge of them, that they had been with Jesus.*

Christ reveals Himself to all His servants in the measure of their desire after Him. . . . And what we *see* we shall certainly *show*. The necessary accompaniment of vision is reflecting the thing beheld. If you look closely enough into a man's eye, you will see in it little pictures of what he beholds at the moment; and if our hearts are beholding Christ, Christ will be mirrored and manifested on our hearts. Our characters will show what we are looking at, and we ought to bear His image so plainly, that men cannot but take knowledge of us that we have been with Jesus. . . . Do beholding and reflecting go together in your case?　　McLAREN.

If I think of the world, I get the impress of the world; if I think of my trials and sorrows, I get the impress of my trials and sorrows; if I think of my failures, I get the impress of my failures; if I think of Christ, I get the impress of Christ.

Thoughts from My Library

They brought forth the sick into the streets . . .   ACTS
that . . . the shadow of Peter passing by might   V.
overshadow some of them. . . . And they were   15, 16.
healed every one.

While Peter was exercising his real self in preaching
the gospel of the risen Christ, his shadow—the direct
reflection of himself—was also busy healing such sick
people as it fell upon. Your bodily shadow may be
very worthless, but your Christian shadow, which is
your influence, may and should be of the utmost
worth. It is all the while falling upon some one, and
he is made better or worse by it. You cannot help
that. God has made it so, that, with the sun upon
one side of you and the ground upon the other, there
will be seen the faithful outline of yourself, according
to the eternal laws of light! God has made it so,
that, with Jesus Christ living within you, and the souls
of men living around you, upon them will fall the
spiritual likeness of yourself, and every one will be
different from what he otherwise would be.

Stephen, a man full . . . of the Holy Ghost.   ACTS
Can I see the dew of heaven as it falls on a summer   vi. 5.
evening? I cannot. It comes down softly and gently,
noiselessly and imperceptibly. But when I go forth in
the morning after a cloudless night, and see every leaf
sparkling with moisture, and feel every blade of grass
damp and wet, I say at once, "There has been a dew."
Just so it is with the presence of the Spirit in the soul.
RYLE.

His face as . . . the face of an angel.   ACTS
It was once said of a Christian man that "His face   vi. 15.

243

was a thanksgiving for past mercies and a love-letter to all mankind."

ACTS vii. 56. *I see the heavens opened and the Son of man standing on the right hand of God.*

There is a volume of tender meaning here. Thirteen times is Christ spoken of in Scripture as "*seated* at the right hand of God"; only *once* is He spoken of as "*standing*," and that once is here. Why, then, this strange exception? Why has the seated Saviour changed His posture so that He is seen "standing" by His dying saint? Oh, blessed testimony to the deathless sympathy and tenderness of that loving Saviour's heart!—Seated though He be—it is as if He had heard the stir in that court on earth;—as if He heard (as indeed He did) every malicious taunt that was hurled at His holy servant. He cannot remain still. He rises;—(or, if we dare use a human expression to give force to the heavenly vision)—He starts from His seat at the call of His injured disciple—He feels the cruelties inflicted on *him* as if they were inflicted on Himself. He, the same gentle, tender Shepherd that He ever was, sees one of the choicest sheep of the fold in the fangs of ravening wolves! Roused by these wild beasts who were scattering His flock;—touched with the tender bleat of that holy and innocent victim of their rage,—the good Shepherd stoops down from the hills of glory; and, as Stephen enters the valley of the shadow of death, He comforts and supports him with His rod and staff!   MACDUFF.

ACTS viii. 26. *Go . . . unto the way . . . which is desert.*

Never fear when the Lord bids us go down to the way "which is desert." The moment we set our foot

Thoughts from My Library

in the wilderness we are the Lord's guests, and He ever keeps His table right royally furnished.

MARK GUY PEARSE.

The Spirit said . . . Go near, and join thyself to this chariot. And Philip ran thither. ACTS viii. 29.

That is not what some of us do. When God gives us a call we begin to creep thither. How many creeping, limping Christians there are! They have got something to do for God's glory, and they crawl instead of running. "I have a natural indisposition to occupy a post of publicity or to excite anything like general observation." My friend, what has thy natural character to do with it? Is it by your natural, or by your supernatural character, that you are going to glorify God? . . . Whenever God intimates His will, run, and you will find the cross will grow very light to willing feet. It is heavy to the man who crawls, but light to the man who runs. AITKEN.

Philip . . . preached unto him Jesus. ACTS viii. 35.

A sermon devoted to metaphysics is a stack of dry cornstalks after the corn has been ripped out with the husking-peg. A sermon given up to sentimental and flowery speech is as a nosegay flung to a drowning sailor. A sermon devoted to moral essay is a basket of chips to help on the great burning. What the world wants now is to be told in the most flatfooted way of Jesus Christ, who comes to save men from eternal damnation. Christ the Light, Christ the Sacrifice, Christ the Rock, Christ the Star, Christ the Balm, Christ the Guide. TALMAGE.

Lord, what wilt thou have me to do? ACTS ix. 6.

Bring your plans, your purposes to God's throne.

245

Test them by praying about them. Do nothing large or new—nothing small or old either, for that matter—till you have asked there, in the silence of the secret place, "Lord, what wilt Thou have me to do?" McLAREN.

ACTS ix. 6. *Arise, and go into the city, and it shall be told thee what thou must do.*

Duty's path always opens for us as we go on—not before we start, but as we obey and move forward. Yet we must not expect there will never be any difficulties to meet or obstacles to surmount. God never has promised that. Too easy a path is often a bane in life, not a blessing. The difficulties and obstacles that remain may be made stepping-stones by which we shall rise to higher things. J. R. MILLER.

ACTS ix. 39. *All the widows stood by him weeping, and shewing the coats and garments which Dorcas made, while she was with them.*

There are no trifles in the moral universe of God. God has placed you in a position in which you can be honest and excel. Do your duty in the present and God will take care of the future. . . . Don't live in the cloudland of some transcendental heaven; do your best to bring the glory of a real heaven down and ray it out upon your fellows in this work-day world.

PUNSHON.

ACTS x. 30, 31. *Cornelius said . . . I prayed in my house; and behold a man stood before me . . . and said, Cornelius, thy prayer is heard.*

If you would have your prayers accepted, they must be arrows shot from the heart; none else reach the throne of God. GUTHRIE.

Thoughts from My Library

God is no respecter of persons.

With God there is no free man but His servant, though in the galleys; no slave but the sinner, though in a palace; none noble but the virtuous, if never so basely descended; none rich but he that possesseth God, even in rags; none wise but he that is a fool to himself and the world; none happy but he whom the world pities. Let me be free, noble, rich, wise, happy, to God. BISHOP HALL.

ACTS x. 34.

Jesus . . . went about doing good.

The finest of all the fine arts is the art of doing good, and yet it is the least cultivated. TALMAGE.

ACTS x. 38.

In the holy land lived a man called Eliab, whom God had blessed with earthly goods. He was also cunning in all the wisdom of the East. But all this could not bring peace to his heart; he was often full of sorrow and wished to die. Then a man of God came to him, and showed him an herb possessed of wonderful powers of healing; but Eliab said: "What is that to me? My body lacks not health; my soul is diseased. It were better for me to die." "The herb will do thy heart good," said the man of God. "Take it, and heal seven sick men and then thou mayest die if thou wilt." Eliab did as he was desired, and sought out misery in its abiding-places. He healed seven sick people and succored the poor with his riches. Then the man of God came again to him and said, "Here is an herb of death; now thou mayest die." But Eliab cried: "God forbid! My soul longeth no more for death, for now I comprehend the meaning and use of life." KRUMMACHER.

247

One Thousand and One

ACTS xv. 18. *Known unto God are all his works from the beginning of the world.*

And if His works were foreknown how much more His saints! . . . The source of a stream must be sought, not where it arises in some green glen among the hills, making a tiny tarn of clear water, where the mountain sheep come down to drink; but in the mighty sea, drawn upward in evaporation, or in the clouds that condense against the cold slopes of the hills. So with the life of God within us. In its earlier stages we are apt to suppose that it originated in our will and choice and return to our Father's House. But as we review it from the eminence of the years, we discover that we chose because we were chosen; that we love because we were first loved; that we left the sepulchre of our selfishness and the cerements of death, because the Son of God flung His majestic word into the sepulchral vault, crying, "Come forth!" All mature piety extols the grace of God—that unmerited love, which each man thinks was magnified most abundantly in his own case. "By the grace of God I am what I am," is a confession which is elicited from every man as he reaches the crest of the hill, and looks back on the cities of the plain from which he has escaped.   F. B. MEYER.

ACTS xvi.25. *And at midnight Paul and Silas prayed, and sang praises unto God.*

While your *salvation* depends on Jesus and His finished work, and on that alone, your *enjoyment* of that salvation depends very much on yourself—on your holy walk with God, on your living a life within the veil—living daily by faith on Him Who loved you and gave Himself for you. Without this you may be a Christian, but you will never be a peaceful, praising, happy Christian.   F. WHITFIELD.

But the Jews which believed not . . . set all the ACTS
city on an uproar.   xvii. 5.

It is a sign we gallop in our way when the dogs follow barking. Slack not your pace, though they do so.
PHILIP HENRY.

These . . . have turned the world upside down.   ACTS
None of these things move me.—Acts xx. 24.   xvii. 6.

The men that move the world are the ones who do not let the world move them.

By the space of three years I ceased not to warn every ACTS
one night and day with tears.   xx. 31.

Why is it that this fount of tears seems denied us? We have tears for all things else than the infinite loss of those who have rejected the Gospel. For this, alas! no single drop trickles along the dry water courses. We are smitten by a terrible drought, our heart a very Sahara: our water springs frozen by remorseless cold or scorched by relentless heat. In losing the power of tears we have lost one great power of causing them. It is by broken hearts that hearts are broken; by wet eyes that eyes are made to brim over with the waters of repentant sorrow.   F. B. MEYER.

The Lord stood by him.   ACTS
The man who stands by Christ will find Christ   xxiii.
standing by him.   TALMAGE.   11.

Herein do I exercise myself, to have always a conscience ACTS
void of offence toward God.   xxiv.
An ill conscience is no comfortable companion to   16.

carry with thee.   An ill conscience is like a thorn in the flesh.   A thorn in the hedge may scratch you as you pass by it; but a thorn in the flesh rankles with you wherever you go: and the conscience, the ill conscience, the conscience that is ill at ease, it makes you ill at ease.   You cannot have peace so long as you have an evil conscience, so long as there is that continual monition flashing across your mind: "Judgment cometh, death cometh: am I ready?"   Many a time when you go to your worldly scenes of pleasure, this conscience, like the finger-writing on the wall of the palace of the King of Babylon, alarms and frightens you.   You tell nobody about it.   Strange thoughts strike across your mind.   You have no rest.   Can a man rest on a pillow of thorns?   Can a man rest with the heartache?   Can a man rest with his soul disturbed with the horrors of guilt?   I tell thee there is no rest to thee till thou comest to Christ.   He alone can calm a conscience.   COLEY.

ACTS xxvi. 28, 29.   *Agrippa said unto Paul, Almost thou persuadest me to be a Christian.   And Paul said, I would to God that not only thou, but also all that hear me . . . were both almost, and altogether such as I am, except these bonds.*

Paul saw two boats; one was called *Altogether* and the other *Almost.*   He saw the *Altogether* go into port, flags flying, and he saw the *Almost* founder at sea.   Not quite a Christian is to be no Christian at all.
                                                    TALMAGE.

ACTS xxvii. 44.   *Some on boards, and some on broken pieces of the ship.*   God often lets His people reach the shore as on the planks of a shipwrecked vessel.   He deprives us of the cisterns in order to make us drink out of the fountains of waters. He frequently takes away our supports, not that we may fall to the ground, but that He may Himself become our rod and our staff. The embarrassments of His people are only the festive scaffoldings on which His might, His faithfulness, and His mercy celebrate their triumphs. KRUMMACHER.

I am not ashamed of the gospel of Christ; for it is the power of God unto salvation to every one that believeth. ROM. i. 16.

Take the Gospel for a sling, and faith and repentance for the smooth stones from the brook; take sure aim, God will direct the weapon, and great Goliaths will tumble before you. TALMAGE.

God . . . will render to every man according to his deeds. ROM. ii. 5, 6.

The most common actions of life, its every day and hour, are invested with the highest grandeur, when we think how they extend their issues into eternity.

GUTHRIE.

Peace with God through our Lord Jesus Christ. ROM. v. 1.

Avaunt, Satan! While I am at peace with God, I am a match for all thy temptations. Thou offerest me silver; I have gold. Thou bringest before me the riches of the earth; I have something more substantial than these. Avaunt, tempter of human kind! Avaunt, thou fiend! Your temptations and blandishments are lost on one who has peace with God. SPURGEON.

Tribulation worketh patience; and patience, experience; and experience, hope; and hope maketh not ROM. v. 3, 4, 5.

251

*ashamed ; because the love of God is shed abroad in
our hearts.*

God is daily searching us, sifting us, trying us to
bring out the evil that is in us, that we may know ourselves, and that He may have fresh opportunities of
bringing out all His supplies and resources. He brings
us, as He did Israel, into danger, poverty, sorrow, and
care that He may get opportunities of displaying all
His love and fullness. Let us not grudge Him these;
they will soon be at an end. It is only here, on this
sad, poor earth, that He can have such opportunities.
When we reach the Kingdom, our sin and emptiness,
and weakness, and grief will be done. It is only *now*
and *here* that God can thus display Himself in His
grace, and long-suffering and plenteousness.

HORATIUS BONAR.

ROM.
v. 5.
*Hope maketh not ashamed, because the love of God is
shed abroad in our hearts.*

Alps on Alps arise, as the believer presses forward
in his course. He beholds a summit and exclaims,
"My God will meet me there, and there will gainsay-
ers be confounded." But when he reaches it, he receives not the expected testimony, and unbelievers
make a mock of his disappointed hopes. He would
be troubled; but in the absence of the external testimony, he receives an inward sweet assurance of the
love and faithfulness of God, and in the very hour of
his disappointment, his face shines with a singular joy.
Looking up he sees a higher mount. "Oh," he exclaims, "it is there, not here, that God should meet
me. I must reach the higher summit." He reaches
it, and it proves to be a new summit of sorrow for

him.   Again, a wave of heavenly bliss rolls over his heart, and he refuses to be confounded.   A still higher peak catches his aspiring eye.   All his disappointments, however, are real conquests.   Those inferior summits mark the way that he must necessarily tread in his course to the hill of transfiguration.   In his *great* hope he is not confounded, only in his lesser hopes that lay hold of time, place, and circumstance.   From every hill of disappointment, he carries off a rich spoil.

BOWEN.

How shall we, that are dead to sin, live any longer ROM.
therein ? vi. 2.

Thy sins after pardon have a blacker circumstance than the sins of devils, or the sins of wicked men, for theirs are not against pardoning mercy nor against special love.   Oh! thaw thy heart every morning with meditation on pardon, and sin will not so easily freeze it in the daytime.   When thou art tempted to sin, consider what thoughts thou hadst when thou wast suing for pardon, how earnest thou wert for it, what promises and vows thou didst make; and consider the love God showed thee in pardoning.   Do not blur thy pardon, or easily wound thy conscience, or weaken thy faith.   CHARNOCK.

Sin shall not have dominion over you. ROM.
vi. 14.

I stood some years ago near the fair city of Geneva, where two great rivers meet, but do not mingle.   Here the Rhône, the arrowy Rhône, rapid and beautiful, pours out its waters of that heavenly blue which it is worth almost a pilgrimage to see, and there the Arve, frantic and muddy, partly from the glaciers from which it is so largely fed, and partly from the clayey soil that it upheaves in its impetuous path, meet and run side by side for miles, with no barriers, save their own innate repulsions, each encroaching now and then into the province of the other, but beaten back again instantly into its own domain. Like mighty rival forces of good and evil do they seem, and for long— just as in the world around us—for long the issue is doubtful; but if you look far down the stream, you find the frantic Arve is mastered, and the Rhône has colored the whole surface of the stream with its own emblematic and beautiful blue. PUNSHON.

ROM.
vi. 23.
The wages of sin is death.

A certain tyrant sent for one of his subjects, and said to him, "What is your employment?" He said, "I am a blacksmith."—"Go home, and make me a chain of such a length." He went home: it occupied him several months; and he had no wages all the time he was making it. Then he brought it to the monarch; and he said, "Go and make it twice as long." He brought it up again; and the monarch said, "Go and make it longer still." Each time he brought it, there was nothing but the command to make it longer still; and, when he brought it up at last, the monarch said, "Take it, and bind him hand and foot with it, and cast him into a furnace of fire." These were the wages of making the chain. Here is a meditation for you to-night, ye servants of the devil. Your master, the devil, is telling you to make a chain. Some have been fifty years welding the links of the chain; and he says, "Go and make it still longer." Next sabbath morning, you will open that shop of yours, and put another link on; next sabbath, you will be drunk, and

put on another link; next Monday, you will do a dis-
honest action: and so you will keep on making fresh
links to this chain; and, when you have lived twenty
more years, the devil will say, "More links on still!"
And then, at last, it will be, "Take him, and bind him
hand and foot, and cast him into a furnace of fire."
"For the wages of sin is death."   SPURGEON.

They that are after the flesh do mind the things of the   ROM.
    flesh; but they that are after the Spirit, the things   viii. 5.
    of the Spirit.

Pampering the flesh is hampering the Spirit.

He . . . searcheth the hearts.   ROM.

It is not the gilded paper and good writing of a   viii. 27.
petition that prevails with a king, but the moving
sense of it: and to the King that discerns the heart,
heart-sense is the sense of all, and that which He alone
regards; He listens to hear what that speaks, and takes
all as nothing where that is silent. All other excellence in prayer is but the outside and fashion of it;
that is the life of it.   LEIGHTON.

All things work together for good to them that love God.   ROM.

In the cathedral at Pisa is a wonderful dome. Spa-   viii. 28.
cious, symmetrical; composed of the choicest marble,
it is a delight to stand beneath, and gaze upon its
beauties. Thus I stood, one sunny April day, when
suddenly the air became instinct with melody. The
great dome seemed full of harmony. The waves of
music vibrated to and fro, loudly beating against the
walls, swelling into full chords like the roll of a grand
organ, and then dying away into soft, long-drawn,
far-receding echoes, melting in the distance into silence.

It was only my guide, who, lingering behind me a moment, had softly murmured a triple chord. But beneath that magic roof every sound resolved into a symphony. No discord can reach the summit of that dome and live. Every noise made in the building, the slamming of seats, the tramping of feet, all the murmur and bustle of the crowd, are caught up, softened, harmonized, blended and echoed back in music. So it seems to me that over our life hangs the great dome of God's providence. Standing, as we do, beneath it, no act in the divine administration toward us, no affliction, no grief, no loss which our heavenly Father sends, however hard to bear it may be, but will come back at last, softened and blended into harmony, within the over-arching dome of His wisdom, mercy and power, till to our corrected sense it shall be the sweetest music of heaven.   J. DORMAN STEELE.

If our circumstances find us in God we shall find God in all our circumstances.

In one thousand trials it is not five hundred of them that work for the believer's good, but nine hundred and ninety-nine of them, AND ONE BESIDES.

GEORGE MÜLLER.

ROM. viii. 37. *In all these things we are more than conquerors through him that loved us.*

Never let us judge of God's love to us or purpose about us by the outward features of our life; only by His personal dealing with our spirits. Do not fear circumstances. They cannot hurt us, if we hold fast by God, and use them as the voices and ministries of His will. Our goodness and our greatness do not consist in what we have but in what we are.   BOWEN.

Thoughts from My Library

More than conquerors. ROM. viii. 37.

It is one thing to WITHSTAND—it is quite another thing to STAND. In the one, we are conquerors, in the other, "more than conquerors through Him that loved us."

They have a zeal of God, but not according to knowledge. ROM. X. 2.

As all zeal without discretion is as an offering without eyes, which was by God forbidden, so, likewise, all blind zeal is a blind offering, which God will never accept. CAWDRAY.

The same Lord over all is rich unto all that call upon him. ROM. X. 12.

The sun does not shine for a few trees and flowers, but for the wide world's joy. The lowly pine on the mountain-top waves its sombre boughs, and cries, "Thou art my sun"; and the little meadow-violet lifts its cup of blue, and whispers with its perfumed breath, "Thou art my sun"; and the grain in a thousand fields rustles in the wind, and makes answer, "Thou art my sun." So God sits effulgent in heaven, not for a favored few, but for the universe of life; and there is no creature so poor or so low, that he may not look up with childlike confidence, and say, "My Father, Thou art mine." BEECHER.

Faith cometh by hearing, and hearing by the word of God. ROM. X. 17.

I prayed for faith and thought that some day faith would come down and strike me like lightning. But faith did not seem to come. One day I read in the tenth chapter of Romans, "Now faith comes by hearing, and hearing by the Word of God." I had closed my Bible and prayed for faith. I now opened my Bible and began to study, and faith has been growing ever since. Now the Bible is the only guidebook that points the way to heaven.   MOODY.

ROM. xii. 1. *Present your bodies a living sacrifice.*

Thanksgiving is a good thing: thanks-living is better.

Self-control reaches its highest discipline in the absolute giving away of the whole life to the care and service of God.   JOSEPH PARKER.

If God had required thee to sacrifice thy son to Him as He required of Abraham, wouldst thou not give him? but now He requireth nothing of thee but thy sins; it is as if He should sue unto thee for thy shame, and thy trouble, and thy guilt, and thy fear, that He might have all which hurts thee. What wilt thou part from if thou wilt not part from thine hurt? Therefore sacrifice thy body, and thou hast sacrificed all that hurts thee.   HENRY SMITH.

ROM. xii. 12. *Continuing instant in prayer.*

Make prayer a holy habit—a cherished privilege. Seek to be ever maintaining inter-communion with Jesus; consecrating life's common duties with His favor and love. Day by day ere you take your flight into the world, night by night when you return from its soiling contacts, bathe your drooping plumes in this refreshing fountain. Let prayer sweeten prosperity and hallow adversity.   MACDUFF.

ROM. xii. 15. *Weep with them that weep.*

Post-mortem sympathy is useless.   HUGH BROWN.

258

Thoughts from My Library

Step very gently around a broken heart. Do you expect, with a thin court-plaister of words, to heal a wound deep as the soul? Talk very softly around those whom God has bereft. Then go your way. Deep sympathy has not much to say.   TALMAGE.

Do that which is good.   ROM. xiii. 3.

Keep as few good intentions hovering about as possible. They are like ghosts haunting a dwelling. The way to lay them is to find bodies for them. When they are embodied in substantial deeds they are no longer dangerous.   ARNOT.

None of us liveth to himself.   ROM. xiv. 7.

An ancient sage illustrated the consequences of sin in this parable: A vessel sailing from Joppa, carried a passenger who, beneath his berth, cut a hole through the ship's side. When the men of the watch expostulated with him, the offender calmly replied, "What matters it to you? The hole I have made lies under my own berth." No man perishes alone in his iniquity; no man can guess the full consequences of his transgression.   SPURGEON.

The character which you are constructing is not your own. It is the building material out of which other generations will quarry stones for the temple of life. See to it therefore that it be granite and not shale.   A. J. GORDON.

Peace and joy.   ROM. xiv. 17.

Peace is the flowing of the brook, but joy is the dashing of the cataract when the brook is filled, bursts its banks, and rushes down the rocks.   SPURGEON.

ROM. *I commend unto you Phœbe. . . . She hath been*
XVI. *a succorer of many, and of myself also.*
1, 2.

A sundial in Spain has this appropriate motto engraved upon it: "*I mark only the bright hours.*" Let this be our motto. In life let us forget the dark days, and remember only the bright ones. Let us forget the evils others have done us, and remember only deeds of kindness.

I COR. *Come behind in no gift.*
i. 7.

The Scripture gives four names to Christians, taken from the four cardinal graces so essential to man's salvation: *Saints* for their holiness, *believers* for their faith, *brethren* for their love, *disciples* for their knowledge. FULLER.

I COR. *The cross is to them that perish, foolishness; but unto*
i. 18. *us which are saved, it is the power of God.*

Damascen likened the cross of Christ to a key of gold which if accepted opens paradise for us; but, if unaccepted, it becomes an iron key, and opens the gates of hell before us.

I COR. *Christ crucified, unto the Jews a stumbling block, and*
i. 23, *unto the Greeks foolishness; but unto them which*
24. *are called . . . Christ the power of God, and*
the wisdom of God.

There are two ways of treating the seed. The botanist splits it up, and discourses on its curious characteristics: the simple husbandman eats and sows; sows and eats. Similarly there are two ways of treating the gospel. A critic dissects it, raises a mountain of debate about the structure of the whole, and relation of its parts; and when he is done with his argument, he is done; to him the letter is dead; he neither lives on it himself, nor spreads it for the good of his neighbors; he neither eats nor sows. The disciple of Jesus, hungering for righteousness, takes the seed whole; it is bread for to-day's hunger, and seed for to-morrow's supply.   ARNOT.

God hath chosen the foolish things of the world to I COR. *confound the wise; and God hath chosen the weak* i. 27. *things of the world to confound the things which are mighty.*

In some of the great halls of Europe may be seen pictures not painted with the brush, but mosaics, which are made up of small pieces of stone, glass, or other material. The artist takes these *little pieces;* and, polishing and arranging them, he forms them into the grand and beautiful picture. Each individual part of the picture may be a little worthless piece of glass or marble or shell; but, with each in its place, the whole constitutes the masterpiece of art. So I think it will be with humanity in the hands of the Great Artist. God is picking up the little worthless pieces of stone and brass, that might be trodden under foot unnoticed, and is making of them His great masterpiece.   BISHOP SIMPSON.

Most of us are too strong for God to use; we are too full of our own schemes and plans and ways of doing things. He must empty us and humble us, and bring us down to the dust of death, so low that we need every straw of encouragement, every leaf of help; and then He will raise us up and make us as the rod of His strength. The world talks of the survival of the fittest; but God gives power to the faint, and increases might to them that have no strength; He perfects His strength in weakness, and uses things that are not to bring to nought things that are. If Ehud had been right handed, he might never have judged Israel; if Gideon had been the greatest instead of the least in his father's house, he would never have vanquished Midian; if Paul had been as eloquent in his speech as he confesses himself to have been contemptible, he would never have preached the gospel from Jerusalem round to Illyricum.   F. B. MEYER.

I COR. ii. 9. *Eye hath not seen, nor ear heard, neither have entered into the heart of man, the things which God hath prepared for them that love him.*

When you survey the spacious firmament, and behold it hung with such resplendent bodies, think—if the suburbs be so beautiful, what must the city be! What is the footstool He makes to the throne whereon He sits!   SECKER.

Great as is the goodness which He has wrought before the sons of men for them that trust in Him, there are far greater treasures of goodness laid up in the deep mines of God for them that fear Him. Bars of uncoined treasure and ingots of massy gold lie in His storehouses, to be put into circulation as soon as we need, and can use, them.   McLAREN.

I COR. ii. 14. *The natural man receiveth not the things of the Spirit of God . . . neither can he know them, because they are spiritually discerned.*

"I remember once being present," says Captain Basil Hall, "at the Geological Society, when a bottle was produced which was said to contain certain Zoöphytes (delicate water-animals, having the form of plants). It was handed round in the first instance among the initiated on the foremost benches, who commented freely with one another on the forms of the animals in the fluid; but when it came to our hands, we could discover nothing in the bottle but the most limpid fluid, without any trace, so far as our eyes could make out, of animals dead or alive, the whole appearing absolutely transparent. The surprise of the ignorant, at seeing nothing, was only equal to that of the learned, who saw so much to admire. Nor was it till we were specifically instructed what it was we were to look for, and the shape, size, and general aspect of the Zoöphytes pointed out, that our understanding began to coöperate with our sight in peopling the fluid which, up to that moment, had seemed perfectly uninhabited. The wonder then was, how we could possibly have omitted seeing objects now so palpable." How many are the things which appear to the illuminated Christians to be palpably revealed, which the unconverted cannot discover to have any place in the Scriptures of truth; and how much surprised does he feel that he could ever have overlooked them!   F. F. TRENCH.

Let every man take heed how he buildeth.   I COR.
iii. 10.

Our business is not to build quickly, but to build upon a right foundation, and in a right spirit. Life is more than a mere competition as between man and man; it is not who can be done first, but who can work best; it is not who can rise highest in the shortest time, but who is working most patiently and lovingly in accordance with the designs of God.

JOSEPH PARKER.

One Thousand and One

The day shall declare it.

You and I write our lives as if on one of those manifold writers which you use. A thin filmy sheet *here*, a bit of black paper below it, but the writing goes through upon the next page, and when the blackness that divides two worlds is swept away *there*, the history of each life written by ourselves remains legible in eternity. And the question is: What sort of autobiography are we writing for the revelation of that day, and how far do our circumstances help us to transcribe fair in our lives the will of our God and the image of our Redeemer?   McLAREN.

It shall be revealed by fire.

As the words that are written with the juice of a lemon cannot be read when they are written, but may be plainly and distinctly seen if you hold the paper to the fire, so the least letters in the book of our conscience, yea, the least notes and points and scratches, which neither any other nor ourselves see well now, shall easily be discerned by the fire of the last judgment.   FEATLEY.

All things are yours . . . and ye are Christ's; and Christ is God's.

I once heard a father tell that when he removed his family to a new residence, where the accommodation was much more ample, and the substance much more rich and varied than that to which they had previously been accustomed, his youngest son, yet a lisping infant, ran around every room, and scanned every article with ecstasy, calling out in childish wonder at every new sight, "Is this ours, father, and is this ours?" The child did not say "yours," and I observed that the father, while he told the story, was not offended with the freedom. You could read in his glistening eye that the infant's confidence in appropriating as his own all that his father had was an important element in his satisfaction. Such, I suppose, will be the surprise and joy, and appropriating confidence, with which the child of our Father's family will count all his own when he is removed from the comparatively mean condition of things present, and enters the infinite of things to come. When the glories of heaven burst upon his view, he does not stand at a distance, like a stranger, saying, "O God, these are Thine." He bounds forward to touch and taste every provision which these blessed mansions contain, exclaiming, as he looks in the Father's face, "Father, this and this is ours!" The dear child is glad of all the Father's riches, and the Father is gladder of His dear child.

ARNOT.

The way to possess unlimited treasure is to give yourself to Christ. BOWEN.

Judge nothing before the time. I COR. iv. 5.

Judge not Christianity even by its most perfect embodiment in the life of its disciples here. The best are imperfect; and Christianity itself teaches this, and points to perfection as yonder. Do not judge the science of that organ-builder by that half-finished instrument in his workshop. There is but little in that to please the eye; and from it scarce a note can be evolved to charm the ear. Judge not the artistic character of that painter by the first rough outline which you discover on the canvas in his studio. There is scarcely a touch of life in it, or any perceptible resemblance to the original. Judge the organ-builder by the instrument as it stands in the great cathedral, pouring forth by the touch of a master-musician pealing strains of music, electrifying the congregated thousands. Judge the artist by the picture as hung up in the Academy of Art; looking, throbbing, and blushing at you as a thing of life; gathering around it a crowd of admiring spectators. Even so judge Christianity. Its organ—the Christian life—is not half finished here in its workshop. Yonder, in the great cathedral of eternity, you will see it in perfection, and feel the inspirations of its harmonies. The painting is not finished here in its studio: its figure is half formed and blotched; and scarcely a feature is accurate. See it in the great gallery of the heavens, finished, and an exact copy of the Son of God Himself, "Who is the image of the Father's glory." THOMAS.

I COR. vi. 17. *He that is joined unto the Lord is one spirit.*

The contact of our spirits with His Spirit is a contact far more real than the touch of earthly hands that grasp each other closest. There is ever some film of atmosphere between the palms. But "he that is joined to the Lord is one spirit" and he that clasps Christ's outstretched hand of help with his outstretched hand of weakness, holds Him with a closeness to which all unions of earth are gaping gulfs of separation. McLAREN.

I COR. vi. 20. *Ye are bought with a price; therefore glorify God in your body, and in your spirit, which are God's.*

Into the slave-market of this world God hath gone in the person of His Son, and paid the tremendous price which authorizes Him to take as many as He can find

266

Thoughts from My Library

willing to go, and create them anew in the image of the Son. . . . It is not a fragment of you that has been purchased; but the whole. You would hardly presume to say that the price was inadequate. Yet do you not seem to say so? How much of your time is the Lord's? Do you dress, feed, employ your body as unto the Lord? Is your tongue, your hand consecrated all to Him? Your memory, imagination, hope? Your love and faith? Your houses and lands? Your influence?   BOWEN.

Let every man abide in the same calling wherein he   I COR.
was called.   vii. 20.

Whatever our place allotted to us by Providence, that for us is the post of duty and honor. God estimates us, not by the position we are in, but by the way in which we fill it.   T. EDWARDS.

The time is short.   I COR.
We all complain of the shortness of time; and yet   vii. 29.
we have more than we know what to do with. Our lives are spent either in doing nothing at all, or in doing nothing to the purpose, or in doing nothing that we ought to do. We are always complaining that our days are few, and acting as though there would be no end of them.   SENECA.

The fashion of this world passeth away.   I COR.
The spirit of the world is forever altering, impalpa-   vii. 31.
ble; forever eluding, in fresh forms, your attempts to seize it. In the days of Noah, the spirit of the world was *violence.* In Elijah's day, it was *idolatry.* In the day of Christ, it was *power,* concentrated and condensed in the government of Rome. In ours, perhaps,

267

it is *the love of money.* It enters in different proportions into different bosoms; it is found in a different form in contiguous towns, in the fashionable watering-places, and in the commercial city; it is this thing at Athens, and another in Corinth. This is the spirit of the world, a thing in my heart and yours to be struggled against, not so much in the case of others as in the silent battle done within our own souls.

F. W. ROBERTSON.

I COR. vii. 32.

I would have you without carefulness.

Do not look forward to the changes and chances of this life in fear, rather look to them with full hope that, as they arise, God, Whose you are, will deliver you out of them. He has kept you hitherto,—do you but hold fast to His dear hand, and He will lead you safely through all things; and when you cannot stand, He will bear you in His arms. Do not look forward to what may happen to-morrow; the same everlasting Father Who cares for you to-day will take care of you to-morrow, and every day. Either He will shield you from suffering, or He will give you unfailing strength to bear it. Be at peace then, and put aside all anxious thoughts and imaginations. FRANCIS DE SALES.

I COR. vii. 32.

The things that belong to the Lord.

The things that belong to men must be understood in order to be loved; the things that belong to God must be loved in order to be understood. PASCAL.

I COR. ix. 24, 25.

So run, that ye may obtain. And every man that striveth for the mastery is temperate in all things.

If it is a small sacrifice, give it up for others, if a great one, for yourself.

Thoughts from My Library

Who will not suffer you to be tempted above that ye are able. I COR. X. 13.

Faith is the better of free air, and of the sharp winter storm in its face. Grace withereth without adversity. The devil is but God's master-fencer, to teach us to handle our weapons. RUTHERFORD.

Whatsoever ye do, do all to the glory of God. I COR. X. 31.

Let us not be Christians as to the few great things of our lives, and atheists as to the many small things which fill up a far greater space of them. God is in both, waiting for the glory we can give Him in them.

Be ye followers of me, even as I also am of Christ. I COR. xi. I.

When in the Mexican War, the troops were wavering, a general rose in his stirrups, and dashed into the enemy's lines, shouting, "Men, follow!" They, seeing his courage and disposition, dashed on after him, and gained the victory. What men want to rally them for God is an example to lead them. All your commands to others to advance amount to nothing so long as you stay behind. To affect them aright, you need to start for heaven yourself, looking back only to give the stirring cry of "Men, follow!" TALMAGE.

For as the body is one, and hath many members, and all the members of that one body, being many, are one body: so also is Christ. I COR. xii. 12.

The Church of Christ is the whole body of those who have heard His voice of love and yielded to it.

MARK GUY PEARSE.

Now we see through a glass darkly; but then face to face. I COR. xiii. 12.

The infinite beauty and glory of our ideal must ever

269

distance our noblest efforts, as the inaccessible heights of the Jungfrau, clad in untrodden snows, rise higher and ever higher above the traveller as he approaches them along the valley at their foot.   F. B. MEYER.

I COR.
xiii. 13
(R. V.).

Now abideth faith, hope, love, these three; but the greatest of these is love.

Joy is love exulting.
Peace is love in repose.
Long-suffering is love untiring.
Gentleness is love in society.
Goodness is love in action.
Faith is love on the battlefield.
Meekness is love at school.
Temperance is love in training.

Love is the greatest thing that God can give us; for Himself is *Love;* and it is the greatest thing we can give to God, for it will give ourselves, and carry with it all that is ours.   JEREMY TAYLOR.

I COR.
XV. 20.

But now is Christ risen from the dead, and become the first-fruits of them that slept.

Death is a dragon, the grave its den; a place of dread and terror; but Christ goes into its den, there grapples with it, and forever overcomes it, disarms it of all its terror; and not only makes it cease to be inimical, but to become the greatest blessing to the saints; a bed of rest, and a perfumed bed; they do but go into Christ's bed, where He lay before them.

FLAVEL.

I COR.
XV. 22.

As in Adam all die, even so in Christ shall all be made alive.

We lost our inheritance by the fall of Adam: we re-

ceive it by the death of Christ, which restores it again
to us by a new and better title.   FLAVEL.

I die daily.   I COR.
XV. 31.

In some respects prayer resembles death. When
man dies his soul returns to God, and when he prays
he does the same thing; and it is this habitual return
of the soul to its maker in acts of devotion that makes
the final return in death so easy. The Christian thus
dies on a small scale every day; and this enables him
to die aright when the appointed time comes.

God giveth it a body as it hath pleased him.   I COR.
XV. 38.

You cannot tell what is in that body of yours; but
wait until all the sin has been removed from it; wait
until its weaknesses and limitations disappear; wait
until it is changed and made like unto His glorious
body, and then it will be seen as it was intended in
the beginning, not a clog nor a hindrance, but a perfect vehicle and medium through which the soul would
have perfect manifestation.   J. WESLEY JOHNSTON.

It is sown in dishonor ; it is raised in glory.   I COR.
XV. 43.

I have stood in a smith's forge and seen him put a
rusty, cold, dull piece of iron into the fire, and, after a
while, he hath taken the very same identical individual
piece of iron out of the fire, but bright, sparkling.
And thus it is with our bodies: they are laid down in
the grave, dead, heavy, earthly; but at that general
conflagration, this dead, heavy, earthly body shall arise
living, lightsome, glorious.   FULLER.

The first man Adam . . . the last Adam.   I COR.
XV. 45.

Jesus kept close to Scripture, and thus conquered:
without any other weapon, save the sword of the Spirit,

271

One Thousand and One

He stood in the conflict, and gained a glorious triumph. What a contrast to the first Adam! The one had every thing to plead against him. The garden, with all its delights, in the one case; the wilderness, with all its privations, in the other: confidence in Satan, in the one case, confidence in God in the other: complete defeat in the one case; complete victory in the other. Blessed forever be the God of all grace, Who has laid our help on One so mighty to conquer, mighty to save! C. H. McINTOSH.

I COR.
XV. 55.

O! death, where is thy sting? O! grave, where is thy victory?

The grave—what is it? It is the bath in which the Christian puts the clothes of his body to have them washed and cleansed. Death—what is it? It is the waiting-room where we robe ourselves for immortality; it is the place where the body, like Esther, bathes itself in spices that it may be fit for the embrace of its Lord. SPURGEON.

I COR.
XV. 57.

God . . . giveth us the victory through our Lord Jesus Christ.

Soldier of the cross, the hour is coming when the note of victory shall be proclaimed throughout the world. The battlements of the enemy must soon succumb; the swords of the mighty must soon be given up to the Lord of lords. What! soldier of the cross, in the day of victory wouldst thou have it said that thou didst turn thy back in the day of battle? Dost thou not wish to have a share in the conflict, that thou mayest have a share in the victory? If thou hast even the hottest part of the battle, wilt thou flinch and fly? Thou shalt have the brightest part of the victory if thou art in the fiercest of the conflict. Wilt thou turn, and lose thy laurels? Wilt thou throw down thy sword? Shall it be with thee as when a standard-bearer fainteth? Nay, man, up to arms again! for the victory is certain. Though the conflict be severe, I beseech you, on to it again! On, on, ye lion-hearted men of God, to the battle once more! for ye shall yet be crowned with immortal glory. SPURGEON.

Be ye steadfast, unmovable, always abounding in the work of the Lord. I COR. xv. 58.

Activity in doing good is one recipe for being cheerful Christians; it is like exercise to the body and it keeps the soul in health. RYLE.

Let not your exertions end in tears; mere weeping will do nothing without action. Get on your feet: ye that have voices and might, go forth and preach the gospel; preach it in every street and lane of this huge city; ye that have wealth, go forth and spend it for the poor and sick and needy and dying, the uneducated, the unenlightened; ye that have time, go forth and spend it in deeds of goodness; ye that have power in prayer, go forth and pray; ye that can handle the pen, go forth and write down iniquity,—every one to his post; every one of you to your gun in this day of battle; now for God and for His truth; for God and for the right; let every one of us who knows the Lord seek to fight under His banner. SPURGEON.

Stand fast in the faith, quit you like men, be strong! I COR. xvi. 13.

The standing fast, the quitting ourselves like men, is the duty that God has laid upon us.

In the days of the Roman persecutions, the edict

went forth from the emperor that every soldier in all the army should be submitted to a test as to his loyalty. He should pour the libation to the emperor, or die such death as his commander should pass upon him. In the northern part of Gaul there was a Julian legion of 100 men, with their centurion. They had become knit together in the dangers and self-sacrifices and hardships of a lonely, arduous, desperate service. The very flower of this band were Christians, who, it was known, would not worship the emperor. But the centurion set up the emperor's image and the libation was prepared. One by one the members of the band filed up, and either poured the libation, or said, "I am a Christian," and turned off to the left. When the test was over, there stood forty men, the very bravest and the best, the most self-sacrificing, and the best-beloved of all that band of men. Sorrowfully the commander sentenced them to death from exposure upon the frozen surface of the lake. As they went forth, a mighty song broke forth, "Forty wrestlers, wrestling for Thee, O Christ, claim for Thee the victory, and from Thee the crown." Far out on the ice they knelt down and raised their voices in thanksgiving to Christ Who had elected them to die for His honor and glory. The centurion caused a great fire to be built on the shore and dismissed the guard, while he, their well-beloved friend, strode up and down, keeping guard, in the hope that they might repent them of this strange faith which he did not understand, but which made them loyal, and true, and gentle, and good beyond their comrades. By and by he saw one dark form separating itself from the rest and come stumbling, creeping up the bank, intent on saving its life by the sacrifice of its soul, but as the traitor fell down before the image of the emperor, the helmet and shield of the centurion clanged upon the ground, and he strode forth and joined himself unto them. Once again the cry went up, "Forty wrestlers, wrestling for Thee, O Christ, claim for Thee the victory, and from Thee the crown."

The God of all comfort who comforteth us in all our tribulations. II COR. i. 3, 4.

The more varied and manifold a man's experiences have become, the more he has the chance to know of God, the more chance God has to show Himself to him. Every new experience is a new opportunity of knowing God. Every experience is like a jewel set in the texture of our life, on which God shines and makes interpretation and revelation of Himself.

PHILLIPS BROOKS.

Who comforteth us in all our tribulation, that we may be able to comfort them which are in any trouble, by the comfort wherewith we ourselves are comforted of God. II COR. i. 4.

A larkspur cannot lecture on the nature of a snowflake—it never saw a snowflake; and those people who have always lived in the summer of prosperity cannot talk to those who are frozen in disaster. TALMAGE.

Give me the comforts of God, and I can well bear the taunts of men. Let me lay my head on the bosom of Jesus, and I fear not the distraction of care and trouble. If my God will give me ever the light of His smile and glance His benediction—it is enough. Come on, foes, persecutors, friends, ay, Apollyon himself, for "the Lord God is my sun and shield." Gather, ye clouds, and environ me, I carry a sun within; blow, wind of the frozen north, I have a fire of living coal within; yea, death, slay me, but I have another life, a life in the light of God's countenance.

SPURGEON.

II COR.
i. 5. *For as the sufferings of Christ abound in us, so our consolation also aboundeth by Christ.*

Surely there is more profound connection than we sometimes discover between the "sufferings" and the "consolation," between the "loss" welcomed for JESUS' sake and the eternal gain that follows after, as harvest follows sowing. "That I may know Him and the power of His resurrection" still stands between that willing *self-emptying* on the one hand, and the deeper *"fellowship with His sufferings"* on the other, for which even the heart of an apostle craved.

Shall we shrink, then, from anything that makes more room for GOD? Let us believe, rather, that if He withhold any earthly blessing, it is only that He may bestow "all spiritual blessings," and remember that He is dealing with us not for our profit merely, but for the good of many and the glory of His own great name, not for time only, but for eternity.

GERALDINE GUINNESS.

II COR.
i. 20. *All the promises of God in him are yea, and in him Amen, unto the glory of God by us.*

The promises of God are to the believer an inexhaustible mine of wealth. Happy is it for him if he knows how to search out their secret veins, and enrich himself with their hid treasures! They are an armory, containing all manner of offensive and defensive

276

weapons. Blessed is he who has learned to enter into the sacred arsenal, to put on the breast-plate and the helmet, and to lay his hand to the spear and to the sword! They are a surgery in which the believer will find all manner of restoratives and blessed elixirs; nor lacks there an ointment for every wound, a cordial for every faintness, a remedy for every disease. Blessed is he who is well skilled in heavenly pharmacy, and knoweth how to lay hold on the healing virtues of the promises of God! The promises are to the Christian a storehouse of food. They are as the granaries which Joseph built in Egypt, or as the golden pot wherein the manna was preserved. Blessed is he who can take the five barley-loaves and fishes of promise, and break them till his five thousand necessities shall all be supplied, and he is able to gather up basketsful of fragments!   SPURGEON.

Our Lord has written the promise of the resurrection, not in books alone, but in every leaf in springtime.   LUTHER.

All the promises in the Bible are so many bills of exchange drawn by God the Father in heaven upon His son Jesus Christ, and payable to every pious bearer,—to every one that comes to the mercy-seat, and offers the promise or bill for acceptance, and pleads in the way of obedient faith and prayer. Jesus, the High Treasurer of heaven, knows every letter of His Father's handwriting, and can never be imposed upon by any forged note. He will ever honor His Father's bills: He accepts them all. It is for His Father's honor that His bills never fail of acceptance and payment.
                                            BEAUMONT.

One Thousand and One

II COR. *By faith ye stand.*
i. 24.

Faith may live in a storm, but it will not suffer a storm to live in it. As faith rises, so the blustering wind of discontented, troublesome thoughts goes down. In the same proportion that there is faith in the heart, there is peace also: they are joined together. "In returning and rest shall ye be saved; in quietness and confidence shall be your strength."

II COR. *Thanks be unto God which always leadeth us in triumph.*
ii. 14
(R. V.).

Those whom Jesus leads in triumph share His triumph. They may be a spectacle to angels and to men. Sometimes in the stocks; often accounted the offscouring of all things; yet, in the spiritual realm, they are made to triumph always. Conquered, they conquer; enslaved, they are free; last in this world, but in the front rank of heavenly society. Poor, beaten, vanquished soul, lift up thy head and rejoice; for if thou art conquered by Jesus, thou shalt be always made to triumph!   F. B. MEYER.

II COR. *God . . . maketh manifest the savour of his knowl-*
ii. 14.   *edge by us in every place.*

A holy life is a silent witness for Jesus—an incense cloud from the heart-altar, breathing odors and sweet spices, of which the world cannot fail to take knowledge. . . . It *must* and *will* manifest its living and influential power. The heart, broken at the cross, like Mary's broken box, begins from that hour to give forth the hallowed perfume of faith, and love, and obedience, and every kindred grace.   MACDUFF.

II COR. *We are unto God a sweet savour of Christ.*
ii. 15.

When we are told that we may be to God a sweet

278

savor of Christ, it must be meant that we may so live as to recall to the mind of God what Jesus was in His earthly career. It is as though, as God watches us from day to day, He should see Jesus in us, and be reminded (speaking after the manner of men) of that blessed life which was offered as an offering, and a sacrifice to God for a sweet-smelling savor. What a test for daily living! Is my life fragrant of Jesus? Do I remind the Father of the blessed Lord? Does He detect Jesus in my walk and speech? and that there are in me the sweet savor of that daily burnt-offering, that delight in God's will, that holy joy in suffering for His glory, that absorption in His purposes which made the life of the Son of Man so well-pleasing to God?   F. B. MEYER.

To the one . . . the savour of death unto death; II COR.
and to the other the savour of life unto life. ii. 16.

The sun and rain will give vigor and growth to a living tree, but the same sun and rain will increase the rot and decay in a dead one.   PENTECOST.

Ye are our epistle . . . known and read of all II COR.
men. iii. 2.

An epistle to be effective must be legible. There are so many that are illegible; what we want is to be epistles distinctly legible—written in a clear, bold hand, so that everybody can read us at once. When that great artist Doré was once travelling in southern Europe, he lost his passport. When he came to the boundary line where he needed to produce it, the official challenged him. Said he, "I have lost my passport; but it is all right—I am Doré, the artist. Please let me go on." "Oh, no," said the officer, "we have plenty of people representing themselves as this or that great one." After some conversation the man said, "Well, I want you to prove it. Here is a pencil and some paper. Now if you are Doré, the artist, draw me a picture." Doré took up the pencil, and with a few master strokes sketched some of the features of the neighborhood. Said the man, "Now I am perfectly sure of it. You are Doré. No other man could do that." It is no use professing to be a servant of Christ unless you are such a disciple that everybody can see what you are. You are to reproduce His life in you.   A. J. GORDON.

A Christian is the world's Bible. In many cases a revised version is much needed.

II COR. *We all, with open face beholding as in a glass the glory*
iii. 18. *of the Lord, are changed into the same image from glory to glory, even as by the Spirit of the Lord.*

The sunshine must fall on us, not as it does on some lonely hillside, lighting up the grey stones with a passing gleam that changes nothing, and fades away, leaving the solitude to its sadness; but as it does on some cloud cradled near its setting, which it drenches and saturates with fire till its cold heart burns, and all its wreaths of vapor are brightness palpable, glorified by the light which lives amidst its mists. So must we have the glory sink into us before it can be reflected from us. In deep inward beholding we must have Christ in our hearts, that He may shine forth from our lives.   McLAREN.

The face is made every day by its morning prayer and by its morning look out of the windows which open upon heaven. All manly grace and nobleness grow as they are used for God in heaven and truth on earth. JOSEPH PARKER.

At present, the believer is like the marble in the hands of the sculptor; but though, day by day, he may give fresh touches, and work the marble into greater emulation of the original, the resemblance will be far from complete until death. Each fresh degree of likeness is a fresh advance toward perfection. It must then be, that when every feature is moulded into similitude; when all traces of feebleness and depravity are swept away forever, the statue breathes, and the picture burns with Deity,—it must be that *then* we "shall be filled." We shall look on the descending Mediator, and, as though the ardent gaze drew down celestial fire, we shall seem instantly to pass through the refiner's furnace, and leaving behind all the dishonor of the grave, and all the dross of corruptible humanity, spring upward, an ethereal, rapid, glowing thing, Christ's image, extracted by Christ's lustre.

MELVILL.

Christ . . . the image of God. II COR. iv. 4.

The moon, a softer but not less beautiful object than the sun, returns, and communicates to mankind, the light of the sun in a gentle and delightful manner, exactly suited to the strength of the human eye: an illustration and most beautiful emblem, in this and other respects, of the Divine Redeemer of mankind, Who, softening the splendor of the Godhead, brings it to the eye of the understanding in a manner fitted to the strength of the mind, so that, without being overwhelmed or distressed, it can thus behold "the light of the knowledge of the glory of God in the face of Jesus Christ." DWIGHT.

One Thousand and One

II COR.
iv. 7.

We have this treasure in earthen vessels that the ex-cellency of the power may be of God and not of us.

Methought I looked and saw the Master standing, and at His feet lay an earthen vessel. It was not broken, not unfitted for service, yet there it lay, powerless and useless, until He took it up. He held it awhile, and I saw that He was filling it, and anon, I beheld Him walking in His garden, whither He had "gone down to gather lilies." The earthen vessel was yet again in His hand, and with it He watered His beauteous plants, and caused their odors to be shed forth yet more abundantly. Then I said to myself, "Sorrowing Christian, hush! hush! peace, be still! thou art this earthen vessel; powerless, it is true, yet not broken, still fit for the Master's use. Sometimes thou mayest be laid aside altogether from active service, and the question may arise, what is the Master doing with me now? Then may a voice speak to thine inmost heart, 'He is filling the vessel, yes, only filling it ready for use.' Dost thou ask in what manner? Nay, be silent. Is it not all too great an honor for thee to be used by Him at all? Be content, whether thou art employed in watering the lilies, or in washing the feet of the saints." Truly, it is a matter of small moment. Enough, surely enough, for an earthen vessel, to be in the Master's hands, and employed in the Master's service.

II COR.
iv. 17.

Our light affliction, which is but for a moment, work-eth for us a far more exceeding and eternal weight of glory.

We write our blessings on the water, but our afflictions on the rock.   GUTHRIE.

Thoughts from My Library

If at any time you feel disposed to say, "It is enough," and that you can bear the burden of life no longer, do as Elijah did, flee into the silence of solitude, and sit under—not the juniper-tree—but under that tree whereon the incarnate Son of God was made a curse for you. Here your soul will assuredly find sweet refreshment, from Christ's acceptable offering to God. . . . At the sight of the cross you will no longer think of complaining of the greatness of your sufferings; for here you behold sufferings, in comparison with which yours must be accounted a light affliction which is but for a moment; here the righteous One suffers for you,—the just for the unjust. . . . Under the cross you are prevented from supposing that some strange thing is happening unto you; "the disciple is not above his Master, nor the servant above his Lord. . . ." At the foot of the cross your grief will soon be lost in that peace and joy of God which drops from this tree of life into the ground of your heart, and the foretaste you will here obtain of heaven, will sweeten the troubles of this life as with the breath of morning. . . . Yea, the cross itself will be transformed into such a medium between heaven and earth, that the most comforting thoughts shall descend into your soul, and the most grateful thoughts shall ascend from your soul to heaven like those angels of God seen in a vision on the plains of Bethel by the solitary and benighted patriarch, Jacob.

KRUMMACHER.

If our earthly house of this tabernacle were dissolved, we have a building of God, an house not made with hands, eternal in the heavens.   II COR. V. 1.

Living is death: *dying* is life.   We are not what we

appear to be. On this side of the grave, we are exiles; on that, citizens: on this side, orphans; on that, children: on this side, captives; on that, freemen: on this side, disguised, unknown; on that, disclosed and proclaimed as the sons of God.   BEECHER.

II COR. *We walk by faith, not by sight.*
v. 7.

"We live by faith," says the apostle, "and not by sight, or by sense." They are as two buckets—the life of faith, and the life of sense; when one goes up, the other goes down; the higher faith rises, the lower sense and reason; and the higher sense and reason, the lower faith. That is true of the schools. Reason going before faith weakens and diminishes it; but reason following upon faith, increases and strengthens it. Luther says well, "If you would believe, you must crucify that question, Why?" God would not have us so full of wherefores. And if you would believe, you must go blindfold into God's command. Abraham subscribes to a blank when the Lord calls him out of his own country.   BRIDGE.

II COR. *The love of Christ constraineth us.*
v. 14.

Ah! Love, what canst thou not do? Thou canst make the timid brave, and the weak strong. The martyr, the patriot, the hero have learned of thee the secret of finding beds of down on stones, and gardens of flowers on barren sands. Thou didst bring the King Himself from the midst of His royalties to the cross, and He counted all things but loss that He might redeem the church on whom He had set His heart. Then self will be dethroned, the cross of daily-dying will be robbed of its bitterness, the furnace floor will become a flower-enamelled pathway, if only thou shalt reign in us supreme! . . . The love that can expel self is not the vague love of a principle or theory, but of a person. It is the love of Christ which passeth knowledge. "I saw," says George Fox, "a sea of light and a sea of ink; and the sea of light flowed into the sea of ink, and swept it away forever." F. B. MEYER.

Love is the blood of the universe. BEECHER.

All things are become new. II COR. V. 17.

One of Goethe's tales is of a rude fisherman's hut which was changed to silver by the setting in it of a little silver lamp. The logs of which the hut was built, its floors, its doors, its roof, its furniture,—all was changed to silver by this magic lamp. The story illustrates what takes place in the home when Christ comes into it. Everything after that is different. The outward conditions and circumstances may be the same, but they shine now with a new beauty.

Just as the sun gleams over the palace, and into the cottage, flushing alike with its splendor the council-chamber of the monarch and the kitchen of the peasant; as the all-pervasive light fills the vast dome of the sky, and the tiny cup of the flower; so religion illumines at once the heaven of our hopes, and the earth of our cares. Secularities become hallowed; toil brightens with the smile of God; business becomes crystalline; light from God comes through it to us; glances from us go through it to God. COLEY.

Workers together with him. II COR. vi. 1.

Christian worker, be clean, pure of heart, and simple in motive. See to it that there be no friction between your will and Christ's. Be adjusted, in gear, well set and jointed. Subdue your own activities as much as your own natural lethargy. Stand still till God impels you. Wait till He works in you to will and to do of His good pleasure. Exercise faith that God should accomplish in you the greatest results possible to the capacity of your nature. Let there be no thought of what you can do for God, but all thought of what God can do through you. Nothing will make you so intense and ceaseless in your activity as this.   F. B. MEYER.

II COR. *Behold, now is the accepted time; behold, now is the*
vi. 2. *day of salvation.*

A minister of the gospel determined on one occasion to preach on the text, "Now is the accepted time; now is the day of salvation." Whilst in his study, thinking, he fell asleep, and dreamed that he was carried into hell, and set down in the midst of a conclave of lost spirits. They were assembled to devise means whereby they might get at the souls of men. One rose, and said, "I will go to the earth, and tell men that the Bible is all a fable, that it is not divinely appointed of God." No, that would not do. Another said, "Let me go: I will tell men that there is no God, no Saviour, no heaven, no hell"; and at the last words a fiendish smile lighted upon all their countenances. "No, that will not do: we cannot make men believe *that*." Suddenly one arose, and with a wise mien, like the serpent of old, suggested, "No: I will journey to the world of men, and tell them that there *is* a God, that there *is* a Saviour, that there *is* a heaven,—yes, and a hell too,—but I'll tell them *there is no hurry;*

TO-MORROW will do, it will be 'even as to-day.'" And
they sent him.

In Nebuchadnezzar's image, the lower the members,
the coarser the metal; the farther off the time, the
more unfit. To-day is the golden opportunity; to-
morrow will be the silver season; next day but the
brazen one; and so on, till at last I shall come but to
the toes of clay, and be turned to dust. FULLER.

As sorrowful, yet alway rejoicing. II COR.
vi. 10.

A Christian man's life is laid in the loom of time to
a pattern which he does not see, but God does; and
his heart is a shuttle. On one side of the loom is
sorrow, and on the other is joy; and the shuttle, struck
alternately by each, flies back and forth, carrying the
thread, which is white or black as the pattern needs.
And in the end, when God shall lift up the finished
garment, and all its changing hues shall glance out, it
will then appear that the deep and dark colors were as
needful to beauty as the bright and high colors.

BEECHER.

What part hath he that believeth with an infidel? II COR.
vi. 15.

Keep clear of any system of religion which con-
founds the world and true believers. RYLE.

Come out from among them, and be ye separate, saith II COR.
the Lord and touch not the unclean thing: and I vi. 17.
will receive you.

Don't roll in the mire to please the pigs.

SPURGEON.

The electrician cannot charge your body with electricity, while a single thread connects you with the
ground, and breaks the completeness of your insula-

tion. The Lord Jesus cannot fully save you whilst there is one point of controversy between you and Him. Let Him have that one last thing, the last barrier and film to a life of .blessedness, and glory will come filling your soul.   F. B. MEYER.

In Brazil, there grows a common plant, which forest-dwellers call the *matador*, or " murderer." Its slender stem creeps at first along the ground; but no sooner does it meet a vigorous tree, than, with clinging grasp, it cleaves to it, and climbs it, and, as it climbs, keeps, at short intervals, sending out arm-like tendrils that embrace the tree. As the murderer ascends, these ligatures grow larger, and clasp tighter. Up, up, it climbs a hundred feet, nay, two hundred if need be, until the last loftiest spire is gained and fettered. Then, as if in triumph, the parasite shoots a huge, flowery head above the strangled summit, and thence, from the dead tree's crown, scatters its seed to do again the work of death. Even thus worldliness has strangled more churches than ever persecution broke.
                                        COLEY.

One cannot honor Christ in one's walk, and at the same time walk with those who dishonor Him.

II COR. *Godly sorrow worketh repentance to salvation not to be*
vii. 10. *repented of.*
        True repentance is that one step that no man ever repented. . . . The way of life is a narrow path, but the footsteps in it are all in one direction,—not one has ever come back and said it was a delusion.
                                        RYLE.

Thoughts from My Library

The gentleness of Christ.   II COR.
X. 1.

The gentleness of Christ is the comeliest ornament
that a Christian can wear.   ARNOT.

The weapons of our warfare are . . . mighty   II COR.
through God.   X. 4.

When the soldier enlists in his country's army, he is
furnished with uniform and arms. . . . So God
arms His recruits, equipping them with both power
and sword. Their business is to use to the best advantage what God bestows upon them. He gave
Moses a rod, David a sling, Samson the jawbone of an
ass, Shamgar an ox-goad, Esther beauty of person,
Deborah the gift of poesy, Dorcas a needle, and
Apollos an eloquent tongue, and to each the ability to
use what each one had, and in so doing each one did
most effective work for God. So He supplies each
one of His disciples to-day with something that when
used will make him useful in His kingdom, and to
each man " to profit withal." Let us use the weapon
that God has given us and not sit down to pine for
the instrument that He has bestowed upon another.
The use of the weapon that we have will make us a
success. The attempt to use another's would make
us a failure.   W. W. DAWLEY.

My grace is sufficient for thee: for my strength is made   II COR.
perfect in weakness.   xii. 9.

God's way of answering His people's prayers is not
by removing the pressure, but by increasing their
strength to bear it. The pressure is often the fence
between the narrow way of life and the broad road to
ruin; and if our Heavenly Father were to remove it, it
might be at the sacrifice of heaven. Oh! if God had

removed that thorny fence in answer, often to earnest prayers, how many of us would now be castaways! How the song of many a saint now in glory would be hushed! How many a harp would be unstrung! How many a place in the mansions of the redeemed would be unfilled! If God answered all the prayers we put up to heaven, we should need no other scourge. Blessed it is that we have One Who is too loving to grant what we too often so rashly ask. F: WHITFIELD.

Every "to-morrow" has two handles. We can take hold of it by the handle of anxiety, or by the handle of faith.

II COR. xiii. 5. *Examine yourselves.*

If your state be good, searching into it will give you the comfort of it. If your state be bad, searching into it cannot make it worse; nay, it is the only way to make it better, for conversion begins with conviction.

BISHOP HOPKINS.

GAL. i. 3, 4. *Our Lord Jesus Christ . . . gave himself for our sins that he might deliver us from this present evil world.*

Attachment to Christ is the only secret of detachment from the world. A. J. GORDON.

GAL. i. 8. *Though we, or an angel from heaven, preach any other gospel unto you than that which we have preached unto you, let him be accursed.*

No matter how infidel philosophers may regard the Bible: they may say that Genesis is awry, and that the Psalms are more than half bitter imprecations, and the Prophecies only the fantasies of brain-bewildered men, and the Gospels weak laudations of an impostor, and the Epistles but the letters of a mad Jew, and that the whole book has had its day, I shall cling to it until they show me a better revelation. The Bible emptied, effete, worn out! If all the wisest men of the world were placed man to man, they could not sound the shallowest depth of the Gospel of John. O philosophers! break the shell, and fly out, and let me hear how you can sing,—not of passion, I know that already; not of worldly power, I hear that everywhere: but teach me, through your song, how to find joy in sorrow, strength in weakness, and light in darkest days; how to bear buffeting and scorn; how to welcome death, and to pass, through its ministration, into the sphere of life; and this, not for me only, but for the whole world that groans and travails in pain. And, until you can do this, speak not to me of a better revelation.   BEECHER.

Neither was I taught it, but by the revelation of Jesus Christ.   GAL. i. 12.

A little from God is better than a great deal from men. What is from men is often tumbled over and over; things that we receive at God's hand come to us as things from the minting house. Old truths are always new to us if they come with the smell of heaven upon them.   BUNYAN.

It pleased God . . . to reveal his Son in me.   GAL. i. 15, 16.

O soul of man, has this revelation ever been thy experience? Dost thou know that Christ is in thee? If thou truly believest in Him, there is no doubt of it. "Know ye not as to your own selves, how that Jesus Christ is in you, except ye be reprobates?" And yet thou mayest be in ignorance of this transcendent possession. Ask God to reveal His Son in thee, to make thee know experimentally the riches of the glory of this mystery. He will rend the veil of the inner life in twain from the top to the bottom, and in the most holy place of thy spirit disclose the Shekinah of His eternal presence. Two conditions only must be fulfilled. Thou must be prepared to yield thine own will to the cross; and to wait before God in the silence and solitude of thy spirit.   F. B. MEYER.

GAL.
ii. 20. *Not I, but Christ.*

Paint Jesus Christ upon your canvas, and then hold Him up to the people ; but so hold Him up, that not even your little finger can be seen.   PAYSON.

I watched an old man trout-fishing once, pulling them out one after another briskly. "You manage it cleverly, old friend," I said. "I have passed a good many below who don't seem to be doing anything." The old man lifted himself up, and stuck his rod in the ground. "Well, you see, sir, there be three rules for trout-fishing; and 'tis no use trying if you don't mind them. The first is keep yourself out of sight. The second is keep yourself further out of sight. And the third is keep yourself further out of sight still. Then you'll do it." "Good for catching men, too," I thought, as I went on my way.   MARK GUY PEARSE.

I was in Italy last year; and, in crossing the Alps with my wife, the sun was so hot, that it scorched her face. She asked me to get her some elder-flower water. I started off to a chemist; and, as I did not know a word of the Italian language, I looked through the jars and bottles in his shop, but could not find anything of

the kind. I tried to jabber something in French; but
he did not understand me, because it was no language
at all. I went down to a little brook that ran through
the town, and, walking along the edge, I came to an
elder-flower-tree. I got a handful of flowers, walked
off to the shop, and held it up to the man; and he
knew in an instant what I meant. I think it is not
easy to convey the gospel to the heart by merely talking of it; but if you can say by your own life, "This
is the life of Christ, this is the joy of being a Christian," you will be much more likely to make converts.

SPURGEON.

You can't jump away from your shadow, but if you
turn to the sun your shadow is behind you, and if you
stand right under the sun your shadow is beneath you.
What we should try to do is to live under the meridian Sun, with our shadow-self under our feet.

F. B. MEYER.

Ye are all one in Christ Jesus.

GAL. iii. 28.

I have seen a field here, and a field there, stand thick
with corn—a hedge or two has separated them. At
the proper season the reapers entered; soon the earth
was disburdened, and the grain was conveyed to its
destined resting-place, where, blended together in the
barn or in the stack, it could not be known that a
hedge had ever separated this corn from that. Thus it
is with the church. Here it grows, as it were, in different fields, and even, it may be, by different hedges.
By and by, when the harvest is come, all God's wheat
shall be gathered into the garner, without one single
mark to distinguish that once they differed in outward
circumstantials of form and order. TOPLADY.

One Thousand and One

GAL.
V. 22. *The fruit of the Spirit is· . . . gentleness.*

It is curious to remark, that wherever the Holy
Ghost is spoken of in the Bible, He is spoken of in
terms of gentleness and love.   We often read of "the
wrath of God" the Father, as Rom. i. 18; and we
read of the wrath of God the Son, as Ps. ii. 12, but we
nowhere read of the wrath of God the Holy Ghost.

M'CHEYNE.

GAL.
vi. 2. *Bear ye one another's burdens, and so fulfill the law*
of Christ.

However perplexed you may at any hour become
about some question of truth, one refuge and resource
is always at hand: you can do something for some one
besides yourself.   When your own burden is heaviest,
you can always lighten a little some other burden.   At
the times when you cannot see God, there is still open
to you this sacred possibility, to *show* God; for it is
the love and kindness of human hearts through which
the divine reality comes home to men, whether they
name it or not.   Let this thought then, stay with you:
there may be times when you cannot find help, but
there is no time when you cannot give help.

G. S. MERRIAM.

There is no anodyne for heart-sorrow like ministry
to others.   If your life is woven with the dark shades
of sorrow, do not sit down in sorrow to deplore your
hapless lot, but arise to seek out those who are more
miserable than you are, bearing them balm for their
wounds and love for their heart-breaks.   And if you
are unable to give much practical help, you may
largely help the children of bitterness by listening to
their tales of woe or to their dreams of foreboding.

Thoughts from My Library

The burdened heart longs to pour out its tale in a sympathetic ear. There is immense relief in the telling out of pain. But it cannot be hurried; it needs plenty of time. If you can do nothing else, listen well, and comfort others with the comfort wherewith you yourself have been comforted by God. And as you listen, and comfort, and wipe the falling tear, you will discover that your own load is lighter, and that a branch or twig of the true tree—the tree of the cross—has fallen into the bitter waters of your own life, making the Marah, Naomi, and the marshes of salt tears will have been healed.   F. B. MEYER.

Whatsoever a man soweth that shall he also reap.   GAL.
vi. 7.

You can't grow the tulips of the kingdom of God unless you get the bulbs from heaven.

Let us not be weary in well-doing: for in due season   GAL.
we shall reap if we faint not.   vi. 9.

Are we preparing for the true heavenly feast of tabernacles—the great reaping-day of glory? That well-known feast and season in the land of Canaan was a joyous one of old only to the Hebrew who had been unremitting in spring and summer toil. To the sluggard who had left his fields unsown, uncultured, untended, there could be no participation in the songs of the jubilant multitude: he had gone forth before the fall of the early or the latter rains, bearing no precious seed; he could not, therefore, on that festive week, come again with rejoicing, bringing his sheaves with him. It was he, who had used with laborious fidelity and drudgery, spade and plough and pruning-hook, who had utilized for field and vineyard the precious rains of heaven, that would bear his palm-branch with

295

most exultant joy, and repose with grateful satisfaction within his shady arbor. If there were no harvest to divide, there could be no gladness. "They joy before Thee according to the joy in harvest, and as men rejoice when they divide the spoil."

It is so, on a vaster scale, with the spiritual sower and reaper in the prospect of immortality. While we never dare lose sight of the foundation-truth of the gospel, that salvation is of grace, not of works; yet neither dare we reject or overlook the great counterpart assertion, which contains at least no paradox or inconsistency to the eye gifted with spiritual discernment, that "faith without works is dead, being alone." No waving of the festal palm, by those who have abandoned their fields of heart and life labor to the thorn and the thistle,—who have left the seed unsown, the ground untilled, the vine to languish; and whom God, the great Husbandman, will address with the withering words on the great day of harvest—"What could I have done more to My vineyard than I have done; wherefore, then, when I looked that it should bring forth grapes, brought it forth wild grapes?" If we would have the joyous song of the heavenly reaper, we must now be among the faithful and diligent sowers.

The rest of the feast of tabernacles above, is only possible to such. No toil here,—no repose, no festal hosanna yonder. "Let us labor, therefore, to enter into that rest." Up! sow your fields and plant your vineyards; do noble work while you have space and opportunity to do it (in your own hearts and in the world around you) for God and His Christ, encouraged by the assurance—"Be not weary in well-doing, for in

Thoughts from My Library

due season ye shall reap if ye faint not." To all such willing and devoted laborers; to all who have listened to the summons of the Master, "Go, work in my vineyard"; to all who have done battle with sin, manfully struggled with temptation, eradicated from the seed-plot of the heart its roots of bitterness; who in a spirit of earnest self-sacrifice have renounced the world, and in a spirit of holy self-consecration and self-surrender have given themselves to God,—the invitation of Christ to the heavy-laden here, will have a new and glorious significance as He welcomes them hereafter at heaven's great harvest-home, the eternal feast of tabernacles—"Come unto Me, I will give you rest!"   MACDUFF.

God forbid that I should glory save in the cross of our Lord Jesus Christ. GAL. vi. 14.

The cross of our Lord Jesus Christ is the centre of human history. It is the sun around which the firmament circles; the key to all Scripture history and type; the fact which gives meaning and beauty to all other facts. To ignore the cross is to repeat the error of the old philosophers, who thought that the earth, and not the sun was the centre of our system, and to whom therefore the very heavens were in confusion. To know and love the cross—to stand beside it as the faithful women did when Jesus died—is to obtain a deep insight into the harmonies of all things in heaven and in earth. . . . The radiance that streams from the cross illumines all events and banishes all darkness. When an artist in music, color, or stone, conceives a beautiful idea he seems reluctant to let it drop: he hints at it before he expresses it in complete beauty;

297

nor is he satisfied until he has exhausted his art by the variety of ways in which he has embodied his thought. The practiced sense may detect it now in the symphony, and then in the chorus; now in the general scheme, and again in the minute detail. It recurs again and again. There is the hint, the outline, the slight symptom, anticipating the fuller, richer revelation. Is not this true also of the death of our beloved Lord ? The Great Artist of all things, enamored with the wondrous cross, filled the world with foreshadowings and anticipations of it long before it stood with outstretched arms on the little hill of Calvary. You may find them in heathen myths, or in ancient sayings and songs. You may find them in touching incidents of human history. You may, above all, find them upon the pages of the Bible. . . . The sun which now shines, so to speak, from the other side of the cross, so as to fling its shadow forward clear and sharp on the canvas of the present, once shone from where we now stand, and flung its shadow backward upon the canvas of the past.   F. B. MEYER.

EPH. *Grace be to you and peace from God.*
i. 2.   Precious as the fruit is, do not put it where the root should be. Peace is not the root of grace in the soul, it is the fruit, and must not be put out of its proper position.   SPURGEON.

EPH. *He hath made us accepted in the beloved.*
i. 6.   There are many locks in my house, and all with different keys; but I have one master-key which opens all. So the Lord has many treasuries and secrets, all shut up from carnal minds with locks which they cannot open; but he who walks in fellowship with Jesus

possesses the master-key which will admit him to all
the blessings of the covenant; yea, to the very heart
of God. Through the Well-beloved we have access
to God, to heaven, to every secret of the Lord.

SPURGEON.

In whom also, after that ye believed, ye were sealed EPH.
with that holy Spirit of promise. i. 13.

Wherever a seal is mentioned in Scripture, you find
that it is something that everybody can see. Everybody could see the seal on the mouth of the cave,
when Daniel was cast into the den of lions. It would
be a seal, perhaps with the king's likeness on it, or, at
any rate, with his name; and this seal, which was
wont to be stamped on a document, would, in the case
of the den, be stamped upon softened clay. . . .
The Lord puts a seal upon His own, that everybody
may know them; and this is done "after . . . ye
believed." This must mean something that marks
you out to the observation of the world as God's people, something that the world can see. The sealing
in your case is the Spirit producing in you likeness to
the Lord,—to the King and to the King's Son. You
have got the seal of God on you when you exhibit
likeness to God's Son. The holier you become, the
seal is the more distinct and plain, the more evident to
every passer-by, for then will men take notice of you
that you have been with Jesus. A seal like that
spoken of in Rev. vii. 2, "on the forehead" is yours.
The sealing is something that cannot be hid. It is not
even on the palm of your hand. It is in your forehead: all men see that you are not what you once
were. The world takes notice that you are like what

they have heard Jesus was. Whenever that takes place, the sealing is begun, and it remains all your lifetime and becomes more and more plain. Every believer is thus "sealed."   BONAR.

EPH.
i. 13,
14.

Ye were sealed with that holy Spirit of promise, which is the earnest of our inheritance.

In the early times, when land was sold, the owner cut a turf from the greensward and cast it into the cap of the purchaser as a token that it was his; or he tore off the branch of a tree and put it into the new owner's hand to show that he was entitled to all the products of the soil; and when the purchaser of a house received seizin or possession, the key of the door, or a bundle of thatch plucked from the roof, signified that the building was yielded up to him. The God of all grace has given to His people all the perfections of heaven to be their heritage forever, and the earnest of His Spirit is to them the blessed token that all things are theirs. The Spirit's work of comfort and sanctification is a part of heaven's covenant blessings, a turf from the soil of Canaan, a twig from the tree of life, the key to mansions in the skies. Possessing the earnest of the Spirit, we have received *seizin* of heaven.
                                        SPURGEON.

EPH.
ii. 4,
5, 6.

God . . . hath quickened us . . . hath raised us up . . . hath made us sit . . . in heavenly places.

A drop of water lay one day in a gutter, soiled, stained, polluted. Looking up into the blue of the sky, it began to wish for purity, to long to be cleansed and made crystalline. Its sigh was heard, and it was

quickly lifted up by the sun's gentle fingers—up, out
of the foul gutter, into the sweet air, then higher and
higher; at length the gentle winds caught it and bore
it away, away, and by and by it rested on a distant
mountain top, a flake of pure, white, beautiful snow.

J. R. MILLER.

Exceeding riches of his grace.   EPH.
Him that is able to do exceeding abundantly.—Eph. ii. 7.
iii. 20.
Love of Chist which passeth knowledge.—Eph. iii. 19.

The Apostle Paul writes not merely of the *exceeding*
greatness of God's power to us-ward who believe
(Eph. i. 19), but of the *exceeding* riches of God's grace
(ii. 7), and of the Father being able to do *exceeding*
abundantly above all that we ask or think (iii. 20).
Again, he prays (verse 19) that we " may know the
love of Christ, which passeth (*exceedeth*) knowledge."
So there is exceeding *grace*—that explains how we
can be God's people; there is exceeding *love*—that
tells us how all these glories can be ours, for He chose
to love us; and then there is exceeding *power*, the exceeding greatness of His power to us-ward who believe.   That is the thing we want, and we get it in this
order.   Come near to the Lord, yield yourselves to
Him, recognize what He wants you for; and then put
yourselves where it flows.   HUBERT BROOKE.

By grace are ye saved through faith ; and that not of EPH.
  yourselves; it is the gift of God: not of works.   ii. 8, 9.

You cannot get to heaven by your works.   You
might as well seek to mount the stars on a tread-
wheel, as to go to heaven by works; for as you get
up a step, you will always come down as low as be-

fore. If you cannot be perfect, God will not save you by works. SPURGEON.

EPH.
ii. 10.

We are his workmanship, created in Christ Jesus unto good works, which God hath before ordained that we should walk in them.

The works are ready, waiting for us, all we have to do is to be willing to be led into them. How many disappointments we should have been spared in life if we had always acted on this conviction. God knows what we are fitted for far better than we know ourselves. He who made us knows whereof we are made. He won't put "square pegs into round holes. . . ." If we would be useful in Christ's service our wisdom is "to have no plan except to enter into His plan for us," and say with Paul, "Lord, what wilt Thou have me to do?" E. W. MOORE.

No man is born into the world whose work is not born with him; there is always work, and tools to work withal, for those who will. LOWELL.

Each redeemed soul should remember that God has sent us into the world with gifts, duties and opportunities, which He Who has ordained them will help us to cultivate, and expects us to improve. All God's ways are consistent with each other, and complete each other. Every one has been sent into the world with a work to do, and with the means for doing it. He who does not see his work, probably has not taken the pains to discover it. He who morosely complains of his scanty opportunities might be surprised to hear that his own negligence has made them scantier. We can't see with our eyes shut. BISHOP THOROLD.

Thoughts from My Library

Jesus Christ . . . in whom all the building fitly EPH. ii. 20, 21.
framed together, groweth unto an holy temple in the
Lord.

A man dreamed that he was trying to build for himself a temple to commemorate his name. He wanted
a whole temple to himself, and an angel came to show
him one that was a model of beauty. But there was
one stone missing from its peak, and the man asked
the angel where it was. "There has never been one
there," replied the angel. "We intended to place you
there, but you say that you want a whole temple to
yourself, and so the place will be filled by some one
else. But you will never have your special temple."
Then the man, aroused by his fears, started up from
his sleep, crying, "O, God, put me in your temple.
Put me in, even though I can be but a chink stone.
Put me in!"

I . . . am less than the least of all saints. EPH. iii. 8.

Christ was an unsurpassable teacher and many were
those who resorted to Him for instruction. But when
He wanted through His servant to teach humility, the
ordinary terms of grammar would not do, and a new
degree of comparison had to be introduced—little, less,
least, and "less than the least."

The love of Christ which passeth knowledge. EPH. iii. 19.

It may seem very strange that the apostle should
bid us undertake to know a love which passes knowledge, and to seek after a peace which passes understanding. And yet there is no contradiction in these
terms. When they were laying the Atlantic cable,
they came to places they were unable to fathom.
They would let down their fathoming line a thousand

fathoms, a second thousand, a third, a fourth, a fifth, and even a sixth thousand fathoms, and the lead would swing clear; and, whenever in the ocean such a place is found, we call it unfathomable; that is, we express our knowledge of those depths by saying that we do not know. And so we express our highest knowledge of the love of God by saying that it passes full comprehension; and so we express our estimate of the peace of God, by saying that it passeth all understanding.

Oh! there is a voice in love; it speaks a language which is its own; it has an idiom and a brogue which none can mimic; wisdom cannot imitate it; oratory cannot attain unto it; it is love alone which can reach the mourning heart; love is the only handkerchief which can wipe the mourner's tears away. And is not the Holy Ghost a loving comforter? Dost thou know, O saint! how much the Holy Spirit loves thee? Canst thou measure the love of the Spirit? Dost thou know how great is the affection of His soul toward thee? Go measure heaven with thy span; go weigh the mountains in the scales; go take the ocean's water, and tell each drop; go count the sand upon the sea's wide shore; and, when thou hast accomplished this, thou canst tell how much He loveth thee. He has loved thee long, He has loved thee well, He loved thee ever, and He still shall love thee: surely He is the person to comfort thee, because He loves.   SPURGEON.

EPH. *Filled with all the fullness of God.*
iii. 19.   Standing on the deck of a ship in mid-ocean, you see the sun reflected from its depths. From a little boat on a mountain lake you see the sun reflected from

its shallow waters. Looking into the mountain spring, not more than six inches in diameter, you see the same great sun. Look into the dewdrop of the morning, and there it is again. The sun has a way of adapting itself to its reflections. The ocean is not too large to hold it, nor the dewdrop too small. So God can fill any man, whether his capacity be like the ocean, like the mountain lake, like the spring, or like the dewdrop. Whatever therefore be your capacity, the text opens to you the possibility of being "Filled with the fullness of God."   A. C. DIXON.

Beware of emptiness. . . . Empty hours, empty hands, empty companions, empty words, empty hearts, draw in evil spirits, as a vacuum draws in air. To be occupied with good is the best defence against the inroads of evil.   ARNOT.

Speaking the truth in love.   EPH.
One way in which disciples wash one another's feet iv. 15. is by reproving one another. But the reproof must not be couched in angry words, so as to destroy the effect; nor in tame, so as to fail of effect. Just as in washing a brother's feet you must not use boiling water to scald them, nor frozen water to freeze them.
                                FINLAYSON.

The best way of eradicating error is to publish and practice truth.   ARNOT.

Speaking the truth in love.   EPH.
Warning . . . and teaching . . . in all wis- iv. 15.
dom.—Col. i. 28.
A Christian, in all his ways, must have three guides —Truth, Charity, Wisdom: Truth to go before him,

Charity and Wisdom on either hand. If any of the three be absent, he walks amiss. I have seen some do hurt, by following a truth uncharitably; and others, while they would salve up an error with love, have failed in their wisdom, and offended against justice.

BISHOP HALL.

EPH.
iv. 30.

Grieve not the Holy Spirit of God.

The Spirit of God is your companion. Most exalted of all beings, He abides with you on the footing of a friend, to teach, persuade, purify and bless. He is particular indeed; but it is for your good. He interferes with you at times;—not to make a display of His authority, but for your preservation. He restrains you at the entrance of some dark pit; it is because a wolf has made its lair there. He stops you as you are stepping into a boat; it is because a whirlwind is rushing to meet it. He hurries you away from some elevated spot: it is because the mountain is heaving, and a volcano is about to burst forth. Dispute not with Him; grieve Him not. He does nothing to grieve you.

BOWEN.

EPH.
iv. 32.

Be ye kind one to another, tender-hearted, forgiving one another, even as God for Christ's sake hath forgiven you.

As a seal leaves a mark of itself in the wax, whereby it is known; so it is with every one who has a readiness to forgive others; for by it the Christian may know that God has sealed the forgiveness of his sins upon his heart.

CAWDRAY.

EPH.
V. I.
(R. V.).

Be ye . . . imitators of God as beloved children and walk in love.

We cannot expect successfully to imitate Christ, unless we contemplate His person, any more than a painter can reproduce a landscape without his studying it and drinking in the spirit which pervades the whole. We must take time to sit at His feet, studying His character as revealed to us in the Gospels, and being transformed, as it were, unconsciously into His image. What we want is not more knowledge of truth, but more practical carrying it out. R. H. SCHOFIELD.

Ye were sometimes darkness, but now are ye light in the Lord: walk as children of light. EPH. v. 8.

A Christian, when he makes a good profession, should be sure to make his profession good. It is sad to see many walk in the dark themselves, who carry a lantern for others. PECKER.

It is only light that can enlighten. It is only fire that can kindle flame. Hence if we would illuminate others, we must have light in ourselves; and if we would kindle the flame of piety in the hearts of others, we must take the "live coal" with which we do so from the burning "altar" of our own spirit.

TAYLOR.

That you may give light, be sure you have light. When the Atlantic cable is *alive,* that is when its insulation is perfect, and it is fitted for its work, a bright light is reflected on a mirror, and thence on a dial, and its movements give the signs. When it is dead—that is when its insulation is destroyed, and the current is running to the earth—that light disappears. So when the soul is alive, its light shines; when it is dead, there is darkness. JOHN HALL.

One Thousand and One

EPH.
V. 11.
Have no fellowship with the unfruitful works of darkness.

The man who goes into the world to level it up will soon find himself levelled down.　　F. B. MEYER.

EPH.
V. 15.
See then that ye walk circumspectly.

There is no such thing as negative influence. We are all positive in the place we occupy, making the world better or making it worse.　　TALMAGE.

EPH.
V. 16.
Redeeming the time.

What possibilities are yours? Every new day that dawns is a fresh opportunity: it is like the marble in the quarry waiting for you to chisel out of it some beautiful thing—some lasting monument of purity and grace that shall stand for you when your earth life is ended. Remember that God gives you the marble to make of it what you will.

EPH.
V. 18.
Be filled with the Spirit.

When the Lord Jesus was carried up into heaven, did not His mantle descend back again to earth? Had it not been promised "Greater things than these shall ye do, because I go to my Father"? Was it not abundantly fulfilled on the day of Pentecost? Is it not still His will that Christians should receive the double portion of His Spirit? Does not the command, "Be filled with the Spirit," still stand on the page of Scripture, and apply to every servant of God?

If so, have you grasped the mantle?

F. S. WEBSTER.

Perhaps we have all of us yet to fathom the meaning of the sentence in the creed, "I believe in the Holy Ghost." I am sure that we have no notion of what

Thoughts from My Library

God could make us to be, and give us to have, and call us to do, and help us to learn, and enable us to suffer, and permit us to enjoy, if we would but try to understand our Lord's own words: "If ye then, being evil, know how to give good gifts unto your children; how much more shall your heavenly Father give the Holy Spirit to them that ask Him?" Whatever hesitation there may be about our other prayers, there need be none with this. It is *enjoined* on us to "be filled with the Spirit."   BOWEN.

Servants of Christ, doing the will of God from the heart.   EPH. vi. 6.

We must never forget that we are learning by doing God's will, and that His will does not all come to us out of a written Bible. Some of it comes fresh from God's own lips in our life's circumstances. In whatever way it may come, we are to do it, and in doing it we will find a blessing. Hard tasks and duties are like nuts: they are rough and unsightly, and the hull is not easy to break; but when it is broken we find it full of rich meat.   J. R. MILLER.

Put on the whole armor of God.   EPH. vi. 11.

In putting on your armor, don't forget that the sword of the Spirit is the Word of God. Not content with merely reading your Bible, study it. Instead of skimming over whole acres of truth, put your spade into the most practical passages, and dig deep.   CUYLER.

The shield of faith, wherewith ye shall be able to quench all the fiery darts of the wicked.   EPH. vi. 16.

A shield is a piece of armor that soldiers were wont to carry with them into the field of battle; so is faith a

309

part of the Christian's armor with which he fights in
the soul's warfare.   A shield is for defence; so is faith.
A shield is not a fixture for any particular part of the
body, as the breast-plate, the helmet, etc., but was for
the hand, to be moved about according to the direction
in which the darts came; so is faith a shield against
the fiery darts of the wicked, coming to whatever part
of the Christian they may.   A shield doth not only de-
fend the whole body, but it is a defence to other parts
of a soldier's armor also; it keeps off the dart from the
helmet and breastplate likewise: so faith is not only a
safeguard to the whole soul, but to all the particular
parts of the Christian life and character.   The shield of
faith protects the girdle of truth, the helmet of salvation, and the breastplate of righteousness.   A shield
hath been of wonderful advantage to soldiers of former
times.   What wonderful things can be said of faith as
a shield in the hands of God's people in all ages!

KEACH.

EPH.
vi. 17.
The sword of the Spirit which is the word of God.

It is said that at the coronation of the boy King of
England, Edward VI., three swords were brought, and
laid before him as emblems of his power.   "Bring
another," said he, "I need most of all the sword of the
Spirit."   The Bible was brought, and has retained its
place in subsequent coronations.   It is the only
symbol used at the inauguration of our Republican
Presidents.

PHIL.
i. 21.
To me to live is Christ and to die is gain.

You can write Paul's estimate of death after nothing
but Paul's estimate of life.   G. CAMPBELL MORGAN.

Thoughts from My Library

To depart and to be with Christ.
PHIL.
i. 23.

The hour of *death* is to the Christian the birthday of endless life.　　　　　　　　　MACDUFF.

Let your conversation be as it becometh the gospel of Christ.
PHIL.
i. 27.

We often miss our Lord's company, because our conversation does not please Him. When our Beloved goes down into His garden, it is to feed there and gather lilies; but if thorns and nettles are the only products of the soil, He will soon be away to the true beds of spices.　　　　　　　　SPURGEON.

Being of one accord.
PHIL.
ii. 2.

When men were of one accord to make themselves a name, God confounded their language; when they were of one accord to glorify Jesus, He gave them to speak with other tongues so that all could understand.

He . . . became obedient unto death, even the death of the cross; wherefore God . . . hath highly exalted him.
PHIL.
ii. 8, 9.

The way to get rid of your cross is to die upon it; there is no other way. Jesus bore no cross in the resurrection.

God hath . . . given him a name which is above every name.
PHIL.
ii. 9.

Cast thine eyes which way thou wilt, and thou shalt hardly look on anything but Christ Jesus hath taken the name of that very thing upon himself. Is it day? and dost thou behold the sun? He is called the Sun of righteousness. Or is it night? and dost thou behold the stars? He is called a star: "There shall come a

One Thousand and One

Star out of Jacob." Or is it morning ? and dost thou
behold the morning-star ? He is called "the bright and
Morning-Star." Or is it noon ? and dost thou behold
clear light all the world over ? He is "that Light that
lighteth every man that cometh into the world."
Come a little nearer: if thou lookest on the earth, and
takest a view of the creatures about thee, seest thou
the sheep ? "As a sheep before her shearers is dumb,
so He opened not His mouth." Or seest thou a lamb ?
"Behold the Lamb of God, which taketh away the sin
of the world." Seest thou a shepherd watching over
his flock ? "I am the good Shepherd, and know My
sheep, and am known of Mine." Or seest thou a
fountain, rivers, waters ? He is called a fountain:
"In that day there shall be a Fountain opened to the
house of David." Or seest thou a tree good for food,
or pleasant to the eye ? He is called "the Tree of life."
Seest thou a rose, a lily, any fair flower in a garden ?
He is "the Rose of Sharon, and the Lily of the valley."
To come a little nearer yet: art thou adorning thyself,
and takest thou a view of thy garments ? He is a garment: "Put ye on the Lord Jesus Christ." Art thou
eating meat, and takest a view of what is on thy table ?
He is the Bread of God; true Bread from heaven; the
Bread of life.   ISAAC AMBROSE.

Christ is a flower, but He fadeth not; He is a river,
but He is never dry; He is a sun, but He knoweth no
eclipse; He is all in all, but He is something more
than all.   SPURGEON.

PHIL.
ii. 12,
13.
*Work out your own salvation . . . for it is God
which worketh in you.*

These two streams of truth are like the rain-shower

that falls upon the water-shed of a country. The one-half flows down the one side of the everlasting hills, and the other down the other. Falling into rivers that water different continents, they at length find the sea, separated by the distance of half the globe. But the sea into which they fall is one, in every creek and channel. And so the truth into which these two apparent opposites converge is "the depth of the wisdom and the knowledge of God," Whose ways are past finding out—the Author of all goodness, Who, if we have any holy thought, has given it us; if we have any true desire, has implanted it; has given us the strength to do the right and to live in His fear; and Who, yet, doing all the willing and the doing, says to us, "Because I do everything, therefore let not *thy* will be paralyzed or *thy* hand palsied; but because I do everything, therefore will *thou* according to My will, and do *thou* according to My commandments!"

MACLAREN.

It is God which worketh in you to will and to do of PHIL.
his good pleasure. ii. 13.

There are several ways of working for God. We may make the wisest plans we can, and then carry them out to the best of our ability. This is perhaps better than working without any plan, but it is by no means the best way to serve our Master.

Or, having carefully laid our plans and determined to carry them through, we may bring them to God, and ask Him to help and prosper us in connection with them.

Yet another way is to *begin* with God, to ask *His* plans, and offer ourselves to Him to help in carrying them out.   J. HUDSON TAYLOR.

One Thousand and One

Do all things without murmurings.

I have read of Cæsar, that, having prepared a great feast for his nobles and friends, it so fell out, that the day appointed was so extremely foul, that nothing could be done to the honor of the meeting: whereupon he was so displeased and enraged, that he commanded all those that had bows to shoot up their arrows at Jupiter, their chief god, as in defiance of him for that rainy weather; which when they did, their arrows fell short of heaven, and fell upon their own heads, so that many of them were very sorely wounded. So all our murmurings, which are as so many arrows shot at God Himself,—they will return upon our own heads: they reach not Him; but they will hit us: they hurt not Him; but they will wound us. Therefore it is better to be mute than to murmur: it is dangerous to provoke a "consuming fire."　　　T. BROOKS.

PHIL.
iii. 1.　*Rejoice in the Lord.*

It honors religion, it proclaims to the world we serve a good Master. Cheerfulness is a friend to grace: it puts the heart in tune to praise God. Uncheerful Christians, like the spies, bring an evil report of the good land; others suspect there is something unpleasant in religion, that they who profess it hang their harps upon the willows, and walk so dejectedly. Be serious, yet cheerful. Rejoice in the Lord always.
　　　T. WATSON.

PHIL.
iii. 8.　*That I may win Christ.*

In Wales and in Scotland, in the mining districts, "winning" the coal, or the mineral, is a common expression, by which they mean sinking a shaft deep down to get out the ore in richer abundance. Let us take that idea. Paul, on the day when he first discovered Christ, found himself to be the possessor of a large estate. He was standing, so to speak, at the opening of this mine, and he saw some of the precious ore. He could not take his eye off what he did see; but, the more he looked, the more he discovered of the inexhaustible riches there. He had only to dig down, to sink his shaft in all directions, and there was no end to what he might bring up out of this mine; and so it was his lifetime's wish, "that I may win Christ." When he had got some of this ore, he was inflamed with a desire to get more. He would stand amid the heaps of his gold and say "That I may win Christ."   BONAR.

I am apprehended of Christ Jesus.   PHIL. iii. 12.

Is this your conception of your life? Captured! Apprehended by Jesus Christ! Set apart for Himself!. Do you realize that you are bound by the most sacred fetters to your Conqueror, and are following His chariot through the earth? Life would assume a new aspect if you realized this, and that all you are in your person, and own in your property, has become Emanuel's.   F. B. MEYER.

This one thing I do.   PHIL. iii. 13.

Men may be divided into two classes,—those who have a "one thing," and those who have no "one thing," to do; those with aim, and those without aim in their lives. . . . The aim in life is what the back-bone is to the body; without it we are invertebrate.   GANNETT.

This one thing I do, forgetting those things which are   PHIL.
behind, and reaching forth unto those things which   iii. 13, 14.

315

are before, I press toward the mark for the prize of the high calling of God in Christ Jesus.

Remembering always tends to become a substitute for doing.   McLAREN.

A heaven-born soul cannot without great peril be content to miss the smallest part of the Master's will or the heavenly prize. Oh, ye who have been lingering in the wilderness and pursuing the endless round of a half-consecrated life awake from the dream of perpetual babyhood, put off the swaddling bands and the infant robes of your childishness and "Leaving the first principles of the doctrine of Christ let us go on unto manhood."   SIMPSON.

PHIL.
iii. 20.
Our conversation [citizenship] *is in heaven.*

Although a wheel turneth about on the ground, yet the greatest part of it is always from the earth, and but little of it toucheth the ground: so, although our body be on earth, yet the conversation of the soul, which is the greater part of us, must be in heaven.

CAWDRAY.

PHIL.
iv. 4.
Rejoice in the Lord alway.

Christians, it is your duty not only to be good, but to shine; and, of all the lights which you kindle on the face, joy will reach farthest out to sea, where troubled mariners are seeking the shore. Even in your deepest griefs, rejoice in God. As waves phosphoresce, let joys flash from the swing of the sorrows of your souls.   BEECHER.

PHIL.
iv. 6.
Be careful for nothing: but in everything by prayer and supplication with thanksgiving let your requests be made known unto God.

As every sacrifice was to be seasoned with salt, so

316

every undertaking and every affliction of the creature must be sanctified with prayer; nay, as it showeth the excellency of gold that it is laid upon silver itself, so it speaketh the excellency of prayer, that not only natural and civil, but even religious and spiritual, actions are overlaid with prayer. We pray not only before we eat or drink our bodily nourishment, but also before we feed on the bread of the word and the bread in the sacrament. Prayer is requisite to make every providence and every ordinance blessed to us; prayer is needful to make our particular callings successful. Prayer is the guard to secure the fort-royal of the heart; prayer is the porter to keep the door of the lips; prayer is the strong hilt which defendeth the hands; prayer perfumes every relation; prayer helps us to profit by every condition; prayer is the chemist that turns all into gold; prayer is the master-workman: if that be out of the way, the whole trade stands still, or goeth backward. What the key is to the watch, that prayer is to religion: it winds it up, and sets it going.

SWINNOCK.

The peace of God.
PHIL. iv. 7.

The peace of God is a heavenly tapestry woven in heavenly looms, and brought down from above by the Holy Spirit, Who adorns with it the inmost being of all who have received and welcomed Himself, that He may show forth in them "the continued life of Jesus upon earth."

Whatsoever things are true . . . pure . . . think on these things.
PHIL. iv. 8.

If we look down, then our shoulders stoop. If our thoughts look down, our character bends. It is only

317

when we hold our heads up that the body becomes erect. It is only when our thoughts go up that our life becomes erect. McKENZIE.

PHIL. iv. 11. *I have learned in whatsoever state I am, therewith to be content.*

He who realizes that he is where God wants him to be, and that he has what God wants him to have, will be contented with his lot and his store, whatever they are; but he who fails to realize this truth would never be contented though he were the most favored man in all the world.

True contentment depends not upon what we have, but upon what we would have: a tub was large enough for Diogenes, but a world was too little for Alexander. COLTON.

PHIL. iv. 13. *I can do all things through Christ which strengtheneth me.*

O, do not pray for easy lives. Pray to be stronger men! Do not pray for tasks equal to your powers. Pray for powers equal to your tasks! Then the doing of your work shall be no miracle. But *you* shall be a miracle. Every day you shall wonder at yourself, at the richness of life which has come in you by the grace of God. PHILLIPS BROOKS.

PHIL. iv. 19. *My God shall supply all your need, according to his riches in glory by Christ Jesus.*

What a source—"God!" What a standard—"His riches in glory!" What a channel—"Christ Jesus!" It is your sweet privilege to place all *your need* over against *His riches*, and lose sight of the former in the presence of the latter. His exhaustless treasury ·is

318

thrown open to you, in all the love of His heart; go
and draw upon it, in the artless simplicity of faith, and
you will never have occasion to look to a creature-
stream or lean on a creature-prop.   C. H. McINTOSH.

Wants are my best riches because I have these supplied by Christ.   RUTHERFORD.

Being fruitful in every good work.   COL.
Praying always with all prayer.—Eph. vi. 18.   i. 10.

Labor is of noble birth; but prayer is the daughter
of heaven.   Labor has a place near the throne, but
prayer touches the golden sceptre.   Labor, Martha-like,
is busy with much serving; but prayer sits with Mary
at the feet of Jesus.   Labor climbs the mountain-peak
with Moses; but prayer soars upward, with Elijah, in
a chariot of fire.   Labor has the raven's wing, yet
sometimes goes forth in vain; but prayer has the
pinions of the dove, and never returns but with the
olive-leaf of blessing!   W. H. GROSER.

Increasing in the knowledge of God.   COL.
Are we growing in the knowledge of what Christ is   i. 10.
to *us?*   It is a happy life this; for it is not a mere
self-emptying—it is a process of *Christ-filling.*

In whom we have redemption through his blood, even   COL.
   the forgiveness of sins.   i. 14.

I once saw the sweetest sight—a little, weary child
falling asleep upon the grass, with a posy of flowers
in its hand.   By degrees the little fingers relaxed their
hold, the little head drooped gently, the little eyelids
closed, and the child slept.   God grant that when I
fall into my last sleep my poor fingers may have in
them some posy, some sweet flowers!   Is there any-

thing in my little garden that I may hold in my hand when I come to die? Righteousness? Ah! that is a poor weed at its best. Genius? What will that do for me in that sublime hour when the babe and the suckling have more knowledge of the things of God than the very wisest of this world. Great riches? Even the man of the world will laugh at you if you propose to hold those in your hand in the hour of death. . . . But there grows sometimes in the deep, shadowed part of a man's heart the sweetest flower—lowliness toward God; and another flower— humbleness toward man. But even that does not make a handful. When a man is sinking to his last sleep let him turn to the fullness of God. Then gathers he, if he be wise, the flower of forgiveness, the great passion-flower of God's love, the crown of thorns, the blood-red rose and the amaranth of the Eternal Realm. G. DAWSON.

COL. i. 29. *I also labor, striving according to his working which worketh in me mightily.*

The more earnestly you are at work for Jesus, the more you need times when what you are doing for Him passes totally out of your mind, and the only thing worth thinking of seems to be what He is doing for you. That is the real meaning of the days of discouragement and self-contempt which come to all of us. PHILLIPS BROOKS.

COL. ii. 3. *In whom are hid all the treasures of wisdom and knowledge.*

The science of Jesus Christ is the most excellent of sciences. Let no one turn away from the Bible because it is not a book of learning and wisdom. It is.

Thoughts from My Library

Would ye know astronomy?—it is here: it tells you of the Sun of Righteousness and the Star of Bethlehem. Would you know botany?—it is here: it tells you of the plant of renown,—the Lily of the Valley and the Rose of Sharon. Would you know geology and mineralogy? —you shall learn it here: for you may read of the Rock of Ages, and the White Stone with the name engraven thereon, which no man knoweth saving he that receiveth it. Would ye study history?—here is the most ancient of all the records of the history of the human race. Whatever your science is, come and bend over this book: your science is here. Come and drink out of this fair fount of knowledge and wisdom, and ye shall find yourselves made wise unto salvation. SPURGEON.

In him dwelleth all the fullness of the Godhead bodily. COL.
And ye are complete in him. ii.9, 10.

Give me ten thousand pounds, and one reverse of fortune may scatter it all away; but let me have a spiritual hold of this divine assurance, " The Lord is my shepherd, I shall not want," then I am all right. I am set up for life. I cannot break with such stock as this in hand. I never can be a bankrupt, for I hold this security, " The Lord is my shepherd, I shall not want." Do not give me ready money now; give me a check book and let me draw what I like. This is what God does with the believer. He does not immediately transfer his inheritance to him, but lets him draw what he needs out of the riches of His fullness in Christ Jesus. SPURGEON.

Set your affection on things above, not on things on COL.
the earth. iii. 2.

The compass on board an iron vessel is very subject

to aberrations; yet for all that, its evident desire is to be true to the pole. True hearts in this wicked world, and in this fleshly body, are all too apt to swerve, but still they show their inward and persistent tendency to point toward heaven and God. On board iron vessels it is a common thing to see the compass placed aloft, to be as far away from the cause of aberration as possible: a wise hint to us to elevate our affections and desires; the nearer to God, the less swayed by worldly influences.   SPURGEON.

COL.
iii. 3.

Ye are dead, and your life is hid with Christ in God.
Live in Christ and you are in the suburbs of heaven. There is but a thin wall between you and the land of praises. Ye are within one hour's sailing of the shore of the new Canaan.   RUTHERFORD.

It is impossible that Satan can touch this life, either in its source, its channel, its power, its sphere, or its duration. God is its source; a risen Christ, its channel; the Holy Ghost, its power; heaven, its sphere; and eternity, its duration.

An established, experienced, hopeful Christian is in the world, like an iceberg in a swelling sea. The waves rise and fall. Ships strain and shiver, and nod on the agitated waters. But the iceberg may be seen from far, receiving the breakers on its snow-white sides, casting them off unmoved, and, where all else is rocking to and fro, standing stable like the everlasting hills. The cause of its steadiness is its depth. Its bulk is bedded in calm water beneath the tumult that rages on the surface. Although, like the ships, it is floating in the water, it receives and throws off the angry waves like the rocks that gird the shore. Behold the condition and attitude of Christians! They float in the same sea of life with other men, and bear the same buffetings; but they are not driven hither and thither, the sport of wind and water. The wave strikes them, breaks over them, and hisses past in foam; but they remain unmoved. They were not caught by surprise while they had a slight hold of the surface. The chief part of their being lies deep beyond the reach of these superficial commotions. Their life, "hid with Christ, in God," bears without breaking all the strain of the storm. ARNOT.

Christ . . . our life. COL. iii. 4.

To be *in* Christ is the secret of our life.

To be *for* Christ is the meaning of our activity.

To be *with* Christ is the hope of our glory.

BISHOP THOROLD.

Christ is all, and in all. COL. iii. 11.

The *service* of Christ is the *business* of my life.

The *will* of Christ is the *law* of my life.

The *presence* of Christ is the *joy* of my life.

The *glory* of Christ is the *crown* of my life.

If thou endurest wrong for Christ's sake, He is a revenger; if sorrow, He is a comforter; if sickness, He is a physician; if loss, He is a restorer; if life, He is a reviver. TERTULLIAN.

Let the peace of God rule in your hearts. COL. iii. 15.

Years ago one of our fleets was terribly shattered by a violent gale. It was found that some of the ships were unaffected by its violence. They were in, what the mariners call "the eye of the storm." While all around was desolation, they were safe. So it is with him who has the peace of God in his heart. PILKINGTON.

One Thousand and One

COL.
iii. 17. *Whatsoever ye do,* . . . *do all in the name of the Lord Jesus.*

My Real is not my Ideal—is that my complaint? One thing at least is in my power: if I cannot realize my Ideal I can at least *idealize my Real.* How? By trying to be perfect in it. GANNETT.

There is some act that you are questioning about. If Jesus were at hand, you would go out and ask Him, "Is it Thy will that I should do it, O my Lord?" Can you not ask Him now? Is the act right? Would He do it? Will it help your soul? It is not often that a man really is in doubt who seriously wants to know the answer to any of these questions. And if the answer to them all is, "Yes," then it is just as truly His command that you should do that act as if His gracious figure stood before your sight and His finger visibly pointed to the task. PHILLIPS BROOKS.

There is an old legend of an enchanted cup filled with poison, and put treacherously into a king's hand. He signed the sign of the cross, and named the name of God over it, and it shivered in his grasp. Do you take this name of the Lord as a test. Name Him over many a cup which you are eager to drink of, and the glittering fragments will lie at your feet, and the poison be spilled on the ground. What you cannot lift before His pure eyes and think of Him while you enjoy, is not for you. McLAREN.

COL.
iii. 23. *Whatsoever ye do, do it* . . . *to the Lord.*

In every act consciously and devoutly done for God's sake, God gives Himself to the soul and feeds it; in the act, not after it and in reward of it, but *in* it.

PHILLIPS BROOKS.

324

Thoughts from My Library

Continue in prayer.
COL. iv. 2.

Our prayers often resemble the mischievous tricks of town children, who knock at their neighbor's houses and then run away; we often knock at heaven's door and then run off into the spirit of the world; instead of waiting for entrance and answer, we act as if we were afraid of having our prayers answered.

WILLIAMS.

Prayerless work will soon slacken, and never bear fruit.   McLAREN.

Study to be quiet and to do your own business.
I THES. iv. 11.

Morning by morning God's great mercy of sunrise steals upon a darkened world in still, slow self-impartation; and the light which has a force that has carried it across gulfs of space that the imagination staggers in trying to conceive, yet falls so gently that it does not move the petals of a sleeping flower, nor hurt the lids of an infant's eyes, nor displace a grain of dust. So should we live and work, clothing all our power in tenderness, doing our work in quietness, disturbing nothing but the darkness, and with silent increase of beneficent power filling and flooding the dark earth with healing beams.   MACLAREN.

It is with narrow-souled people as with narrow-necked bottles,—the less they have in them, the more noise they make in pouring out.   POPE.

Ye sorrow not, even as others which have no hope.
I THES. iv. 13.

The heathen sorrowed without hope. A shattered pillar; a ship gone to pieces; a race lost; a harp lying on the ground with snapped strings, with all its music lost; a flower-bud crushed with all its fragrance in it,

—these were the sad utterances of their hopeless grief. The thought that death was the gate of life came not in to cheer the parting, or brighten the sepulchre.

BONAR.

I THES.
iv. 16.
The Lord himself shall descend from heaven with a shout, with the voice of the archangel, and with the trump of God.

Did you ever hear the sound of the trumpets which are blown before the judges as they come into a city to open the assizes? Did you ever reflect how different are the feelings which those trumpets awaken in the minds of different men? The innocent man, who has no cause to be tried, hears them unmoved. They proclaim no terrors to him. He listens and looks on quietly, and is not afraid. But often there is some poor wretch waiting his trial, in a silent cell, to whom those trumpets are a knell of despair. They tell him that the day of trial is at hand. Yet a little time, and he will stand at the bar of justice, and hear witness after witness telling the story of his misdeeds. Yet a little time and all will be over,—the trial, the verdict, the sentence; and there will remain nothing for him but punishment and disgrace. No wonder the prisoner's heart beats when he hears the trumpet's sound! So shall the sound be of the archangel's trump.

RYLE.

I THES.
v. 14.
Be patient toward all.

Endeavor to be patient in bearing with the defects and infirmities of others, of what sort soever they be; for that thyself also hast many failings which must be borne with by others. How seldom we weigh our neighbor in the same balance with ourselves.

THOMAS À KEMPIS.

Thoughts from My Library

Pray without ceasing.

I THES. V. 17.

Life is a constant want, therefore it should be a constant prayer.

Quench not the Spirit.

I THES. V. 19.

In order that you may not quench the Spirit, you must make it a constant study to know what is the mind of the Spirit. You must discriminate with the utmost care between His suggestions and the suggestions of your own deceitful heart. You must be on your guard against impulsive movements, inconsiderate acts, rash words. You must abide in prayer. Search the Word. Confess Christ on all possible occasions. Seek the society of His people. Shrink from conformity to the world, its vain fashions, unmeaning etiquette. Be scrupulous in your reading. "Watch and pray." Have oil in your lamps. "Quench not the Spirit."   BOWEN.

The very God of peace sanctify you wholly.

I THES. V. 23.

It is much more easy to profess holiness in a general way, than to carry it out in particulars; and I fear that many talk familiarly of sanctification in the *lump*, who know but little of it in the *piece*.   RYLE.

Be not weary in well doing.

II THES. iii. 13.

When the battle of Corioli was being won through the stimulus given to the soldiers by the impassioned vigor of Caius Marcius, they mourned to see their leader covered with wounds and blood. They begged him to retire to the camp, but with characteristic bravery he exclaimed, "It is not for conquerors to be tired!" and joined them in prosecuting the victory to its brilliant end. Such language might well become the Christian warrior. He is tempted to lie down and rest before the conquest is complete and the triumph thoroughly achieved. But his conquests should but stir him with a holy zeal and fire him with a sublime courage, that he may be faithful unto death, and then receive a crown of life.

I TIM.
i. 5.
Charity out of a pure heart, and of a good conscience, and of faith unfeigned.

In the Cathedral of St. Mark, in Venice—a marvellous building, lustrous with an Oriental splendor far beyond description—there are pillars said to have been brought from Solomon's Temple; these are of alabaster, a substance firm and durable as granite, and yet transparent, so that the light glows through them. Behold an emblem of what all true pillars of the Church should be—firm in their faith, and transparent in their character; men of simple mould, ignorant of tortuous and deceptive ways, and yet men of strong will, not readily to be led aside or bent from their uprightness.   SPURGEON.

I TIM.
ii. 6.
Who gave himself a ransom for all.

The Jews would not willingly tread upon the smallest piece of paper in their way, but took it up; for possibly, said they, the name of God may be on it. Though there was a little superstition in that, yet much good may be learned from it, if we apply it to men. Trample not on any: there may be some work of grace there that thou knowest not of. The name of God may be written upon that soul thou treadest on; it may be a soul that Christ thought so much of as to give His precious blood for it: therefore despise it not.   LEIGHTON.

Thoughts from My Library

Be thou an example of the believers.

Be such a man and live such a life that if every man were such as you and every life such as yours this earth would be Paradise.

I TIM. iv. 12.

Be what you wish others to become. Let yourself, and not your words, preach for you.   AMIEL.

Meditate upon these things: give thyself wholly to them ; that thy profiting may appear to all.

Meditation is a going up into the mount of the Lord, into its ampler air, where earth recedes and sinks into the mists, and God comes down to talk with us, and to make His goodness pass before us.

I TIM. iv. 15.

                         MARK GUY PEARSE.

Follow after . . . patience.

Impatient people water their miseries and hoe up their comforts; sorrows are visitors that come without invitation, but complaining minds send a wagon to bring their troubles home in.   SPURGEON.

I TIM. vi. 11.

Life . . . in Christ Jesus.

A Christian lives in two worlds at one and the same time—the world of flesh and the world of Spirit. It is possible to do both. There are certain dangerous gases, which from their weight fall to the lower part of the place where they are, making it destructive for a dog to enter, but safe for a man who holds his head erect. A Christian, as living in the world of flesh, is constantly passing through these. Let him keep his head erect in the spiritual world, and he is safe. He does this so long as the Son of God is the fountain whence he draws his inspiration, his motives, encouragement, and strength.   GEORGE PHILIP.

II TIM. i. 1.

One Thousand and One

II TIM. i. 6. *Stir up the gift of God, which is in thee.*

The fire within us needs constant stirring, as well as feeding, to keep it bright.   RYLE.

II TIM. i. 12. *I know whom I have believed.*

Personal acquaintance with Christ is a living thing, like a tree that uses every hour for growth. It thrives in sunshine, it is refreshed by rain—even the storm drives it to fasten its grip more firmly in the earth for its support. So, troubled heart, in all experience, say, "This comes that I may make closer acquaintance with my Lord."

A soldier lay dying in the hospital, in terrible agony. A visitor asked him, "What church are you of?"— "Of the church of Christ," he replied. "I mean of what persuasion are you?"—"Persuasion," said the dying man, as his eyes looked heavenward, beaming with love to the Saviour,—"I am persuaded that neither death, nor life, nor angels, nor principalities, nor powers, nor things present, nor things to come, nor height, nor depth, nor any other creature, shall be able to separate me from the love of God which is in Christ Jesus."

II TIM. ii. 1. *Be strong in the grace that is in Christ Jesus.*

Grace is the ladder to glory, and on every step of it man must die to *self* or he can never reach its summit.

F. WHITFIELD.

II TIM. ii. 3. *Thou therefore endure hardness, as a good soldier of Jesus Christ.*

Of all work that produces results, nine-tenths must be drudgery.   BISHOP OF EXETER.

Do not let the warmth by the camp-fire, or the

pleasantness of the shady place where your tent is pitched, keep you there when the cloud lifts. Be ready for change, be ready for continuance, because you are in fellowship with your Leader and Commander; and let Him say, Go, and you go; Do this, and you gladly do it, until the hour when He will whisper, Come; and, as you come, the river will part, and the journey will be over. And "the fiery, cloudy pillar," that "guided you all your journey through," will spread itself out an abiding glory, in that higher home where "the Lamb is the light thereof."

McLAREN.

It is the daily drill which makes the battle hero.

PUNSHON.

If we suffer we shall also reign within him.   II TIM.
ii. 12.
The highest bidder for the crown of glory is the lowliest bearer of the cross of self-denial.

A. J. GORDON.

Bless God for the wilderness; thank God for the long nights; be thankful that you have been in the school of poverty and have undergone the searching and testing of much discipline. Take the right view of your trials. You are nearer heaven for the graves you have dug if you have accepted bereavements in the right spirit; you are wiser for the losses you have bravely borne, you are nobler for all the sacrifices you have willingly completed. Sanctified affliction is an angel that never misses the gate of heaven.

JOSEPH PARKER.

The foundation of God standeth sure, having this seal,   II TIM.
The Lord knoweth them that are his.   ii. 19.

This is said with reference to some that appear unto

331

men to be the children of God and afterward fall away. Christians have no promise that they shall be kept from misconception on this point; and they are sometimes greatly shocked to find the court of God's house strewn with columns. God is the architect of His temple, and is cognizant of His own plans; He allows stones and pillars to be placed in the edifice which He knows do not permanently belong to it; but for the places they temporarily occupy, there are other materials known to Him; and no chasms, no unlovely vacancies shall after all appear. Let this console us. The Lord knoweth them that are His. These pseudo-Christians that figure for a while upon the platform, and then pass away in the whirlwind of sin, amid the triumphs of a scoffing world, were never known to Him for anything but what they really were.

BOWEN.

II TIM.
iii. 5.

Having a form of godliness.

I was walking one day in Westminster Abbey. As I paused to survey the monuments of the illustrious departed that are gathered there, my attention was arrested by the appearance of the pavement near to where I stood. A beautiful many-colored light rested upon it, and gave it an aspect that I could not but linger to behold. The cause was apparent. A painted window above me explained the reason. And the pavement, beautiful as it appeared, had no color in itself: it was the window above that gave it the beauteous hue. How many are like that pavement! they appear beautiful, and we are apt to mistake it for "the beauty of holiness"; but it is in a borrowed light, —contact with the wise and good it may be: remove that, and their true color appears.

332

Thoughts from My Library

The time will come when they will not endure sound doctrine.   II TIM. iv. 3.

Well-bred people now do not talk about "the world, the flesh, and the devil"; they speak of "environment, heredity, and circumstances."

I have fought a good fight.   II TIM. iv. 7.

In early times in America when writing for a minister to go out west the message was "Send us one who can swim." The question was asked what was meant by such a request as that. The reply came, "The last man we had, in order to keep an appointment, had to cross a fierce, rushing stream, and he was drowned in the attempt. Send us a man who can swim."   TALMAGE.

They profess that they know God; but in works they deny him.   TIT. i. 16.

Religion is the best armor a man can have, but it is the worst cloak.   BUNYAN.

Zealous of good works.   TIT. ii. 14.

If we travel slowly, and loiter on the road, Jesus will go on before us, and sin will overtake us. If we are dilatory and lazy in the vineyard, the Master will not smile on us when He walks through His garden. Be active, and expect Christ to be with thee: be idle, and the thorns and briers will grow so thickly, that He will be shut out of thy door.   SPURGEON.

God . . . hath in these last days spoken unto us by his Son.   HEB. i. 1, 2.

An old writer says, "God in the types of the last dispensation, was teaching His children their letters.

333

In this dispensation He is teaching them to put these letters together, and they find that the letters, arrange them as we will, spell Christ, and nothing but Christ."

HEB. *Forasmuch then as the children are partakers of flesh*
ii. 14. *and blood, he also himself likewise took part of the same; that through death he might destroy him that had the power of death, that is, the devil.*

I like these words exceedingly; they present a desirable view of matters—the children at the top, Christ in the middle, and the devil at the bottom.

HEB. *He is able to succor them that are tempted.*
ii. 18.
I see the unclean spirit rising like a winged dragon, circling in the air, and seeking for a resting-place. Casting his fiery glances toward a certain neighborhood, he spies a young man in the bloom of life, and rejoicing in his strength, seated on the front of his cart, going for lime. "There he is!" said the old dragon: "his veins are full of blood, and his bones of marrow; I will throw into his bosom sparks from hell; I will set all his passions on fire; I will lead him from bad to worse, until he shall perpetrate every sin; I will make him a murderer, and his soul shall sink, never again to rise, in the lake of fire." By this time, I see it descend, with a fell swoop, toward the earth; but, nearing the youth, the dragon heard him sing,

> "Guide me, O thou great Jehovah!
> Pilgrim through this barren land:
> I am weak, but Thou art mighty;
> Hold me with Thy powerful hand.
> Strong Deliverer,
> Be Thou still my strength and shield."

"A dry, dry place, this," says the dragon; and away he goes. But I see him again hovering about in the air, and casting about for a suitable resting-place. Beneath his eye there is a flowery meadow, watered by a crystal stream; and he descries among the kine a maiden, about eighteen years of age, picking up here and there a beautiful flower. "There she is!" says Apollyon, intent upon her soul: "I will poison her thoughts; she shall stray from the paths of virtue; she shall think evil thoughts, and become impure; she shall become a lost creature in the great city, and, at last, I will cast her down from the precipice into everlasting burnings." Again he took his downward flight; but he no sooner came near the maiden, than he heard her sing the following words, with a voice that might have melted the rocks:

> "Other refuge have I none;
> Hangs my helpless soul on Thee:
> Leave, ah! leave me not alone;
> Still support and comfort me."

"This place is too dry for me," says the dragon; and off he flies. Now he ascends from the meadow, like some great balloon, but very much enraged, and breathing forth "smoke and fire," and threatening ruin and damnation to all created things. "I *will* have a place to dwell in," he says, "in spite of decree, covenant, or grace." As he was thus speaking, he beheld a woman, "stricken in years," busy with her spinning-wheel at her cottage-door. "Ah, I see!" says the dragon: "she is ripe for destruction; she shall know the bitterness of the wail which ascends from the burning marl of hell!" He forthwith alights on the roof of her cot; when he hears the old woman repeat with trembling voice, but with heavenly feeling, the words, "For the mountains shall depart, and the hills be removed; but My kindness shall not depart from thee." "This place is too dry for me," says the dragon; and away he goes again. . . . "In yonder cottage lies old William, slowly wasting away. He has borne the heat and the burden, and altogether has had a hard life of it. He has very little reason to be thankful for the mercies he has received, and has not found serving God a very profitable business: I know I can get him to 'curse God and die.'" Thus musing, away he flew to the sick man's bedside; but, as he listened, he heard the words, "Though I walk through the valley of the shadow of death, I will fear no evil, for Thou art with me: Thy rod and Thy staff, they comfort me." Mortified and enraged, the dragon took his flight, saying, "I will return to the place from whence I came." CHRISTMAS EVANS.

HEB. iv. 3.

We which have believed do enter into rest.

There is a rest that is *given*, a rest that is *found*, and a rest that *remaineth* to the people of God. The first brings relief to the troubled conscience, the second to the troubled heart, and the third brings to the believer the fullness of joy that is in the presence of the Lord, the pleasures that are at His right hand forevermore. The first is directly connected with the Son as the Saviour of sinners; the second is more immediately related to the Holy Spirit as our abiding Comforter; and the third is associated with the "Father's house," in which "are many mansions."

HEB. iv. 9.

There remaineth . . . a rest to the people of God.

How sweet the music of this first heavenly chime floating across the waters of death from the towers of the new Jerusalem! *Pilgrim,* faint under thy long

336

and arduous pilgrimage, hear it! It is REST. *Soldier,* carrying still upon thee the blood and dust of battle, hear it! It is REST. *Voyager,* tossed on the waves of sin and sorrow, driven hither and thither on the world's heaving ocean of vicissitude, hear it! The haven is in sight; the very waves that are breaking on the shore seem to murmur—*So giveth He His beloved* REST. It is the long-drawn sigh of existence at last answered. The toil and travail of earth's protracted week is at an end. The calm of its unbroken Sabbath is begun. Man, weary man, has found at last the long sought-for *rest* in the bosom of his God.

MACDUFF.

O weary sons and daughters of Adam! you will not have to drive the ploughshare into the unthankful soil in heaven; you will not need to rise to daily toils before the sun hath risen, and labor still when the sun hath long ago gone to his rest: but ye shall be still, ye shall be quiet, ye shall rest yourselves. Toil, trouble, travail, and labor are words that cannot be spelled in heaven: they have no such things there; for they always rest. SPURGEON.

The word of God is . . . sharper than any two- HEB.
edged sword. iv. 12.

Cling to the whole Bible, not a part of it. A man is not going to do much with a broken sword.

MOODY.

He . . . was in all points tempted like as we are, HEB.
yet without sin. iv. 15.

All the saints must go to the proving house; God had one Son without sin, but He never had a son without trial. SPURGEON.

337

One Thousand and One

Let us . . . come boldly unto the throne of grace that we may obtain mercy and find grace to help in time of need.

However early in the morning you seek the gate of access, you find it already open, and however deep the midnight moment when you find yourself in the sudden arms of death, the winged prayer can bring an instant Saviour; and this wherever you are. It needs not that you ascend some special Pisgah or Moriah. It needs not that you should enter some awful shrine, or pull off your shoes on some holy ground. Could a memento be reared on every spot from which an acceptable prayer has passed away, and on which a prompt answer has come down, we should find *Jehovah Shammah*, "the Lord hath been here," inscribed on many a cottage hearth, and many a dungeon floor. We should find it not only in Jerusalem's proud temple and David's cedar galleries, but in the fisherman's cottage by the brink of the Gennesaret, and in the upper chamber where Pentecost began. And whether it be the field where Isaac went down to meditate, or the rocky knoll where Israel wrestled, or the den where Daniel gazed on the hungry lions, and the lions gazed on him, or the hillside where the Man of Sorrows prayed all night, we should still discern the ladder's feet let down from heaven—the landing place of mercies, because the starting place of prayer.

J. HAMILTON.

HEB. vi. 1. *Dead works.*

Dead works are those which do not spring from the life-giving principle of faith.

Thoughts from My Library

Hope . . . an anchor of the soul, both sure and HEB.
steadfast. vi. 19.

On the margin of the ocean that surrounds and laves
our island home, an object of absorbing interest may
often be observed,—a ship riding at anchor near a lee
shore in an angry sea. She has drifted, ere she was
aware, too near a rockbound coast; the wind is blowing direct on shore; there is not room to tack; whether
she should point her prow north or south, she will
strike a projecting headland ere she can escape from
the bay. One resource remains,—to anchor where she
is till the wind change. There she lies. Stand on this
height and look down upon her through the drifting
spray. I scarcely know in nature a more interesting
or suggestive sight. The ship is dancing on the waves;
she appears to be in their power and at their mercy.
Wind and water combine to make her their sport.
Destruction seems near; for if the vessel's hull is
dashed by these waves upon the rocks of the coast, it
will be broken into a thousand pieces. But you have
stood and looked on the scene awhile, and the ship
still holds her own. Although at first sight she seemed
the helpless plaything of the elements, they have not
overcome—they have not gained upon her yet. She is
no nearer destruction than when you first began to
gaze in anticipation of her fate. The ship seems to
have no power to resist the onset of wind and wave.
She yields to every blast and every billow. This moment she is tossed aloft on the crest of a wave, and
the next she sinks heavily into the hollow. Now her
prow goes down beneath an advancing breaker, and
she is lost to view in the spray; but anon she emerges,
like a sea-fowl shaking the water from her wings and

rejoicing in the tumult. As she quivered and nodded giddily at each assault, you thought, when first you arrived in sight, that every moment would prove her last; but now that you have watched the conflict long, it begins to assume in your mind another aspect, and promise another end. These motions of the ship now, instead of appearing the sickly movements of the dying, seem to indicate the calm, confident persever-ance of conscious strength and expected victory. Let winds and waves do their worst, that ship will meet them fearless, will hold her head to the blast, and maintain her place in defiance of their power. What is the secret of that ship's safety? No other ship is in sight to which she may cling; no pillar stands within reach to which she may be moored. The bond of her security is a line that is unseen. The ship is at anchor. The line on which she hangs does not depend on the waters, or anything that floats there; it goes through the waters, and fastens on a sure ground beyond them. The soul, considered as a passenger on the treacherous sea of Time, needs an anchor; and an anchor " sure and steadfast" is provided for the needy soul.

ARNOT.

HEB.
vii. 25. *He ever liveth.*

Many reformations have expired with the reformer. But our Great Reformer " ever liveth" to carry on His reformation.

HEB.
viii. 5. *See . . . that thou make all things according to the pattern shewed to thee in the mount.*

God never gives a man a pattern without making Himself responsible for the provision of all materials needed for its execution. Take God's plan, and then trust God utterly for the needful grace; it is there; it only awaits the claim of your faith. All things are added to the man who seeks first and only the kingdom of God. If the materials are not forthcoming, you may seriously question whether you are not working on a plan of your own. God will not provide for a single tassel of your own addition to His scheme.

F. B. MEYER.

From henceforth expecting till his enemies be made his HEB.
footstool. X. 13.

The wrath of man shall praise God. I believe the last song of the redeemed, when they shall ultimately triumph, will celebrate in heavenly stanzas the wrath of man overcome by God. Sometimes, after great battles, monuments are raised to the memory of the fight; and of what are they composed? They are composed of weapons of death and of instruments of war which have been taken from the enemy. Now, to use that illustration, as I think it may be properly used, the day is coming when fury and wrath and hatred and strife shall all be woven into a song; and the weapons of our enemies, when taken from them, shall serve to make monuments to the praise of God. Rail on, rail on, blasphemer! Smite on, smite on, tyrant! Lift thy heavy hand, O despot! Crush the truth, which thou canst not crush; knock from His head the crown,—the crown that is far above thy reach, poor, puny, impotent mortal as thou art! Go on, go on! But all thou doest shall but increase His glories. For aught we care, we bid you still proceed with all your wrath and malice. Though it shall be worse for you, it shall be more glorious for our Master: the greater your preparations for war, the more

splendid shall be His triumphal chariot when He shall
ride through the streets of heaven in pompous array.
The more mighty your preparations for battle, the
more rich the spoil which He shall divide with the
strong. O Christian, fear not the foe! Remember,
the harder his blows, the sweeter thy song; the greater
his wrath, the more splendid thy triumph; the more
he rages, the more shall Christ be honored in the day
of His appearing. SPURGEON.

HEB.
X. 19. *Having . . . boldness to enter into the holiest by
the blood of Jesus.*
*The Holy Ghost . . . shall teach you all things.—
John xiv. 26.*

This is our title to enter. Our capacity to worship,
when we have entered, will depend upon our spiritual
energy. Christ is our title. The Holy Spirit is our
capacity. Self has nothing to do with either the one
or the other. What a mercy! We get in by the blood
of Jesus; we enjoy what we find there by the Holy
Spirit. The blood of Jesus opens the door; the Holy
Spirit conducts us through the house. The blood of
Jesus opens the casket; the Holy Spirit unfolds the
precious contents. The blood of Jesus makes the
casket ours; the Holy Spirit enables us to appreciate
its rare and costly gems. C. H. McINTOSH.

HEB.
X. 19,
22. *Having boldness to enter into the holiest by the blood of
Jesus . . . let us draw near with a true heart.*

Oh, the glory of the message! For fifteen centuries
Israel had a sanctuary with a Holiest of All, into which,
under pain of death, no one might enter. Its one witness was: Man cannot dwell in God's presence; cannot abide in His fellowship. And now how changed

is all! As then the warning sounded: "No admittance! enter not!" so now the call goes forth: "Enter in! the veil is rent; the Holiest is open; God waits to welcome you to His bosom; henceforth you are to live with Him." This is the message. Child! thy Father longs for thee to enter, to dwell, and to go out no more forever.   ANDREW MURRAY.

Let us draw near . . . in full assurance of faith. HEB.
    Faith, let us remember, is the root, and assurance is X. 22.
the flower.   Doubtless you can never have the flower
without the root; but it is no less certain you may
have the root and not the flower.   Faith is that poor
trembling woman who came behind Jesus in the press,
and touched the hem of His garment; Assurance is
Stephen standing calmly in the midst of his murderers,
and saying, "I see the heavens opened, and the Son
of man standing on the right hand of God."   Faith is
the penitent thief, crying, "Lord, remember me ;" Assurance is Job sitting in the dust, covered with sores,
and saying, "I know that my Redeemer liveth";
"Though He slay me, yet will I trust in Him."   Faith
is Peter's drowning cry, as he began to sink, "Lord,
save me!"   Assurance is that same Peter declaring before the council, in after-times, "This is the stone
which was set at naught by you builders, which is become the head of the corner.   Neither is there salvation in any other; for there is none other name under
heaven given among men whereby we must be saved."
Faith is the anxious, trembling voice, "Lord, I believe;
help Thou mine unbelief;" Assurance is the confident
challenge, "Who shall lay anything to the charge of
God's elect?   Who is he that condemneth?"   Faith is

One Thousand and One

Saul praying in the house of Judas at Damascus, sorrowful, blind, and alone; Assurance is Paul, the aged prisoner, looking calmly into the grave, and saying, "I know whom I have believed. There is a crown laid up for me." Faith is life. How great the blessing! Who can tell the gulf between life and death? And yet life may be weak, sickly, unhealthy, painful, trying, anxious, worn, burdensome, joyless, smileless to the very end. Assurance is more than life. It is health, strength, power, vigor, activity, energy, manliness, beauty.　　　　　　　　　　　RYLE.

HEB.
X. 23.
Let us hold fast the profession of our faith.

Faith is the cable which binds our boat to the shore, and by pulling at it we draw ourselves to the land; faith unites us to God, and then draws us near to Him.　　　　　　　　　SPURGEON.

HEB.
X. 23.
He is faithful that promised.

I would sooner walk in the dark and hold hard to a promise of my God, than trust in the light of the brightest day that ever dawned.　　　SPURGEON.

HEB.
X. 28,
29.
He that despised Moses' law died without mercy: of how much sorer punishment . . . shall he be thought worthy, who hath trodden under foot the Son of God?

Disheartened by the extraordinary dangers and difficulties of their enterprise, a Roman army lost courage, and resolved on a retreat. The general reasoned with his soldiers. Expostulating with them, he appealed to their love of country, to their honor, and to their oaths. By all that could revive a fainting heart he sought to animate their courage and shake their resolution.

Thoughts from My Library

Much they trusted, they admired, they loved him; but his appeals were all in vain. They were not to be moved; and, carried away, as by a panic, they faced round to retreat. At this juncture they were forcing a mountain-pass, and had just cleared a gorge where the road, between two stupendous rocks on one side and the foaming river on the other, was but a foot-path, broad enough for the step of a single man. As a last resort, he laid himself down there, saying, "If you will retreat, it is over this body you go, tramping me to death beneath your feet." No foot advanced. The flight was arrested. His soldiers could face the foe, but not mangle beneath their feet one who loved them, and had often led their ranks to victory, sharing like a common soldier all the hardships of the campaign, and ever foremost in the fight. The sight was one to inspire them with decision. Hesitating no longer to advance, they wheeled round to resume their march; deeming it better to meet sufferings, and endure even death itself, than to trample under foot their devoted and patriotic leader. Their hearts recoiled from such an outrage. But for such as have named the name of Christ not to depart from iniquity, for such as have enlisted under His banner to go back to the world, for such as have renounced sin to return to its pleasures, involves a greater crime. A more touching spectacle bars our return. Jesus, as it were, lays Himself down on our path; nor can any become backsliders, and return to the practice and pleasure of sin, without tramping Him under their feet.

GUTHRIE.

Ye endured a great fight of afflictions.   HEB.
X. 32.

There is a way in which the lapidary tells whether a

345

diamond is genuine or not. He breathes on it, and if the breath linger there, it is a false diamond; if the breath immediately vanish, it is a real diamond. Then he has the grinding process afterward, if the first fail. So you can tell God's jewel. If the breath of temptation comes on it, and soon vanishes, it is a real diamond; if that breath lingers, and continues to blur it, it is a false diamond. But better than all is the grinding machine of affliction. If a soul can go through that and keep bright, it is one of God's jewels.

TALMAGE.

HEB. x. 38. *The just shall live by faith.*

Faith links us to eternal life; obedience keeps the life full. C. I. SCOFIELD.

HEB. xi. 4. *He, being dead, yet speaketh.*

The sun sets behind the western hills, but the trail of light he leaves behind him guides the pilgrim to his distant home. The tree falls in the forest; but in the lapse of ages it is turned into coal, and our fires burn now the brighter because it grew and fell. The coral insect died, but the reef it raised breaks the surge on the shores of great continents, or has formed an isle in the bosom of the ocean to wave now with harvests for the good of man, and to be a gem hereafter for the diadem of the great Redeemer. We live, and we die; but the good or evil that we do lives after us, and "is not buried with our bones." CUMMING.

It was a touching memorial to their comrade, the warrior of Breton birth, La Tour d' Auvergne, the first grenadier of France, as he was called, when, after his death, his comrades insisted that, though dead, his name should not be removed from the rolls. It was still regularly called, and one of the survivors regularly answered for the departed soldier, "Dead on the field." The eleventh chapter of the Epistle to the Hebrews is such a roll-call of the dead. It is the register of a regiment, which will not allow death to blot names from its page, but records the soldiers who have, in its ranks, won honorable graves and long abiding victories.   W. R. WILLIAMS.

Without faith it is impossible to please God.   HEB. xi. 6.

When a man hath liberty to go into the treasure-house of a king, to enrich himself, he will first seek the keys wherewith to open the doors; so, if we desire to be enriched with God's grace, we must first labor to have faith, which is the only key of God's treasure-house, and secures us all graces needful both for body and soul.   CAWDRAY.

By faith Abraham . . . went out, not knowing whither he went.   HEB. xi. 8.

Whither he went, he knew not; it was enough for him to know that he went with God. He leaned not so much upon the promise as upon the Promiser: he looked not on the difficulties of his lot—but on the King eternal, immortal, invisible, the only wise God; Who had deigned to appoint his course, and would certainly vindicate Himself. . . .

Ah, glorious faith! this is thy work, these are thy possibilities! contentment to sail with sealed orders, because of unwavering confidence in the love and wisdom of the Lord High Admiral: willinghood to arise up, leave all, and follow Christ, because of the glad assurance that earth's best cannot bear comparison with heaven's best.   F. B. MEYER.

One Thousand and One

HEB.
xi. 27. (*Moses*) *endured, as seeing him who is invisible.*

When Scoresby was selecting his men to accompany him in his Arctic explorations, he needed sailors that could stand the severest exposures, and who had nerve to bear the worst trials. So every man who applied to accompany the expedition was made to stand barefooted on a great block of ice while the surgeon examined his body, and Scoresby inquired into his past history. Scores were rejected at once, as they had not nerve to endure the test. The men who stood the trial made up a band of the most glorious heroes. So sometimes God tries us when he has in store for us some great undertaking. Many faint and excuse themselves from the start. Some endure, and make the heroes and leaders of the church.

VAIL.

HEB.
xi. 33. *Through faith . . . obtained promises.*

God's promises were never meant to ferry our laziness. Like a boat, they are to be rowed by our oars; but many men, entering, forget the oar, and drift down more helpless in the boat than if they had staid on shore. There is not an experience in life by whose side God has not fixed a promise. There is not a trouble so deep and swift-running, that we may not cross safely over, if we have courage to steer and strength to pull.   BEECHER.

HEB.
xi. 40. *They without us should not be made perfect.*

The Church of Christ, which is partly militant and partly triumphant, resembles a city built on both sides of a river. There is but the stream of death between grace and glory.   TOPLADY.

Thoughts from My Library

Let us lay aside every weight, . . . *looking unto* HEB.
   Jesus.   xii. 1, 2.

To know the Lord Jesus is the only cure for worldliness.   MARK GUY PEARSE.

Despising the shame.   HEB.

And how is that to be done? In two ways. Go   xii. 2.
up the mountain, and the things in the plain will look
very small; the higher you rise, the more insignificant
they will seem. Hold fellowship with God, and live
up beside your Master, and the threatening foes here
will seem very, very unformidable.

Another way is—pull up the curtain and gaze on
what is behind it. The low foot-hills that lie at the
base of some Alpine country may look high when
seen from the plain, as long as the snowy summits
are wrapped in mist, but when a little puff of wind
comes and clears away the fog from the lofty peaks,
nobody looks at the little green hills in front. So the
world's hindrances and the world's difficulties and
cares, look very lofty till the cloud lifts. But when
we see the great white summits, everything lower
does not seem so very high after all. Look to Jesus
and that will dwarf the difficulties.   MACLAREN.

Consider him that endured such contradiction of sin- HEB.
   ners against himself, lest ye be wearied and faint in xii. 3.
   your minds.

One thing which contributed to make Cæsar's soldiers invincible, was their seeing him always ready to
take his share in danger, and never desire any exemption from labor and fatigue. We have a far higher
incentive in the war for truth and goodness when we

consider Him Who endured such contradiction of sinners against Himself.   SPURGEON.

HEB.
xii. 6.

Whom the Lord loveth he chasteneth.

Lawns which we would keep in the best condition are very frequently mown; the grass has scarcely any respite from the scythe.   Out in the meadows there is no such frequent cutting, they are mown but once or twice in the year.   Even thus the nearer we are to God, and the more regard He has for us, the more frequent will be our adversities.   To be very dear to God involves no small degree of chastisement.

SPURGEON.

As a father in a sunny garden stoops down to kiss a child the shadow of his body falls upon it ; so many of the dark misfortunes of our life are not God going away from us, but our Heavenly Father stooping down to give us the kiss of His infinite and everlasting love.

TALMAGE.

HEB.
xii. 11.

Now no chastening for the present seemeth to be joyous, but grievous: nevertheless, afterward it yieldeth the peaceable fruit of righteousness unto them which are exercised thereby.

There are three ways of meeting divine chastening. We may " *despise*" it, as something commonplace—something that may happen to any one; we do not see the hand of God in it.   Again, we may "*faint*" under it, as something too heavy for us to bear—something entirely beyond endurance; we do not see the Father's heart in it, or recognize His gracious object in it, namely to make us partakers of His holiness. Lastly, we may be "*exercised*" by it.   This is the way to reap "the peaceable fruit of righteousness" afterward. . . . Every stroke of His rod is a proof of His love. C. H. McINTOSH.

Why should I start at the plough of my Lord that maketh deep furrows on my soul? I know He is no idle husbandman, He purposeth a crop.

RUTHERFORD.

God wants iron saints; and since there is no way of imparting iron to the moral nature other than by letting His people suffer, He lets them suffer. . . . The iron crown of suffering precedes the golden crown of glory. F. B. MEYER.

Follow . . . holiness without which no man shall see the Lord. HEB. xii. 14.

Holiness, which is the dress of heaven, is ready to fall, like Elijah's mantle, from the hand of Him Who hath said—"Turn unto Me and I will pour out My spirit upon you." CHALMERS.

Let brotherly love continue. HEB. xiii. 1.

As the spokes of a carriage-wheel approach their centre, they approach each other: so also, when men are brought to Jesus Christ, the centre of life and hope, they are drawn toward each other in brotherly relationship, and stand side by side journeying to their heavenly home. J. F. SERJEANT.

I will never leave thee nor forsake thee. HEB. xiii. 5.

God Almighty never failed a man. We fail one another and deceive each other, but God will never fail us. God never made a fish with fins until He made an ocean to put him in. God never made a bird with wings until He made an atmosphere for it to fly in, and God never planted the instincts of life immortal in our soul until He had built a heaven for our souls to dwell in.   SAM JONES.

HEB. xiii. 8.

Jesus Christ the same yesterday, and to-day, and for-ever.

Religious systems naturally circle around the priest. Christianity finds its centre in Jesus. What He is, it must be; and since He is unchangeably the same, it can never be superseded or pass away; it can never wane as the stars of the old dispensation did in the growing glory of the new; it must abide as the one final revelation of God to man, and the way by which man may enter into fellowship with God.   F. B. MEYER.

HEB. xiii. 14.

Here have we no continuing city, but we seek one to come.

A Christian, being only a traveller through the world, must expect a traveller's fare,—bad roads sometimes, bad weather, and bad accommodation; but since his journey is short, and his city is in heaven, all his actions, sufferings, prayers, and conversation turn that way.   BOGATSKY.

HEB. xiii. 15.

By him therefore, let us offer the sacrifice of praise to God continually, that is, the fruit of our lips giving thanks to his name.

Praise is contentment rippling over into gladness, like the music of the brook.   MARK GUY PEARSE.

HEB. xiii. 20.

The everlasting covenant.

Our union with Christ is the union of the covenant, and therefore not dependent upon frames and feelings.

A. L. NEWTON.

Thoughts from My Library

If any of you lack wisdom, let him ask of God . . . JAS.
and it shall be given him. i. 5

The natives of India had a saying about Sir Henry
Lawrence—"When Sir Henry looked up twice to
heaven and once down to earth, and then stroked his
beard, he knew what to do." If we may utilize the
saying, it seems to express the attitude of mind with
which all life's work and study should be done. The
reverence which looks up, and the observation which
looks around, combined with the judgment that can
reflect, become safeguards against the falsehoods of
extremes. There is an observation which is keen
enough, but which, never looking upward, has no
reverence; there is a pious reverence which, in its
rapt and heavenward gaze, forgets to look earthward,
and so loses touch with humanity; but he who, while
regarding heaven, does not forget the world in which
he lives and seeks to know also the man within, will
avoid alike the dogmatism which is irreverent and the
mysticism which is unpractical. BISHOP OF RIPON.

God . . . *giveth to all men liberally.* JAS.
Our Lord does everything on the largest and most i. 5.
generous scale. Does Christ, our Creator, go forth to
make leaves? He makes them by the whole forest
full—notched like the fern, or silvered like the aspen,
or broad like the palm; thickets in the tropics. Does
He go forth to make flowers? He makes plenty of
them; they flame from the hedge, they hang from the
top of the grapevine in blossoms, they roll in the blue
wave of the violets, they toss their white surf into the
spirea—enough for every child's hand a flower, enough
to make for every brow a chaplet, enough with beauty

to cover up the ghastliness of all the graves. Does He go forth to create water? He pours it out, not by the cupful, but by a river-full, a lake-full, an ocean-full, pouring it out until all the earth has enough to drink, and enough with which to wash. Does Jesus, our Lord, provide redemption? It is not a little salvation for this one, a little for that, and a little for the other; but enough for all. "Whosoever will, let him come." Each man an ocean-full for himself. Promises for all, pardon for all, comfort for all, mercy for all, heaven for all. TALMAGE.

JAS.
i. 6.
Ask in faith, nothing wavering.

Take the bow of faith and the arrow of prayer.
MACDUFF.

God cares not for the length of our prayers, or the number of our prayers, or the beauty of our prayers, or the place of our prayers. It is the *faith* in them that tells. TALMAGE.

Never was faithful prayer lost at sea. No merchant trades with such certainty as the praying saint. Some prayers, indeed, have a longer voyage than others; but then they come with the richer lading at last.
GURNALL.

JAS.
i. 12.
Blessed is the man that endureth temptation: for when he is tried, he shall receive the crown of life, which the Lord hath promised to them that love him.

Let Satan's fiery darts inflame your love rather than your lust, and, like a skillful pilot, make use of the violence of the winds and raging of the sea to further you in your spiritual voyage. CHARNOCK.

Thoughts from My Library

The Father of lights, with whom is no variableness, JAS.
neither shadow of turning. i. 17.

There be many Christians most like unto young
sailors who think the shore and the whole land doth
move when the ship and they themselves are moved.
Just so, not a few imagine that God moveth, and
saileth, and changeth places because their giddy souls
are under sail and subject to alteration, to ebbing and
flowing. But the foundation of the Lord abideth sure.

RUTHERFORD.

Pure religion and undefiled before God and the Father JAS.
is this, To visit the fatherless and widows in their i. 27.
affliction, and to keep himself unspotted from the
world.

The purest lives I have known have not been those
carefully screened from the world, but which, coming
up in it, have kept themselves unspotted. The sweetest and truest have grown and ripened under conditions, you would say, most hostile, but which have
been wrought into the means of a grandly elevated
faith and life. WARE.

Whosoever shall keep the whole law and yet offend in JAS.
one point, he is guilty of all. ii. 10.

A chain is no stronger than its weakest link.

Faith, if it hath not works, is dead, being alone. JAS.

Faith is a noble duchess; she ever hath her gentle- ii. 17.
man usher going before her, the confessing of sins;
she hath a train after her, the fruits of good works,
the walking in the commandments of God. He that
believeth will not be idle; he will walk, he will do his
business. Have ever the gentleman usher with you.

355

So if you will try Faith, remember this rule, consider whether the train is waiting upon her.   LATIMER.

JAS.
ii. 20.

Faith without works is dead.

Workless faith God never regards,
Faithless work God never rewards.

JAS.
ii. 22.

Faith wrought with (Abraham's) works, and by works was faith made perfect.

As ciphers, added one by one in an endless row to the left hand of a unit, are of no value, but, on the right hand, rapidly multiply its power, so, although good works are of no avail to make a man a Christian, yet a Christian's good works are both pleasing to God and profitable to men.   ARNOT.

That was a very good illustration of the harmony between Paul and James on the subject of faith and works, used by the late Frederick W. Robertson, of Brighton, Eng.: "Paul says, 'Faith justifies without works.' James says, 'Faith without works is dead.'" Robertson thus reconciles them: "A tree cannot be struck without thunder; that is true, for there is never destructive lightning without thunder. But, again, if I say, The tree was struck by lightning without thunder, that is true, too, if I mean that the lightning alone struck it, without the thunder striking it. Put it in one sentence—faith alone justifies, but not the faith which is alone. Lightning alone strikes, but not the lightning which is alone, without thunder; for that is only summer lightning, and harmless."

JAS.
iii. 15.

Earthly, sensual, devilish.

The ladder that leads down to hell has three steps; on the first, there is written "earthly"; on the second,

356

"sensual"; and down there, just at hell's door comes the third, and on it is written "devilish." AITKEN.

The friendship of the world is enmity with God. JAS. iv. 4.

It is like the ivy with the oak. The ivy may give the oak a grand, beautiful appearance, but all the while it is feeding on its vitals. Are we compromising with the enemies of God? Are we being embraced by the world, by its honors, its pleasures, its applause? This may add to us in the world's estimation, but our strength becomes lost. DENHAM SMITH.

God . . . giveth grace unto the humble. JAS. iv. 6.

Many a poor man makes a bright Christian; God keeps him humble that He may dwell in his heart, and that the beams of His grace may shine in his heart. See yon evening star, how bright it shines, how pure and steady are its rays; but look, it is lower in the heavens than those stars which sparkle with a restless twinkling in the higher region of the skies. God keep you low, that you may shine bright. SALTER.

Purify your hearts, ye double minded. JAS. iv. 8.

How foolish are we if we attempt to entertain two guests so hostile to one another as Christ Jesus and Satan! Rest assured, Christ will not live in the parlor of our hearts if we entertain Satan in the cellar of our thoughts. SPURGEON.

Ye know not what shall be on the morrow. JAS. iv. 14.

"To-morrow" is the devil's great ally—the very Goliath in whom he trusts for victory. "Now" is the stripling sent forth against him. . . . The world will freely agree to be Christians to-morrow, if Christ will permit them to be worldly to-day. ARNOT.

One Thousand and One

JAS.
iv. 17.

To him that knoweth to do good, and doeth it not, to him it is sin.

Thousands of men pass off the stage of life, and are heard of no more. Why? they do not partake of good in the world, and none were blessed by them; none could point to them as the means of their redemption; not a line they wrote, not a word they spake, could be recalled; and so they perished: their light went out in darkness, and they were not remembered more than insects of yesterday. Will you thus live and die, O man immortal? Live for something. Do good, and leave behind you a monument of virtue that the storm of time can never destroy. Write your name in kindness, love, and mercy, on the hearts of thousands you come in contact with year by year: you will never be forgotten. No! your name, your deeds, will be as legible on the hearts you leave behind you as the stars on the brow of evening. Good deeds will shine as the stars of heaven.

CHALMERS.

JAS.
v. 16.

The effectual fervent prayer of a righteous man availeth much.

A man dreamed he was travelling, and came to a little church, and on the cupola of that church there was a devil fast asleep. He went along further, and came to a log cabin, and it was surrounded by devils all wide awake. He asked one of them what it meant; said the devil, "I will tell you. The fact is, that whole church is asleep and one devil can take care of all the people; but here are a man and woman who pray, and they have more power than the whole church."

Thoughts from My Library

Blessed be the God and Father of our Lord Jesus I PET.
Christ, which according to his abundant mercy hath i. 3.
begotten us again unto a lively hope by the resurrec-
tion of Jesus Christ from the dead.

The resurrection of Jesus Christ is the amen of God
to all His deeds for the salvation of men.

E. KAUTZCH.

Kept by the power of God through faith unto salva- I PET.
tion. i. 5.

A kite soaring on high is in a situation quite foreign
to its nature; as much as the soul of man is, when
raised above this lower world to high and heavenly
pursuits. A person at a distance sees not how it is
kept in its exalted situation; he sees not the wind that
blows it, nor the hand that holds it, nor the string by
whose instrumentality it is held. But all of these
powers are necessary to its preservation in that pre-
ternatural state. If the wind were to sink, it would
fall. It has nothing whatever in itself to uphold itself:
it has the same tendency to gravitate to the earth that
it ever had, and, if left for a moment to itself, it would
fall. Thus it is with the soul of every true believer.
It has been raised by the Spirit of God to a new, a pre-
ternatural, a heavenly state; and in that state it is upheld by an invisible and almighty hand, through the
medium of faith. And upheld it shall be, but not by
any power in itself. If left for a moment, it would
fall as much as ever. The whole strength is in God
alone; and its whole security is in the unchangeable-
ness of His nature, and in the efficacy of His grace. In
a word, "it is kept by the power of God, through
faith, unto salvation." SALTER.

I PET.
i. 7.

The trial of your faith, being much more precious than of gold that perisheth, though it be tried with fire, might be found unto praise and honor and glory at the appearing of Jesus Christ.

When the devil tries our faith it is that he may crush it or diminish it; but when God tries our faith it is to establish and increase it.   MARCUS RAINSFORD.

God has settled in heaven certain trials of our faith, which will as surely befall us as the crown of glory be given us at Christ's appearing.   God's purposes of grace are a golden chain; not a link must be missing.

Unfaithfulness will be to our souls as the deluge to the world,—a flood to drown us in perdition.   Persecution will be to us as the deluge to the ark,—a flood to lift us toward heaven.   PUNSHON.

I PET.
i. 14.

Obedient children.

Understanding what the will of the Lord is.—Eph. v. 17.

There is nothing like an obedient to-day to reveal God's will to-morrow.

I PET.
i. 16.

Be ye holy; for I am holy.

The highway of holiness is along the commonest road of life—along your very way.   In wind and rain, no matter how it beats—it is only going hand in hand with Him.   MARK GUY PEARSE.

I PET.
i. 19.

A lamb without blemish and without spot.

The Lamb for an individual.—GEN. iv. 4.
The Lamb for a household.—EX. xii. 3.
The Lamb for a nation.—NUM. xxiii. 4.
The Lamb for the world.—JOHN i. 29.

Thoughts from My Library

The word of God, which liveth and abideth forever. I PET. i. 23.

The Word abideth. The Jew hated it—but it lived on, while the veil was torn away from the shrine which the Shekinah had forsaken, and while Jerusalem itself was destroyed. The Greek derided it,—but it has seen his philosophy effete and his Acropolis in ruins. The Romans threw it into the flames—but it rose from its ashes, and swooped down upon the falling eagle. The reasoner cast it into the furnace, which his own negligence had heated "seven times hotter than its wont," but it came out without the smell of fire. The formalist fastened serpents around it to poison it, but it shook them off and felt no harm. The infidel cast it overboard in a tempest of sophistry and sarcasm—but it rode gallantly upon the crest of the proud waters. And it is living still—yet heard in the loudest swelling of the storm—it has been speaking all the while—it is speaking now. PUNSHON.

The word of the Lord endureth forever. I PET. i. 25.

The empire of Cæsar is gone; the legions of Rome are mouldering in the dust; the avalanches that Napoleon hurled upon Europe have melted away; the pride of the Pharaohs is fallen; the Pyramids they raised to be their tombs are sinking every day in the desert sands; Tyre is a rock for bleaching fishermen's nets; Sidon has scarcely left a wreck behind; but the word of God still survives. All things that threatened to extinguish it have only aided it; and it proves every day how transient is the noblest monument that man can build, how enduring is the least word that God has spoken. Tradition has dug for it a grave, intolerance has lighted for it many a fagot; many a Judas has

361

betrayed it with a kiss; many a Peter has denied it with an oath; many a Demas has forsaken it, but the word of God still endures. CUMMING.

I PET.
ii. 16.

Servants of God.

God has three kinds of servants in the world—(1) slaves, who serve Him from a principle of fear; (2) hirelings, who serve Him for the sake of wages; (3) sons, who serve Him under the influence of love.

I PET.
ii. 17.

Love the brotherhood. Fear God.

Yesterday is no mausoleum of dead deeds, no storehouse of mummies. Yesterday holds the full store of to-day's civilization; contains our tools, conveniences, knowledges; contains our battlefields and victories; above all gives us Bethlehem and Calvary. But alone man's yesterday is impotent; his to-morrow insufficient. The true man binds all his days together with an earnest, intense, passionate purpose. His yesterdays, to-days and to-morrows march together, one solid column, animated by one thought, constrained by one conspiracy of desire, energizing toward one holy and helpful purpose—to serve man and love God. NEWELL DWIGHT HILLIS.

I PET.
ii. 21,
22.

Christ also suffered for us, leaving us an example, that ye should follow his steps: who did no sin.

Never fear to suffer; but oh! fear to sin. If you must choose between them, prefer the greatest suffering to the smallest sin. GUTHRIE.

I PET.
ii. 24.

Who his own self bare our sins in his own body on the tree, that we, being dead to sins, should live unto righteousness.

Suppose a large graveyard, surrounded by a high wall,

362

with only one entrance by a large iron gate which is fast bolted. Within these walls are thousands and tens of thousands of human beings, of all ages and of all classes, by one epidemic disease bending to the grave. The grave yawns to swallow them, and they must all die. There is no balm to relieve them, no physician there: they must perish. This is the condition of man as a sinner: all, all have sinned, and the soul that sinneth shall die. While man was in this deplorable state, Mercy, an attribute of Deity, came down and stood at the gate, looked at the scene, and wept over it, exclaiming, "Oh that I might enter! I would bind up their wounds; I would relieve their sorrows; I would save their souls." While Mercy stood weeping at the gate, an embassy of angels, commissioned from the court of heaven to some other world, passing over, paused at the sight; and Heaven forgave that pause. Seeing Mercy standing there, they cried, "Mercy, Mercy, can you not enter? can you look upon this scene, and not pity? can you pity, and not relieve?" Mercy replied, "I can see;" and in her tears she added, "I pity, but cannot relieve."— "Why can you not enter?"—"Oh!" said Mercy, "Justice has barred the gate against me, and I cannot, must not, unbar it." At this moment, Justice himself appeared, as it were to watch the gate. The angels inquired of him, "Why will you not let Mercy in?" Justice replied, "My law is broken, and it must be honored: die they or Justice must." At this, there appeared a form among the angelic band, like unto the Son of God, Who, addressing Himself to Justice, said, "What are thy demands?" Justice replied, "My terms are stern and rigid. I must have sickness for their health; I must have ignominy for their honor; I must have death for life; without the shedding of blood, there is no remission."—"Justice," said the Son of God, "I accept thy terms. On Me be this wrong, and let Mercy enter."—"When," said Justice, "will you perform this promise?" Jesus replied, "Four thousand years hence, upon the hill of Calvary, without the gates of Jerusalem, I will perform it in My own person." The deed was prepared and signed in the presence of the angels of God. Justice was satisfied; and Mercy entered, preaching salvation in the name of Jesus. The deed was committed to the patriarchs; by them to the kings of Israel and the prophets; by them it was preserved till Daniel's seventy weeks were accomplished; and, at the appointed time, Justice appeared on the hill of Calvary, and Mercy presented to him the important deed. "Where," said Justice, "is the Son of God?" Mercy answered, "Behold Him at the bottom of the hill, bearing His own cross;" and then he departed, and stood aloof at the hour of trial. Jesus ascended the hill, while in His train followed His weeping Church. Justice immediately presented Him with the important deed, saying, "This is the day when this bond is to be executed." When He received it, did He tear it in pieces, and give it to the winds of heaven? No: He nailed it to His cross, exclaiming "It is finished!" Justice called on holy fire to come down, and consume the sacrifice. Holy fire descended: it swallowed His humanity; but, when it touched His divinity, it expired, and there was darkness over the whole heavens; but, glory to God in the highest! on earth peace, and good-will to men.

CHRISTMAS EVANS.

Thoughts from My Library

The answer of a good conscience toward God. I PET. iii. 21.

Conscience is God's king, that He puts in a man's breast; and conscience ought to reign. You may get up a civil war to fight against conscience; but you cannot kill the king. You may dethrone him for a while; but he struggles and fights for the mastery. COLEY.

Live according to God in the spirit. I PET. iv. 6.

Take care of your *life:* the Lord will take care of your *death.* F. WHITFIELD.

Watch unto prayer. I PET. iv. 7.

Prayer is the chalice in which we fetch the water from the rock. It is the ladder on which we climb up to pick the grapes hanging over the wall of heaven. It is the fire that warms the frigid soul. It is the ship that carries away our wants, and comes back with a return cargo of Divine help. Archimedes said, if he could only find a fulcrum for his lever, he could move the world. Ah! we have found it! Prayer is the lever. The divine promise is the fulcrum. Pushing down on such a lever, we move not only earth, but also heaven. TALMAGE.

Prayer is the conduit-pipe between my soul and heaven. It is the *outlet* upward for gratitude, and yearning desires for blessing; it is the *inlet* through which the supplies of grace pour downward into the heart. CUYLER.

As every man hath received the gift, even so minister the same one to another, as good stewards of the manifold grace of God. I PET. iv. 10.

Each of God's saints is sent into the world to prove some part of the divine character. Perhaps I may be one of those who shall live in the valley of ease, having much rest, and hearing sweet birds of promise singing in my ears. The air is calm and balmy, the sheep are feeding round about me, and all is still and quiet. Well, then, I shall prove the love of God in sweet communings. Or perhaps I may be called to stand where the thunderclouds brew, where the lightnings play, and tempestuous winds are howling on the mountain-top. Well, then, I am born to prove the power and majesty of our God: amid dangers He will inspire me with courage; amid toils He will make me strong. Perhaps it shall be mine to preserve an unblemished character, and so prove the power of sanctifying grace in not being allowed to backslide from my professed dedication to God. I shall then be a proof of the omnipotent power of grace, which alone can save from the power as well as the guilt of sin.

SPURGEON.

I PET.
iv. 13.

Rejoice, inasmuch as ye are partakers of Christ's sufferings; that, when his glory shall be revealed, ye may be glad also with exceeding joy.

Christ and His cross are not separable in this life, howbeit Christ and His cross part at heaven's door; for there is no house-room for crosses in heaven. One tear, one sigh, one sad heart, one loss, one thought of trouble, cannot find lodging there. They are but the marks of our Lord Jesus down in this wide inn and stormy country on this side death. Sorrow and the saints are not married together; or, suppose it were so, heaven would make a divorce.   RUTHERFORD.

I PET.
v. 5.

Be clothed with humility.

Humility—the fairest and loveliest flower that grew

366

in paradise, and the first that died—has rarely flourished since on mortal soil. It is so frail and delicate a thing that it is gone if it but looks upon itself, and they who venture to believe it theirs prove by that single thought they have it not.

Casting all your care upon him, for he careth for you. I PET v. 7.
Whatsoever it is that presses thee, go, tell thy Father, put over the matter into His hand, and so thou shalt be freed from that dividing, perplexing care that the world is full of. When thou art either to do or suffer anything, when thou art about any purpose or business, go tell God of it, and acquaint Him with it; yea, burden Him with it, and thou hast done for matter of caring; no more care, but quiet, sweet diligence in thy duty, and dependence on Him for the carriage of thy matters. Roll thy cares, and thyself with them, as one burden, all on thy God.   R. LEIGHTON.

Have you one anxious thought you do not bring to Jesus ? Have you one care you deem too light, too small to lay before Him ? It is then too small to give you one moment's concern. Either cast your care upon Him. that careth for you, or cast it away from you altogether; if it be unfit for His sympathy, it is unworthy of you.

Men do not avail themselves of the riches of God's grace. They love to nurse their cares, and seem as uneasy without some fret, as an old friar would be without his hair girdle. They are commanded to cast their cares upon the Lord; but, even when they attempt it, they do not fail to catch them up again, and think it meritorious to walk burdened. They take

God's ticket to heaven, and then put their baggage on their shoulders, and tramp, tramp the whole way there afoot.   BEECHER.

II PET.
i. 4.

Exceeding great and precious promises.

The promises of God scattered throughout the Bible are like the stars in the firmament; if it were always day we should not know that the sky is so full of them, but when night approaches they begin to shine. When the night of affliction overtakes the child of heaven the promises of God are seen to shine forth one after another in the firmament of His Word.

II PET.
i. 10,11.

Give diligence to make your calling and election sure . . . for so an entrance shall be ministered unto you abundantly into the everlasting kingdom of our Lord and Saviour Jesus Christ.

You see yonder ship. After a long voyage, it has neared the haven, but is much injured; the sails are rent to ribbons, and it is in such a forlorn condition that it cannot come up to the harbor: a steam-tug is pulling it in with the greatest possible difficulty. That is like the righteous being "scarcely saved." But do you see that other ship? It has made a prosperous voyage; and now, laden to the water's edge, with the sails all up and with the white canvas filled with the wind, it rides into the harbor joyously and nobly. That is an "abundant entrance"; and if you and I are helped by God's Spirit to add to our faith, virtue, and so on, we shall have at the last an "abundant entrance into the kingdom of our Lord Jesus Christ."

SPURGEON.

Though the wheels move slowly, yet they will

reach the goal! You are not the men you were twenty years ago. The most of the desert-road is now *behind* some of you. Your future on earth is narrowing itself to a point. How is it with your souls? Your *feet* are sore with the long journey; are your *wings* ready for flight into the kingdom of the crystal river and the unsetting sun?   JOSEPH PARKER.

A . . . sure word of prophecy.   II PET. i. 19.

Dr. Cyrus Hamlin, the venerable missionary and educator, tells the following story. While he was in Constantinople, soon after the Crimean War, a colonel in the Turkish army called to see him and said: "I want to ask you one question. What proof can you give me that the Bible is what you claim it to be—the Word of God?"

Dr. Hamlin evaded the question and drew the officer into conversation, during which he learned that his visitor had travelled a great deal, especially in the East in the region of the Euphrates. "Were you ever in Babylon?" asked the doctor. "Yes, and that reminds me of a curious experience I had there," replied the visitor, who then related the following account of his visit to the ancient capital of the world:

"I am very fond of sport, and having heard that the ruins of Babylon abound in game I determined to go there for a week's shooting. Knowing that it was not considered safe for a man to be there except in the company of several others—and money being no object to me—I engaged a sheik with his followers to accompany me for a large sum. We reached Babylon and pitched our tents. A little before sundown I took my gun and strolled out to have a look around. The

369

holes and caverns among the mounds which cover the ruins are infested with game, which, however, is rarely seen except at night. I caught sight of one or two animals in the distance, and then turned my steps toward our encampment, intending to begin my sport as soon as the sun had set. What was my surprise to find the men striking the tents. I went to the sheik and protested most strongly. I had engaged him for a week and was paying him most handsomely, and here he was starting off before our contract had scarcely begun.

"Nothing I could say, however, would induce him to remain. 'It isn't safe,' he said, 'no mortal flesh dare stay here after sunset. In the dark ghosts, goblins, ghouls, and all sorts of things come out of the holes and caverns, and whoever is found here is taken off by them and becomes one of themselves.' Finding I could not persuade him, I said, 'Well, as it is, I'm paying you more than I ought to, but if you'll stay I'll double it.' 'No,' he said, 'I couldn't stay for all the money in the world. No mortal flesh has ever seen the sun go down on Babylon and lived to tell the tale. But I want to do what is right by you. We'll go off to a place about an hour distant and come back at daybreak.' And go they did and my sport had to be given up."

"As soon as he had finished," said Dr. Hamlin, "I took my Bible, and read from the thirteenth chapter of Isaiah: 'And Babylon, the glory of kingdoms, the beauty of the Chaldees' excellency, shall be as when God overthrew Sodom and Gomorrah. It shall never be inhabited, neither shall it be dwelt in from generation to generation: neither shall the Arabian pitch tent there: neither shall the shepherds make their fold there: but wild beasts of the desert shall be there: and their houses shall be full of doleful creatures: and owls shall dwell there, and satyrs shall dance there. And the wild beasts of the islands shall cry in their desolate houses, and dragons in their pleasant palaces: and her time is near to come, and her days shall not be prolonged.'

" 'That's it exactly,' said the Turk when I had finished, 'but that's history you have been reading.' No," answered Dr. Hamlin, "it's prophecy. Come, you're an educated man. You know that the Old Testament was translated into Greek about 300 years before Christ." He acknowledged that it was. "And the Hebrew was given at least 200 years before that?" "Yes." "Well, wasn't this written when Babylon was in its glory, and isn't it prophecy?" "I'm not prepared to give you an answer now," he replied, "I must have time to think it over." "Very well, do so, and come back when you're ready and give me your answer," said Dr. Hamlin. "From that day to this I have never seen him," continued the doctor, "but what an unexpected testimony to the truth of the Bible in regard to the fulfillment of prophecy did that Turkish officer give!"

Holy men of God spake as they were moved by the Holy   II PET.
    Ghost.   i. 21.

In the diamond fields of South Africa a diamond was found, celebrated lately under the title of flystone; placed under a magnifying-glass, you see enclosed in all its brilliancy a little fly, with body, wings, and eyes in a most perfect state of preservation. How

One Thousand and One

it came there no one knows, but no human skill can take it out. So in Holy Scripture the Spirit of God is found in a place from which no power of man can remove it. M'EWAN.

II PET. iii. 9. *The Lord is not slack concerning his promise.*

When the Spirit renews in our minds a Gospel truth, let us turn it into a present plea, and be God's remembrancer of His own promises, as the Spirit is our remembrancer of Divine truths. We need not doubt some rich fruit of the application at such a season.

CHARNOCK.

II PET. iii. 18. *Grow in grace.*

Five degrees of growth in grace:
New born babes.—1 PET. ii. 2.
Weaned child.—Is. xxviii. 9.
Little children.—1 JOHN ii. 12.
Young men.—1 JOHN ii. 13.
Fathers.—1 JOHN ii. 13.

I JOHN i. 3. *Truly our fellowship is with the Father, and with his Son Jesus Christ.*

The life of fellowship with God cannot be built up in a day. F. B. MEYER.

Crucified with Him.—ROM. vi. 6.
Died with Christ. (Alford's Trans.).—ROM. vi. 8.
Buried with Him.—ROM. vi. 4.
Planted together in the likeness of His death.—ROM. vi. 5.
Planted together in the likeness of His resurrection.—ROM. vi. 5.
Quickened together.—EPH. ii. 5.
Raised up together.—EPH. ii. 6.

Thoughts from My Library

Sitting together in heavenly places.—EPH. ii. 6.
Living together.—I THESS. v. 10.
Working together.—MARK xvi. 20.
Suffering together.—ROM. viii. 17.
Glorified together.—ROM. viii. 17.

If we walk in the light, as he is in the light, we have I JOHN
fellowship one with another, and the blood of Jesus i. 7.
Christ his Son cleanseth us from all sin.

When a man walketh in the sun, if his face be toward it, he hath nothing before him but bright shining
light, and comfortable heat; but, let him once turn his
back to the sun, what hath he before him but a
shadow? And what is a shadow but the privation of
light, and heat of the sun? Yea: it is but to behold
his own shadow, defrauding himself of the other.
Thus there is no true wisdom, no true happiness, no
real comfort, but in beholding the countenance of God:
look from that, and we lose these blessings. And
what shall we gain? a shadow, an empty image,—instead of a substantial, to gain an empty image of ourselves, and lose the solid image of God. SPENCER.

You have seen two thunderclouds meet. One cloud
from this mountain, and another cloud from that
mountain, coming nearer and nearer together, and re-
sponding to each other, crash to crash, thunder to
thunder, boom! boom! And then the clouds break
and the torrents pour, and they are emptied perhaps
into the very same stream that comes down so red at
your feet, that it seems as if all the carnage of the
storm-battle has been emptied into it. So in this Bible
I see two storms gather, one above Sinai, the other
above Calvary, and they respond one to the other—

flash to flash, thunder to thunder, boom! boom! Sinai thunders, "The soul that sinneth, it shall die;" Calvary responds, "Save them from going down to the pit, for I have found a ransom." Sinai says, "Woe! woe!" Calvary answers, "Mercy! mercy!" And then the clouds burst, and empty their treasures into one torrent, and it comes flowing to our feet, red with the carnage of our Lord—in which, if thy soul be plunged, it shall go forth *free—free!*   TALMAGE.

I JOHN i. 9. *If we confess our sins he is faithful and just to forgive us our sins.*

"If we *confess* our sins," not, "If we *ask to be forgiven.*" We must face the fact of sin, fully, and not try to excuse ourselves.   J. HUDSON TAYLOR.

He that repents every day for the sins of every day, when he comes to die will have the sin but of one day to repent of.   P. HENRY.

I JOHN ii. 15. *Love not the world, neither the things that are in the world.*

An eagle, flying over a valley of ice, discovered a carcass, upon which it descended, and feasted so long, that its wings became frozen to the ice. In vain it struggled to mount upward: a vivid emblem of worldly desires.

If you will go to the banks of a little stream, and watch the flies that come to bathe in it, you will notice, that, while they plunge their *bodies* in the water, they keep their wings high out of the water; and, after swimming about a little while, they fly away with their wings unwet through the sunny air. Now,

Thoughts from My Library

that is a lesson for us. Here we are immersed in the cares and business of the world; but let us keep the wings of our soul, our faith, and our love, out of the world, that, with these unclogged, we may be ready to take our flight to heaven. J. INGLIS.

The world passeth away, and the lust thereof: but he that doeth the will of God abideth forever. I JOHN ii. 17.

See all things, not in the blinding and deceitful glare of the world's noon, but as they will seem when the shadows of life are closing in. At evening the sun seems to loom large on the horizon, while the landscape gradually fades from view; and then the sunset reveals the infinitude of space crowded with unnumbered worlds, and the firmament glows with living sapphires. Even so, let the presence of God loom large upon the narrow horizon of your life, and the firmament of your souls glow with the living sapphires of holy thoughts. Ah! try now to look at the world and its allurements as they will seem in the last hour; to look at unlawful pleasure as it shall then seem, not only a disappointing, but a depraving and an envenomed thing; to look at the small aims of ambition as they shall seem when they have dwindled into their true paltriness. FARRAR.

In the age succeeding the flood, they piled old Babel's tower, and said, "This shall last forever." But God confounded their language: they finished it not. Old Pharaoh and the Egyptian monarchs heaped up their Pyramids, and they said, "They shall stand forever": and so, indeed, they do stand; but the time is approaching when age shall devour even these. The most stable things have been evanescent as shadows and the bubbles of an hour, speedily destroyed at God's bidding. Where is Nineveh? and where is Babylon? Where the cities of Persia? Where are the high places of Edom? Where are Moab and the princes of Ammon? Where are the temples of the heroes of Greece? Where the millions that passed from the gates of Thebes? Where are the hosts of Xerxes? or where the vast armies of the Roman emperors? Have they not passed away? And though in their pride they said, "This monarchy is an everlasting one, this queen of the seven hills shall be called the eternal city," its pride is dimmed; and she who sat alone, and said, "I shall be no widow, but a queen forever,"—she hath fallen, hath fallen; and in a little while she shall sink like a millstone in the flood, her name being a curse and a byword, and her site the habitation of dragons and of owls. Man calls his works eternal; God calls them fleeting; man conceives that they are built of rock; God says, "Nay, sand; or, worse than that, they are air." Man says he erects them for eternity; God blows but for a moment, and where are they? Like baseless fabrics of a vision, they are passed and gone forever.   SPURGEON.

I saw a temple reared by the hands of man, standing with its high pinnacle in the distant plain. The streams beat about it, the God of Nature hurled His thunder-bolts against it; yet it stood as firm as adamant. Revelry was in the hall; the gay, the happy, the young, the beautiful, were there. I returned, and, lo! the temple was no more. Its high walls lay in scattered ruin; moss and grass grew rankly there; and, at the midnight hour, the owl's long cry added to the solitude. The young and gay who had revelled there had passed away. I saw a child rejoicing in his youth, the idol of his mother, and the pride of his father. I returned, and that child had become old. Trembling with the weight of years, he stood, the last of his generation, a stranger amidst all the desolation around him. I saw an old oak standing in all its pride upon the mountain: the birds were carolling in its boughs. I returned, and saw the oak was leafless and sapless: the winds were playing at their pastime through the branches. "Who is the destroyer?" said I to my guardian angel. "It is Time," said he. "When the morning-stars sang together for joy over the new-made world, he commenced his course, and when he has destroyed all that is beautiful on the earth, plucked the sun in his sphere, veiled the moon in blood; yea, when he shall have rolled the heavens and the earth away as a scroll, then shall an angel from the throne of God come forth, and, with one foot upon the land, lift up his hand toward heaven, and swear by heaven's Eternal, time was, but time shall be no more."   PAULDING.

They went out from us, but they were not of us.   I JOHN
                                                      ii. 19.
One evening I went out with a shepherd to collect his sheep. After they had been gathered together, and were being driven off the moor, I observed that there were some among them who did not belong to his flock. I particularly noticed, also, that he paid no attention whatever to these wandering strangers, urged forward, though they were, by the barking dog, further and further from their rightful companions. At last, thinking I must have been mistaken in supposing they were not his, I pointed to one or two of

them, and said, "Are those your sheep?" And he answered, "No." I said unto him, "Why, then, do you not separate them from the flock?" And he answered, and said, "They will find out directly they are not of us, and then they will go away of themselves." And immediately I remembered the words of John, and how he had said, "They went out from us, but they were not of us; for if they had been of us, they would no doubt have continued with us; but they went out that they might be made manifest that they were not all of us."

I JOHN
iv. 16.

We have known and believed the love that God hath to us. God is love.

When one who has never sailed out upon the ocean stands on its shore and watches the trembling waves as they surge and break upon the sands, how little does he know of the majesty and grandeur of the great deep, of its storms, of its power, of its secrets, of its unfathomable chambers, of its unweighed treasures? He sees only the little silver edge that breaks at his feet. So we stand but where the Spirit of God breaks upon the shore of our world. We see its silver edge. We feel the plash of its waves upon our hearts. But of its infinite reaches and outgoings beyond our shores we know almost nothing. Yet blessed are they who even stand by the shore and lave their hearts in even the shallowest eddies of this divine ocean.

J. R. MILLER.

I JOHN
iv. 18.

Perfect love casteth out fear.

Fear and love rise up in antagonism to each other as motives in life, like those two mountains from which respectively the blessings and curses of the old law

378

were pronounced—the Mount of Cursing, all barren and stony, without verdure and without water; the Mount of Blessing, green, and bright with many a flower, and blessed with many a trickling rill. Fear is barren. Love is fruitful. The one is a slave, and its work is little worth. The other is free, and its deeds are great and precious. From the blasted summit of the mountain which gendereth to bondage may be heard the words of the law, but the power to keep all these laws must be sought on the sunny hill where liberty dwells in love and gives energy to obedience. Therefore, Christian man, if you would use in your own life the highest power that God has given us for our growth in grace, draw your arguments not from fear but from love. And if you would win the world, melt it, do not hammer it. If you would grow in power, holiness, blessedness, remember this—"love is the fulfilling of the law."

McLAREN.

Whatsoever is born of God overcometh the world. I JOHN
v. 4.

He that "is born of God overcometh the world"; rising above the storms, and disturbing elements of flesh and nature, and all out of which Christ has risen, it seeks its own native element springing up into everlasting life, like the frigate bird which, when the storms agitate the surface of the ocean, when winds and waves rage in contempt of life on every side, rises aloft into the calm above the storms, and floats securely and tranquilly in that peaceful atmosphere, where it finds itself at home and at rest!

Keep yourselves from idols. I JOHN
v. 21.

When Alexander the Great visited the Greek philos-

379

opher, Diogenes, he asked him if there was anything that he could give him. He got this short answer, "I want nothing but that you should stand from between me and the sun." One thing there is which should never satisfy and content us; and that is, "anything that stands between our souls and Christ."   RYLE.

II JOHN 8.
Look to yourselves.

"I cannot sweep the darkness out, but I can shine it out," said John Newton. We cannot scourge dead works out of the church, but we can live them out. If we accuse the church with having the pneumonia, let us who are individual air-cells in that church breathe deeply and wait patiently and pray believingly, and one after another of the obstructed cells will open to the Spirit till convalescence is reëstablished in every part.

A. J. GORDON.

JUDE 21.
Keep yourselves in the love of God.

I once saw a dark shadow resting on the bare side of a hill. Seeking its cause, I saw a little cloud, bright as the light, floating in the clear blue above. Thus it is with our sorrow. It may be dark and cheerless here on earth; yet look above, and you shall see it to be but a shadow of His brightness Whose name is love.

ALFORD.

REV. i. 8.
I am Alpha and Omega, the beginning and the ending.

What are the two characteristics of what is enclosed by Alpha and Omega? These: All-needed and all-sufficient. The Bible opens with a book of beginnings, and its last book is a book of endings; they enclose a revelation, *all-needed and all-sufficient.* We cannot do without a page of it, or it would not have been

here. The practical thing is this: Do not put anything before Alpha, and do not put anything after
Omega. I have a righteous indignation against pref-
aces to the Gospel of Christ, and an equally righteous
indignation as to any supplement or appendix to that
Gospel. Christ is the Alpha and Christ is the Omega,
and I do not want to put anything before Him; and if
I am to live the Christian life I dare not put anything
after Him. All-needed and all-sufficient!

GEORGE WILSON.

I was in the Spirit on the Lord's day. REV. i. 10.

Never had John such a Sabbath, and never could he
see such again, until the earnest and emblem were ex-
changed for the full vision and fruition of the eternal
Sabbath above. What sights! what sounds! what
forms! what scenery!—fit recompense surely for years
of conflict and toil. The solitary place was made
glad. What Christian Church was ever consecrated
like this? Where the most magnificent Sanctuary
made with hands that has ever witnessed such glory?
The worshipper—one lonely exile. His temple—a
rock in mid-ocean. The theme he listens to—the
Church-militant,—its sufferings—its triumphs—its
eternal rewards. The Preacher, no earthly ambassador
—but his adorable Lord, arrayed in the lustre of His
exalted humanity. Oh! never did the tones of the
Sabbath-bell fall so joyfully on the ear, as when the
expatriated Pilgrim was startled from his bended knees
by the trumpet-voice exclaiming, " I am Alpha and
Omega, the first and the last ! " MACDUFF.

Fear none of those things. REV. ii. 10.

Above the voices of many waters, the mighty

breakers of the sea, the Lord sits as king upon the flood; yea, the Lord sitteth as king forever. A storm is only as the outskirts of His robe, the symptom of His advent, the environment of His presence. His way lies through, as well as *in* the sea, His path amid mighty waters, and His footsteps are veiled from human reason. Dare to trust Him; dare to follow Him! Step right down into the ooze of the sea, to find it rock; go down into the mighty depths, to discover that the very forces which barred your progress and threatened your life, at His bidding become the materials of which an avenue is made to liberty.

F. B. MEYER.

REV.
ii. 10.
Be thou faithful unto death.

On one of those battlefields where Austria suffered disastrous defeat when the bloody fight was over, and the victors were removing the wounded, they came on a young Austrian stretched on the ground, whose life was pouring out in the red streams of a ghastly wound. To their astonishment he declined their kind services. Recommending others to be removed, he implored them, though he might still have been saved, to let him alone. On returning some time afterward, they found him dead—all his battles o'er. But the mystery was explained. They raised the body to give it burial, and there, below him, lay the colors of his regiment. He had sworn not to part with them, and though he clung to life, would not purchase recovery at the price of his oath, and the expense of a soldier's honor.

GUTHRIE.

REV.
iii. 1.
Thou hast a name that thou livest, and art dead.

Have you ever read " The Ancient Mariner " ? I dare

382

say you thought it one of the strangest imaginations ever put together, especially that part where the old mariner represents the corpses of all the dead men rising up to man the ship,—dead men pulling the rope, dead men steering, dead men spreading sails. I thought what a strange idea that was. But do you know that I have lived to see that time? I have seen it done. I have gone into churches, and I have seen a dead man in the pulpit, a dead man as deacon, and a dead man handling the plate, and dead men sitting to hear. SPURGEON.

A man may be a living churchman but a dead Christian. RYLE.

Hold that fast which thou hast.   REV.

We can only hold fast what we have by constantly   iii. 11.
using it. If we have a measure of love, we must daily study the means of manifesting it. It is easily recovered from yesterday, but not from the day before. If we have joy, we must persevere in rejoicing; every day must have its spiritual joy. Our peace too, we must daily see to it that it is with us. So with long suffering, gentleness, goodness, faith, meekness, temperance. Each day is to be considered a stage, and we must ascertain regularly that none of our treasures have been left behind. Christians are ready to think, until they have learned the contrary, that their graces are safe when they are slumbering, but their slumber is fatal. Whatever we would retain we must keep near our consciousness; our will, our memory, our understanding, all must be conversant with it.

BOWEN.

REV.
iii. 17.

Thou sayest, I am rich, and increased with goods, and have need of nothing; and knowest not that thou art wretched, and miserable, and poor, and blind, and naked.

We need help from God to know our helplessness. The greatest of all our enemies is in the royal chamber of our inmost being and rules us with a rod of iron, though it be bound about with ivy leaves. We need help from God Himself to become aware of the true character of this enthroned enemy, and to see the desolations he has wrought in our heritage. Alas for them who know not their need of help. The triumph of their foe is complete. They are led captive at his will, even though we see them occupying the high places of the earth, admired and followed by vast crowds.

BOWEN.

REV.
iii. 20.

Behold, I stand at the door, and knock: if any man hear my voice, and open the door, I will come in to him, and will sup with him, and he with me.

Behold the *dignity* of man! The heart is a palace, barred and bolted, kept by man, and Christ his Maker allows him to hold the key, and will not force a way in. Behold the *interest* in man! Gracious powers from above gather about him in pity and love, and out of the midst of these, Christ knocks and asks admission. No other being is the centre of such interest. Behold the *privilege* of man! If he hear the entreaty and open the door, the Son of God will come in and dwell with him. Behold the *blessedness* of man! The soul into which Christ thus enters has Christ sup with him and he with Christ. Note the order: Christ first comes down and sups with him, and then takes him

384

up to sup with Himself—Christly communion with
Christ as leader up the ever higher Christly ranges.
Here is the highest bliss and Christ stands at the door
of our hearts and knocks, offering it.   I. E. DWINELL.

A man once stopped a preacher in a street of London, and said, "I once heard you preach in Paris, and
you said something which I have never forgotten, and
which has, through God, been the means of my conversion." "What was that?" said the preacher. "It
was that the latch was on our side of the door. I had
always thought that God was a hard God, and that we
must do something to propitiate Him. It was a new
thought to me that Christ was waiting for me to open
to Him."

*To him that overcometh will I grant to sit with me in
my throne.*   REV.
iii. 21.

At the close of the war of 1866, the triumphant army
of Prussia came to Berlin for a reception of welcome.
As each regiment approached the city gate from the
Thiergarten, it was halted by a choir, demanding by
what right it would enter the city. The regiment replied in a song, reciting the battles it had fought, the
victories it had won; then came a welcome from the
choir, "Enter into the city." And so the next came
up, reciting its deeds, and another, and another, each
challenged and welcomed. They marched up the
Linden between rows of captured cannon, with the
banners they had borne and the banners they had
taken, and they saluted the statue of grand old Frederick, the creator of Prussia. So, when all the fierce
warfare of earth shall have been accomplished, and
the kingdom of Christ assured, the phalanxes of His

church shall go up to the city with songs and tokens of victory. They shall march in together, singing hallelujahs, and shall lay their trophies at the feet of Him upon whose head are many crowns—King of kings and Lord of lords. THOMPSON.

REV. *They rest not day and night.*
iv. 8.
O blessed rest! when we "rest not day and night, saying, Holy, holy, holy, Lord God Almighty!"—when we shall rest from sin, but not from worship—from suffering and sorrow, but not from joy! O blessed day! when I shall rest with God—when I shall rest in knowing, loving, rejoicing and praising! when my perfect soul and body shall together perfectly enjoy the most perfect God—when God, Who is love itself, shall perfectly love me, and rest in His love to me, and I shall rest in my love to Him—when He shall rejoice over *me* with joy, and joy over me with singing, and I shall rejoice in Him. BAXTER.

REV. *They sung a new song.*
v. 9.
Peter Mackenzie, a Wesleyan preacher in England was once preaching from the text, "And they sung a new song," and he said: "Yes, there will be singing in heaven, and when I get there I shall want to have David with his harp, and Paul and Peter and other saints, gather round for a sing. And I will announce a hymn from the Wesleyan Hymnal. Let us sing hymn No. 749, 'My God, my Father, while I stray.'

"But some one will say: 'That won't do. You are in heaven, Peter; there is no straying here. And I will say, Yes that is so. Let us sing No. 651, 'Though waves and storms go o'er my head.' But another saint will say, 'Peter, you are in heaven now, you forget that there are no storms here.' Well, I will try again. No. 536, 'Into a world of ruffians sent.' 'Peter! Peter!' some one will say; 'we will put you out unless you stop giving out inappropriate hymns,' and then I will ask, 'What shall we sing?' And they will all say, 'Sing the new song, the song of Moses and the Lamb.'"

A great multitude . . . stood before the throne, and before the Lamb, clothed with white robes, and palms in their hands.   REV. vii. 9.

A station *on the feet* in front of the throne in *heaven* is the effect of being often *on the knees* before the throne on *earth.*

These are they which came out of great tribulation, and have washed their robes, and made them white in the blood of the Lamb.   REV. vii. 14.

Who are they that I see triumphing in the heavenly host? They that lived in ceiled houses? They that walked the earth with crowns upon their heads? They that knew no sorrow? No. "These are they which came out of great tribulation, and have washed their robes and made them white in the blood of the Lamb"; they that cried from under the altar, "How long, O Lord, how long?"—these are they that stand highest in the kingdom of God. Heaven is just before you. And many of you that seem to have a long and weary path of suffering will soon be done with your period of trial, and will rise to honor and glory in Christ Jesus.   BEECHER.

The angel . . . sware . . . that there should be time no longer.   REV. x. 5, 6.

Time's one great day begins with the creation of

man, and ends with the coming of the Lord; but already in God's sight that expanse is nothing more than a point; and to ourselves, when from eternity we look back, it will seem a speck upon the infinite. As one star differeth from another star in glory, this day will shine more brightly than all the rest, for it is the bride's birthday; it is the date attached to every name in the Lamb's book of life. ARNOT.

REV. xiv. 16. *He that sat on the cloud thrust in his sickle on the earth; and the earth was reaped.*

Jesus Christ always uses expressions with regard to His people, which impute their death to Him alone. You will recollect the expression in the Revelation—"Thrust in thy sickle, and reap: for the time is come for thee to reap; for the harvest of the earth is ripe." But when He begins to reap, not the vintage, which represents the wicked that were to be crushed, but the harvest which represents the godly; then it is said, "He that sat on the cloud thrust in the sickle." He did not leave it to His angels, He did it Himself.

SPURGEON.

REV. xxi. 4. *There shall be no more death.*

Death is the black servant who rides behind the chariot of life. SPURGEON.

REV. xxi. 7. *He that overcometh shall inherit all things.*

At the battle of Crecy, where Edward the Black Prince, then a youth of eighteen years of age, led the van, the king, his father, drew up a strong party on a rising ground, and there beheld the conflict, in readiness to send relief where it should be wanted. The young prince, being sharply charged, and in some danger, sent to his father for succor; and as the king delayed to send it, another messenger was sent to crave immediate assistance. To him the king replied, " Go, tell my son, I am not so inexperienced a commander as not to know when succor is wanted, nor so careless a father as not to send it." He intended the honor of the day should be his son's, and therefore let him with courage stand to it, assured that help should be had when it might conduce most to his renown. God draws forth His servants to fight in the spiritual warfare, where they are engaged not only against the strongholds of carnal reason, and the exalted imaginations of their own hearts, but also in the pitched field against Satan and his wicked instruments. But they, poor hearts, when the charge is sharp, are ready to despond, and cry with Peter, " Save, Lord, we perish "; but God is too watchful to overlook their exigencies, and too much a Father to neglect their succor. If help, however, be delayed, it is that the victory may be more glorious by the difficulty of overcoming.

SPURGEON.

I am . . . the bright and morning star.　REV. xxii. 16.

The " bright and morning star " is more to our soul's firmament than all the constellations of the sky.

JOHN KER.

The Spirit and the bride say, Come. And let him that heareth say, Come. And let him that is athirst come : and whosoever will, let him take the water of life freely.　REV. xxii. 17.

I have heard that in the deserts, when the caravans are in want of water, they are accustomed to send on a camel, with its rider, some distance in advance; then, after a little space, another follows; and then, at a short interval, another. As soon as the first man finds water, almost before he stoops down to drink he shouts aloud, "Come!" The next one, hearing the voice, repeats the word, "Come!" while the nearest again takes up the cry, "Come!" until the whole wilderness echoes with the word "Come!" SPURGEON.

Index

Index

Index

Index

Joy in heaven, 205.
—— want of, 63.
Judging, 265.
Judgment, 127, 147, 264.

KINDNESS, 201, 202, 294, 358.
Kingdom of God, the, 114.
Knowledge of God, the, 30, 48, 145, 158.

LAMB of God, the, 360.
Labor and prayer, 319, 325.
Law and the Gospel, the, 212, 373.
—— of God, the, 147, 355.
Liberality, 120.
Life, a loom, 49, 287.
—— purpose in, 135, 315.
—— uncertainty of, 86.
Likeness to Christ, 14, 151, 182, 281, 295, 300, 306.
Little things, 24, 69, 73, 123, 127, 128, 162, 176, 187, 217, 260.
Looking to Christ, 72, 79, 80, 111, 189, 242, 373.
Love, 270, 284, 285.

MAN, the image of God, 164.
Manna, 28, 36.
Meditation, 109, 329.
Meekness, 114.
Mercy and judgment, 102, 136, 185.
—— and justice, 362.
Misuse of God's gifts, 125.
Morning hour, the, 31, 32, 71, 98, 280.
Murmuring, 314, 329.

NAMES of Christians, the, 260.
Nearness to God, 321.

Neglect of salvation, 125, 242.
"Now," 100, 286, 357.

OBEDIENCE, 17, 38, 39, 50, 52, 157, 213, 215, 360.
Omnipotence of God, the, 9, 48, 183, 192, 224.
Opportunity, 100, 308.

PASSING through life, 124, 260.
Patience, 208, 326.
Peace, 259, 298.
—— of God, the, 188, 234, 238, 317, 323.
—— with God, 251.
Personal work, 213.
Pharisaism, 181.
Pharisee and the publican, the, 207.
Poverty, 195.
Praise, 84, 94, 352.
Prayer, 18, 47, 63, 71, 78, 100, 101, 105, 107, 120, 152, 164, 179, 180, 189, 200, 203, 246, 255, 258, 271, 316, 325, 327, 338, 358, 365.
—— and praise, 96.
Pride, 119, 121.
Priesthood, 30.
Procrastination, 100, 127, 286.
Prophecy, fulfilled, 369.
Prosperity, 116.
Providence of God, the, 255, 256.
Psalm xxiii., 75.

QUIETNESS, 131, 156, 325.

REFLECTING Christ, 304,
Regeneration, 212, 213.
Religion, 190, 215, 285, 287, 333.
Repentance, 288, 374.

Index

Index

Date Due

Code 4386-04, CLS-4, Broadman Supplies, Nashville, Tenn., Printed in U.S.A.